Demons of Urban Reform

Palgrave Historical Studies in Witchcraft and Magic

Series Editors: **Jonathan Barry, Willem de Blécourt and Owen Davies**

Titles include:

Edward Bever
THE REALITIES OF WITCHCRAFT AND POPULAR MAGIC IN EARLY MODERN
EUROPE
Culture, Cognition and Everyday Life

Alison Butler
VICTORIAN OCCULTISM AND THE MAKING OF MODERN MAGIC
Invoking Tradition

Julian Goodare, Lauren Martin and Joyce Miller
WITCHCRAFT AND BELIEF IN EARLY MODERN SCOTLAND

Jonathan Roper (*editor*)
CHARMS, CHARMERS AND CHARMING

Alison Rowlands (*editor*)
WITCHCRAFT AND MASCULINITIES IN EARLY MODERN EUROPE

Rolf Schulte
MAN AS WITCH
Male Witches in Central Europe

Laura Stokes
DEMONS OF URBAN REFORM
Early European Witch Trials and Criminal Justice, 1430–1530

Forthcoming:

Johannes Dillinger
MAGICAL TREASURE HUNTING IN EUROPE AND NORTH AMERICA
A History

Soili-Maria Olli
TALKING TO DEVILS AND ANGELS IN SCANDINAVIA, 1500–1800

Palgrave Historical Studies in Witchcraft and Magic
Series Standing Order ISBN 978–1403–99566–7 Hardback
978–1403–99567–4 Paperback
(*outside North America only*)

You can receive future titles in this series as they are published by placing a standing order.
Please contact your bookseller or, in case of difficulty, write to us at the address below with
your name and address, the title of the series and one of the ISBNs quoted above.

Customer Services Department, Macmillan Distribution Ltd, Houndmills, Basingstoke,
Hampshire RG21 6XS, England

Demons of Urban Reform

Early European Witch Trials and Criminal Justice, 1430–1530

Laura Stokes
Assistant Professor,
Department of History,
Stanford University, USA

palgrave
macmillan

First published 2011 by
PALGRAVE MACMILLAN

Palgrave Macmillan in the UK is an imprint of Macmillan Publishers Limited, registered in England, company number 785998, of Houndmills, Basingstoke, Hampshire RG21 6XS.

Palgrave Macmillan in the US is a division of St Martin's Press LLC, 175 Fifth Avenue, New York, NY 10010.

Palgrave Macmillan is the global academic imprint of the above companies and has companies and representatives throughout the world.

Palgrave® and Macmillan® are registered trademarks in the United States, the United Kingdom, Europe and other countries.

ISBN: 978-1-4039-8683-2 hardback

This book is printed on paper suitable for recycling and made from fully managed and sustained forest sources. Logging, pulping and manufacturing processes are expected to conform to the environmental regulations of the country of origin.

A catalogue record for this book is available from the British Library.

A catalog record for this book is available from the Library of Congress.

10 9 8 7 6 5 4 3 2 1
20 19 18 17 16 15 14 13 12 11

Printed and bound in Great Britain by
CPI Antony Rowe, Chippenham and Eastbourne

Contents

Figures

Acknowledgments

The questions that eventually grew into this book began at Reed College nearly fifteen years ago, as part of a senior thesis investigating the social construction of deviance. Accordingly, the first thanks go to my advisors there: Ray Kierstead, who inspired my love for the early modern, and David Sacks, who showed me how to be a historian. At the University of Virginia my interest matured through a series of seminar papers and a master's thesis on Johannes Nider that owed much to the assistance of Ted Lendon. This book appeared in its first draft as a dissertation under the mentorship of Erik Midelfort, with the advice and support in particular of Anne Schutte, Paul Halliday, and Sönke Lorenz.

With invaluable input from many friends and colleagues, this project has changed much in the years since its appearance as a dissertation. I am grateful to engaged and interrogative audiences at the Arbeitskreis interdisziplinäre Hexenforschung conference (2003), the Sixteenth Century Society & Conference (2005, 2006, 2007, and 2009), the "Boundaries of Witchcraft" conference at Oxford (2008), and the "Devil in Society in the Premodern World" conference in Toronto (2008). I am also indebted to audiences at Bucknell University (2006) and the University of Minnesota (2008) and to innumerable individuals who have taken the time to listen and offer their thoughts along the way. In particular I am grateful for the collegial friendship of an emerging cohort of young demonographers and witchcraft researchers, especially Mike Bailey, Tamar Herzig, and Maryse Simon. I have also benefitted from the intellectual community at Stanford, where I have enjoyed opportunities to present my thoughts in various forums, including workshops of the Stanford Humanities Center. This book has been improved by a long list of readers along the way, to whom I remain grateful: Erik Midelfort, Anne Schutte, Paul Halliday, Alison Weber, Philippe Buc, Desi Hopkins, Willem de Blécourt, and Sara Beam.

This book is dedicated to the entire community of witchcraft scholars, who have welcomed me into their ranks and encouraged my work. I hope this book proves an interesting contribution to the grand conversation.

Introduction

In July of 1519, Andreas from Tschafel was condemned to die in Lucerne along with two accomplices: Hans Stächli from Meerschwand and Barbel Vermeggerin from König in the territory of Bern. Under what tortures the three confessed their supposed crimes is unknown to us, but their confessions bear all the marks of creativity inspired by torment. Andreas confessed first to one theft, then to several more. His interrogators, clearly unsatisfied with the list, pressed him further. Under pressure, Andreas not only confessed generally to more thefts than he could remember, but to a whole litany of anti-religious and anti-social crimes:

> He has confessed that he has stolen so much money that he cannot remember the amount. He has admitted to having had sex with a cow, and he has confessed to having florentinized six boys. Also he has confessed how he was gambling once and could not win, and so he gave the little finger on his left hand to the Devil, that he might make him win. But it never helped him. Also he has admitted that he has not been to confession in fifteen years. Moreover, he has confessed that he has renounced God, His worthy mother, and the whole heavenly host, and has given himself to the Devil and believed in him. [The Devil] instructed him, taught him how to make hail and overcome good. He has confessed that he made a storm in Güns, not far from Chur, but it was not a big storm. This he attempted often; at times he succeeded, others not.[1]

Even then, Andreas's confession was not at an end. He went on to tell of a quarrel with a shoemaker whose dog had tried to bite him. He said he stabbed the shoemaker and ran off, not knowing if he lived or died.

1

Last of all, Andreas confessed to having chanced upon a sleeping man, murdered him in his sleep, and stolen his money.

Andreas's confessions raise compelling questions. What was the Devil doing in the confessions of a thief? Historians of the witch hunts have long recognized that interrogators in witch trials often sought confessions of diabolism and that it was usually in the process of interrogation that the Devil and the more fantastic elements of witchcraft entered the trials. The Devil was central to the elite concept of witchcraft, and in many jurisdictions investigators may have felt they needed a confession of diabolism to ensure a conviction. This was certainly not what motivated Andreas's interrogators. As a foreigner, his confession of habitual theft would have guaranteed execution in Lucerne during the early sixteenth century. His questioners seem to have sought confessions of every crime Andreas had ever committed, a complete biography of crime and sin. The combination of charges such as theft and murder with those of sodomy and witchcraft was more pronounced in this case than in many others, but the appearance of witchcraft in conjunction with other crimes was not unusual. This might come as something of a surprise if one approached the subject with a mental image of witchcraft as a kind of heresy, a particularly religious crime. Andreas's trial, however, was conducted entirely by a secular, urban court. His judge and interrogators were members of the Lucerne city council, yet they did not hesitate to prosecute him for religious transgressions like avoidance of confession. At Andreas's execution, where his confession would likely have been read aloud, they demonstrated their authority to the gathered people by establishing their power to control and punish both crime and sin, and thus to protect the community from the wrath of God.

The story of how such a powerful demonstration came to take place stretches back a full century before this trial, to a time when criminal justice in Lucerne almost never ended in execution and the main focus of the council's efforts at social control was the maintenance of civic harmony through the prevention and mediation of interpersonal conflict. Over the years there have been calls to examine witch trials in the context of other forms of prosecution, but the project has rarely been undertaken.[2] Andreas Blauert did so for the Hochstift Speyer, and his results in that study are similar to my own; he concludes that witchcraft prosecution, criminal justice generally, and the policing of indecent behavior were interrelated phenomena.[3] The story of how this interrelationship developed in Lucerne is central to the argument of this book because, as we shall see, the origins of witchcraft prosecution and its subsequent establishment were inextricably bound up with fifteenth-century developments in criminal justice and other modes of social control. The unusual nature of these developments in Lucerne, moreover, will help us understand how witchcraft prosecution became established in that city, while in both Basel and Nuremberg it was ultimately rejected.

The question of the definition of witchcraft is a particularly important one. It is a question that has dominated the scholarship on the early witch trials, but the definition that I choose to employ here diverges substantially from the general consensus of that scholarship. Whereas most scholars of early witchcraft prosecution understand witchcraft as by definition a *crimen mixti fori*, necessarily involving both the secular crime of harmful magic and the religious heresy of diabolism, I use a much simpler definition. In this work, I define a *witch* as a person who is believed to use magic for malicious purposes.[4] When discussing the specific mixture of sorcery and heresy, I will refer to *diabolic witchcraft.*

This simpler definition of witchcraft facilitates an examination of early witch trials – with and without diabolism – as a collective phenomenon within a broader context. One of the first details that becomes clear when examining the early witch trials is a shift in punishment. In the early years of the fifteenth century, a woman accused of being a witch in Basel or Lucerne would most likely have been banished, if she were punished at all. By the last decades of the fifteenth century in these two cities, however, a woman accused of the same crime faced a high probability of being executed at the stake. This transformation has been interpreted as the effect of the new concept of the diabolic witch. Yet even within formal, legal formulations of the crime and its punishment, diabolism was not necessary for the application of the death sentence. It seems, therefore, that other forces may have been at play in the increased judicial severity vis-à-vis crimes of magic. In order to place this shift in punishment within a broader context, this study examines the handling of witchcraft alongside the treatment of other kinds of crime within a secular, urban context.

An urban context is provided in this work through three case studies: the cities of Basel, Lucerne, and Nuremberg, of which Lucerne emerges as the case of primary interest. Although not constitutionally identical, these three cities shared basic structural similarity; they were governed by city councils, possessed a fair degree of legal autonomy, and had predominantly German-speaking populaces. In each case there were also factors of particular interest to the history of witchcraft which aided my choice of these cities. Basel and Lucerne shared a regional, indigenous witchcraft concept. Lucerne, despite its relatively small size, has a marked history of early witch trials, providing an exceptionally rich source-base for examining those early trials in a secular context. Basel, which experienced fewer witch trials during the fifteenth century than Lucerne, is of particular interest because it played host to the Council of Basel. As will be further discussed below, the Council has been identified as a point of dissemination for demonological ideas associated with the developing stereotype of the diabolic witch. Having entered the Swiss Confederation in 1501, Basel is also interesting as a bridge between Swiss Lucerne and Imperial Nuremberg. The third city, Nuremberg, serves mainly as a negative case. Nuremberg did not execute accused witches during the fifteenth century, and only very rarely thereafter. The sources from the city are rich enough, however, to demonstrate that witchcraft accusations did arise and cases of magical crime were handled before the courts from time to time. We also know that the idea of the diabolic witch was present in the city, as the Nuremberg city council commissioned an abbreviated translation of the witch-hunting manual *Malleus Maleficarum* in the 1490s. The early witch trials have already been examined for each of these cities; this project builds on existing studies by examining those trials in a new comparative framework.[5]

The most important comparative innovation of this study is not a comparison among the three cities but within each city, between the treatment of witchcraft and the handling of other crimes and moral transgressions. As such, this study restores witch trials to their prosecutorial context, alongside other capital crimes and within the broad spectrum of social control. One might be inclined to ask if we can even compare accused witches to, say, accused thieves. After all, we would all agree that theft really does take place. Witchcraft, however, is impossible from the standpoint of Western, twenty-first-century law. Yet as historians, we must acknowledge that witchcraft was legally as real as theft five hundred years ago. It may even have had real, physical effects.[6] Conversely, when we push the question, all crime has a constructed nature. Representations of crime – be they news reports or the carefully orchestrated products of official justice – have a profound effect on how the public perceives the reality and probability of particular crimes.[7] What is or is not a crime is defined by legal codes that change over time and can also be the subject of great ambiguity, as is made clear by the controversy over the constitutionality of sodomy laws in America today. Then, too, there is the uncertainty created by the procedures of justice. When a man is tortured into a confession of theft, can we trust that he is truly a thief? What if he is only threatened with torture? Or forced to sit three days without food? Or left for a month in a dank dungeon without contact with the outside world? The usual procedures of fifteenth-century criminal justice are such as to undermine any confidence in the relation between the confession of a given individual and the truth of his guilt or innocence. From the sources remaining to us, we can be no more certain of the guilt of a thief than the guilt of a witch. What we can seek to know is how they were imagined, prosecuted, and punished.

By placing witch trials in the context of other legal proceedings, I have been able to examine both the persecution and prosecution of witchcraft. The idea of persecution is one that we impose on the past, but in this case, we have good reason to do so. The persecution of witches in the fifteenth century in Basel and Lucerne was paralleled by a growing persecution of sodomy. The social foundations of these persecutions must be understood; the forces that drove them and the fear and hate that fueled them must be examined. Alternately, there are persecutory elements in the prosecution of certain classes of persons more heavily for crimes like theft, especially given the greater vulnerability of the poor and the stranger to the harsh procedures of criminal justice. But the idea of persecution is limited, because the trials that I examine were not chaotic witch hunts where legal procedure was thrown to the wind. It is difficult to look on torture and recognize any procedural rationality, but it did indeed grow from the very rationalization of legal procedure. It is in the legal transformations of the fifteenth century, as much as in the demonological ones, that we must seek the roots of witchcraft prosecution.

The history of criminal prosecution in Germany has long been told from the standpoint of legal history. That narrative emphasized the fifteenth century as a time of procedural transformation under the general rubric of the "reception" of Roman law into Germany.[8] Recent legal-historical work has highlighted the slow, spotty, and incomplete nature of this transformation.[9] Meanwhile, work in the relatively new field of German criminal history has radically challenged the assumptions about practice that this old narrative entailed.[10] While the present work takes into account both legal-historical and praxis-oriented literature, at its heart lies a story of fifteenth-century procedural transformation. Rather than assuming that this transformation simply derived from the availability of new legal concepts, I ask why the men in power chose to avail themselves of new procedures when and how they did.

The intersection of witchcraft with ordinary crime during the fifteenth century, its definition, the use of torture and execution, and the meaning of the wave of prosecution which peaked with Andreas's trial comprise the context for a new attempt to answer an old question: how did the crime and prosecution of witchcraft emerge during the fifteenth century? Witch hunts did not occur prior to the fifteenth century, but they marked the three centuries that followed, in a pattern that has been called the great European witch hunt. Why? What had changed? Where did the pattern of witch hunting originate? The simplest answer to this question, based on the best scholarship available, is that the change took place in what is now western Switzerland during the 1430s.

The doctrine of diabolic witchcraft coalesced during the years of the Council of Basel.[11] The Council itself must have played a decisive role in the development of the diabolic witch concept and its subsequent distribution. Several key figures were present at the Council of Basel, not least of whom was Duke Amadeus VIII of Savoy, whom the Council elected as Pope Felix V. The Duchy of Savoy was the site of some of the earliest cases of diabolic witchcraft, including the trials in the diocese of Lausanne. Pope Eugene IV, who was reigning when the duke of Savoy was elected pope by the Council and who ultimately successfully defended his claim to the papacy, lambasted Savoy as a land brimming with heretics, *Waudenses* – the term at that time could mean either Waldensians or witches.[12] The political power struggles that centered on the Council of Basel and the theological development of the idea of diabolic witchcraft were intimately linked.

Recent research into the impact of the Basel convocation of clerics on the development of demonology demonstrates that an active exchange of demonological ideas took place at the Council. Reflections of this exchange appear after the Council in the works of various participants.[13] The Council of Basel also appears to have been crucial to the dissemination of the diabolic witch doctrine that had been developed among inquisitors, judges, and theologians in the western Alpine region. Beginning in the 1440s, the diabolic witch appeared throughout western Europe, mostly in isolated trials but occasionally in small witch panics.[14] In the fifth book of his *Formicarius*, Johannes Nider discussed the witch trials in the Duchy of Savoy. Andreas Blauert argues that we should read this as an example of the reception of the west-Swiss diabolic witch concept into the international milieu of the Council. University towns and bishops' cities then became centers of distribution for the witch doctrine in other regions.[15]

The most pronounced spread of witch trials during and after the Council of Basel, however, was within the Alpine region. Some of the earliest trials in the region took place within the diocese of Lausanne. In Neuchâtel, the earliest witch trials were linked with these; in 1439 an inquisitor of Lausanne conducted witch trials there.[16] In the southern Alpine Leventine valley, the diabolic witch stereotype, which had appeared there in an inquisitorial trial in the early 1430s, resurfaced during the 1450s in a locally-run, secular witch panic which claimed about twenty lives.[17] In the same decade, the diabolic witch also appeared in Lucerne and Basel for the first time. The confession of Else of Meersburg, recorded around 1450 in Lucerne, included explicit elements of diabolism. In describing how she raised a hailstorm, Else testified that she had thrown water in the air "in the names of all the devils," in particular Beelzebub and her own special demon, Krütli.[18] A similar element of diabolism appeared in the trial of Gret Frölicherin and Verena Symlin in the territory of Basel in 1458:

> Verena Symlin of Pratteln, [...] stood before an open country court, [...] on account of much evil and many misdeeds which she has practiced and committed in her days, especially that she denied almighty God and His worthy mother, and gave herself to the Devil and his spirit and therewith committed her evil with her companion Gret Frölicherin.[19]

Such diabolism appears to support the argument that the stereotype of the diabolic witch was the primary fuel for the trials that began in these regions around the mid-century.

This contention is central to the only comparative study that has been made of the early witch trials in the last twenty years, Andreas Blauert's *Frühe Hexenverfolgungen*. Blauert argues that the diabolic witch doctrine migrated during the 1440s from the west-Swiss region of its inception into German-speaking Alpine territories where it gained ground within secular jurisdictions. He places Heinrich Kramer's *Malleus Maleficarum* at the end of this process, as Kramer integrated earlier formulations of the witch doctrine with his own practical experience of witch hunting in the region around Lake Constance. Blauert points to the Lucerne chronicle of Hans Fründ regarding witch hunts in the Valais around 1428 as evidence of the reception of the witch stereotype. Fründ's report, probably written around 1450, contained a full-blown reflection of the diabolic witch stereotype from western Switzerland:

> There were [...] some among them who came together at a secret place at night for the school [the witches' sabbath]. Then the evil

spirit came in the manner of a teacher and preached to them against the Christian faith and forbade them to confess and do penance. [...] There were also some among them who killed their own children and roasted them and ate and drank. [...] And they went to see their neighbors, and where they placed their evil hands, the children turned black or blue; they had rubbed evil poison on their hands.[20]

Yet Fründ's description, Blauert argues, was anachronistic. Fründ was reflecting the witch concept as he knew it around 1450, and his chronicle thus provides us better evidence of the ideas current at the mid-century than of confessions in the Valais from 1428.[21] Blauert's argument is generally compelling and well-grounded, but it offers no explanation for the absence of diabolism from many witch trials.

I do not intend to argue that diabolism played no important role in the early witch trials. It was precisely in the study of the fifteenth-century origins of European witch hunting that the theological distinction between witch and sorcerer became so important to historians. The emergence of diabolic witchcraft was of profound importance to witch hunting in Europe. It was the role of the Devil that provided the theoretical context for mass witch hunting. The fantasy of the diabolic conspiracy gave interrogators a reason to seek denunciations; the witches' sabbath provided the structure for those denunciations. Thus in seeking the roots of the witch hunts in the fifteenth century, historians have searched especially for the roots of diabolism. Yet this has had the unfortunate side-effect of eclipsing from view those magical crimes which preceded and ran parallel to diabolic witchcraft, especially in the fifteenth century. The appearance of diabolic witchcraft is insufficient to fully explain the development of witchcraft prosecution. For all of these reasons, the definition used for *witch* in this study is much broader and more encompassing than the usual definition within historical witchcraft research. Following Wolfgang Behringer, the *witch* in this work is defined simply as a person who maliciously uses evil magic.[22]

Armed with this simpler definition of witchcraft, we quickly find that the fear of witches long predated the arrival of the diabolic witch. The chronological brackets of this study, 1430–1530, were selected to encompass roughly the first century following the introduction of the diabolic witch concept. My research soon revealed to me that the earlier prosecution of witchcraft was an important part of the story, so I have stretched back in time earlier than 1430 to gather evidence on earlier witchcraft concepts. In my last chapter I stretch forward in time, to place the developments described in the rest of this text in a longer historical context. In general, however, I have remained within the somewhat arbitrary confines of the titular century.

I begin my analysis in Chapter 1 with an essay in defining witchcraft for the specific historical context of this work. There I introduce the theological and judicial innovation of the diabolic witch as well as the indigenous witch concept that existed earlier in Basel and Lucerne. Part I presents the proper subject of the book, the urban witch trials in Basel, Nuremberg, and Lucerne. The first two cases follow a pattern common to the free cities of the Holy Roman Empire: each experienced deadly witch trials over a few generations but generally resisted the model of witch hunting followed elsewhere. Lucerne presents a quite different pattern, with hundreds of witch trials across the centuries and several distinct periods of witch hunting. The case of Lucerne in particular demands a deeper and more nuanced explanation than that offered by current models of urban witch hunting. Accordingly, as the book progresses, the initial comparison becomes less important and my emphasis shifts to explaining the unusual circumstances in Lucerne. Part II turns to the judicial context of early witch trials. Together these two chapters present the fifteenth-century transformation of criminal justice in both structure and practice. The strong coincidence between general prosecutorial zeal and the timing of witch trials makes clear the importance of this context for understanding the history of those trials. Once again, Lucerne stands out; with the long transformation to an early modern mode of criminal justice packed into a shorter period, its effects seem to have been more intense. Part III focuses in on the case of Lucerne to offer an explanation of the particular convergence of prosecutorial zeal, urban reform, social control, and witch trials that took place there. Chapter 7 is an examination of late medieval urban social control. The German cities pioneered innovations that became more widespread after the Reformation. Chapter 8 is a close analysis of the trial that opens this book, and provides a bridge between the early witch trials discussed in Part I and the later history of witch hunting in Lucerne. In the conclusion I will return to a broader focus, first discussing all three cities and then providing some reflections on the implications of this study both for witchcraft research and for our understanding of the role of witch hunts in early modern history.

1
Evil by Any Other Name: Defining Witchcraft

Over a hundred years ago, Cologne archivist Joseph Hansen essayed an answer to the question of the origins of witch hunting in Europe.[1] Hansen argued that the late medieval Inquisition essentially invented the witch doctrine: the idea of the diabolic witch who had forged a pact with the Devil and sealed it with her flesh, who flew through the night to the witches' sabbath, was the sworn enemy of ordinary society, and together with an invisible legion of other witches exercised her undying malice through individual acts of evil magic. This witch doctrine was expressed clearly in Heinrich Kramer's infamous *Malleus Maleficarum* of 1486, but had already coalesced in trials and demonology by 1440. Although Hansen's thesis has been much revised and the roles of popular ideas and secular courts have since been emphasized, an examination of the events between 1420 and 1440 lends much strength to his contention. Three interrelated events in particular, in the western Alpine region, bear examination in this regard. The first is a series of heresy trials in Fribourg, a persecution of Waldensians which metamorphosed into witch trials. The second is the anonymous *Errores Gazariorum*, a manuscript that is one of the earliest known articulations of the composite doctrine of the diabolic witch. The third is a series of witch trials in the area of Lausanne.

The persecution of Waldensians by the Inquisition was a central part of Hansen's argument. In the pursuit of Waldensians, who had taken refuge in the mountains and were able to maintain strong communities there, the Inquisition encountered folk superstitions and magical beliefs. In trying to understand such beliefs within a systemized scholastic worldview, Hansen argued, inquisitors fused sorcery and heresy into the new crime of witchcraft.[2] The Fribourg Waldensian trials allow the closest examination of how such a fusion might have played out.

Kathrin Utz Tremp has comprehensively analyzed two generations of heresy persecutions in Fribourg.[3] The words used for witches in western Switzerland heighten the ambiguity of these transitional trials; the *Vaudois* in Fribourg were first Waldensians and later witches. Because of this, the transition from heresy to witchcraft cannot be identified in the expense records, which contain the most reliable traces of these trials. Nonetheless, Utz Tremp has been able to demonstrate that elements of magic and diabolic witchcraft entered the Fribourg *vaudoisie* trials in 1429/30.[4] Still carrying with it all the baggage of heresy, the term *vaudoisie* had been definitively linked to *maleficia*, acts of harmful magic.[5]

The trials in Fribourg in 1429 and 1430 were directed by Ulric de Torrenté, inquisitor of the diocese of Lausanne. Andreas Blauert has proposed that Ulric wrote the anonymous *Errores Gazariorum*. The *Errores*, a brief manuscript with a rich description of a diabolic heretical sect, contains one of the earliest descriptions of the witches' sabbath. Blauert revises Pierrette Paravy's dating of the document between 1431 and 1437, arguing instead that the *Errores* was probably written within the circle of Lausanne inquisitors around 1438.[6] In a recent edition of key demonological texts from the fifteenth century, Martine Ostorero and Utz Tremp have resolved this controversy by dating the two extant manuscripts of the *Errores* to the two periods; the key passage which Blauert used to ascertain the later date is not present in the earlier manuscript.[7] Internal evidence makes it clear that the text was written by someone who had detailed knowledge of the early witch trials being conducted by the Dominicans of Lausanne. Of particular interest is a witch trial conducted by Ulric as inquisitor in Vevey in 1438, which included a distinctive hailstorm that made its way into the later manuscript of the *Errores*. Was Ulric de Torrenté the author of the *Errores Gazariorum*? Blauert argued that he was, and Bernard Andenmatten and Utz Tremp have recently demonstrated that he possessed a copy of the manuscript and that the witch doctrine that it expressed was one of his tools as an inquisitor. Yet their close examination of his itinerary demonstrates that he was probably not the author of the *Errores*. Ostorero has shown that the Savoyard Franciscan Ponce Feugeyron is a more likely candidate.[8]

Regardless of who wrote the *Errores*, it is clear that the manuscript was present and circulating among the inquisitors at Lausanne. The importance of the witch doctrine in that diocese can be seen from a remarkable series of trials that took place there, beginning in 1438. The records of these trials, which were conducted by the Dominican inquisitors of Lausanne, have been edited under the direction of Agostino Paravicini Bagliani at the University of Lausanne and published in the series

Cahiers lausannois d'histoire médiévale.[9] The primary source for these trials is a single, bound collection of testimonies and confessions contained in the cantonal archive of Lausanne, a source remarkably rich in detail. The elements of the witches' sabbath and especially of diabolism abound, beginning with the 1438 trial of a man named Aymonet, son of Jaquet Mangetaz. Aymonet confessed to having attended the sabbath and paid homage to the Devil.[10] Georges de Saluces, bishop of Lausanne from 1440 to 1461, played a crucial role in continuing the prosecution of diabolic witchcraft after this first trial.[11] Motivated by a desire for both moral and administrative reform and armed with a copy of the *Errores*, the bishop presided over an ongoing series of trials in which mostly male subjects were prosecuted for magic and diabolism.

Thus the excellent sources from Lausanne seem to confirm Hansen's original thesis that the crime of diabolic witchcraft was an invention of the late medieval Inquisition. To leave the story there, however, would be to ignore the key role of secular judges in the development of the crime of diabolic witchcraft during the early fifteenth century. The best evidence of this role comes from the career of Claude Tholosan, high judge in the Dauphiné from 1426 through 1449.[12] During his time as judge, Tholosan presided over the trials of 258 accused witches. In 1436, with about half of these trials already behind him, Tholosan decided to summarize his experience with the sect of the witches; this was around the same time that the *Errores Gazariorum* was being composed by an inquisitor in the diocese of Lausanne. Like the *Errores*, Tholosan's *Ut magorum et maleficiorum errores* includes a detailed description of the sect of the witches, charging them with ritual renunciation of Christianity and veneration of the Devil, gathering at a witches' sabbath, creating foul and poisonous potions, and causing infertility and sickness by means of these potions and with the aid of the Devil. Not only did Tholosan describe the witches' society as a heretical sect, he also warned that they sought converts with missionary zeal. After describing the crimes of the witches, Tholosan – an educated jurist – made the case for secular jurisdiction and the death penalty.

In light of the witch hunt that Tholosan apparently conducted, as well as the evidence of the *Ut magorum et maleficiorum errores*, it is difficult to argue that the crime of witchcraft was an invention of the Inquisition, unless the moment of that invention came earlier. At any rate, the transformation of heresy trials against Waldensians in Fribourg into witch trials around 1429 was probably not the decisive moment. The strong parallels between the *Errores Gazariorum* and the *Ut magorum et maleficiorum errores* as well as their near-simultaneous authorship lead me to believe that their authors were both drawing on a pre-existing tradition, a development which is lost to us.

A third treatment of the question of witches that was written at the same time as the *Errores* and *Ut magorum* offers some insight into what that development may have been. This was the *Formicarius* of Johannes Nider, at the time a Dominican prior in Basel.[13] Nider's *Formicarius* was not primarily a treatment of witchcraft or demonology. It was a theological treatise on spiritual dangers of all kinds, and Nider's primary purpose – even in discussing the threat of witchcraft – was to call each believer to personal, spiritual reform, not to advocate the prosecution of witches.[14] That a discussion of witchcraft even enters into Nider's *Formicarius* is probably an indication of how current the subject was at the time, especially at the religious and intellectual hub of the Council of Basel. Indeed, in Nider's treatment of witchcraft it is clear that he was not drawing on his own experiences but on those of acquaintances and on matters of public knowledge.

Unlike Tholosan and the author of the *Errores Gazariorum*, both of whom drew upon events of the immediate past, Nider referred to cases from the preceding forty years. Some of the best known stories he tells of witchcraft – stories which Kramer later re-told in the *Malleus* – were related to him by his friend Peter of Greyerz. The Upper Simme Valley in the territory of Bern, where Greyerz had been a judge as a young man, was "the scene of the first Alpine witch trials," in the words of Arno Borst.[15] Borst argues that at the root of these trials lay the loss of economic independence for the farmers in the Upper Simme Valley, as they converted from mixed agriculture to husbanding cattle at the end of the fourteenth century, as well as a simultaneous transformation of political relations as the valley was brought under the control of the city of Bern. It was at that time, around 1400, that Greyerz was appointed as the Bernese governor of the area, in which capacity he oversaw a series of witch trials.[16]

There are at least two layers to the story as Nider related it in the *Formicarius*. On the one hand there are events which probably had taken place in the Simme Valley over thirty years earlier; on the other there are elements which Andreas Blauert argues were added later, either by Greyerz or by Nider himself. The trials in the Simme Valley apparently began with a single man called Staedelin. Staedelin was considered a sorcerer by his neighbors, who suspected him of manipulating the weather and magically stealing crops. Staedelin's relationship with other sorcerers, as first introduced, does not reflect the stereotype of diabolic witchcraft that developed in the fifteenth century. Greyerz claimed that Staedelin had learned sorcery from a certain Hippo, who in turn had been taught by a man called Scabius. The two older sorcerers were apparently dead by the time of Staedelin's trial, Scabius having been murdered by his enemies. Accused by his neighbors, Staedelin was tried and confessed under torture to invocation of demons, weather sorcery, and magical theft of crops.[17] This trial probably took place, even as Nider related it.

Peter of Greyerz, however, also reported having burned numerous witches, members of a diabolic sect. These witches purportedly confessed to having murdered children, committed cannibalism, venerated the Devil, and engaged in dark sorcery. These elements reflect the hereticized witchcraft of two generations later. Andreas Blauert has argued that the diabolic witchcraft was interpolated by Nider, who infused Greyerz's stories with current ideas.[18] There is, however, no need to imagine that the multiple burnings of members of a diabolic sect were invented; a persecution of Waldensians in the territory of Bern in 1399 included many victims "in the city and the countryside." The only element which may have been added was the ascription of sorcery to these heretics. The diabolism of which they were accused was already an established theme in the late medieval persecution of heretics.[19]

Where does this leave the so-called first Alpine witch trials? For one, the story from Greyerz demonstrates that accusations of diabolism against heretics could easily be fused with sorcery. More interesting, however, is the sorcery trial which lies at the heart of Greyerz's recollections. Staedelin, and Scabius before him, were feared and persecuted by their neighbors. The black magic of which they were suspected was believed to be the cause of the primary evils suffered by the peasants: failed crops, devastating hailstorms, loss of livestock, and stillborn children. The absence of the diabolic sect from witch trials before the 1430s did not mean the absence of evil. It is the continuity between the fear and persecution of men like Staedelin and the witch trials of the second half of the fifteenth century which form the proper subject of this work, rather than the intervening development of diabolic witchcraft.

Defining witchcraft can be difficult; it has a tendency to slip out from under the best made definitions. Local beliefs in early modern Europe were highly various, and in practice the influence of demonology could be slight. In addressing this problem, historians of the European witch hunts have settled on a definition of witchcraft that works well for the purposes of scholarship, a definition that provides categories into which various cases can be fit. Scholars have adopted the idea of witchcraft that had emerged in the witch doctrine of the 1430s. Witchcraft under this rubric is necessarily conceived of as diabolic in nature, although not all the elements of the diabolic witch stereotype must be present. In the absence of the Devil, cases of maleficent magic are referred to simply as sorcery.

There are numerous problems with this handy dichotomy, however. It fails to explain, for example, the absence of diabolism in many witch trials. Despite this absence, the danger of execution (at least after the mid-fifteenth century) was quite real. For the early trials, one might argue that the paucity of descriptive sources is partially to blame for the Devil's truancy. Many of the cases which make up the material examined for this book lack both witness testimonies and confessions; the only evidence we have of them is mere notations in council minutes or city expense books. Even if we assume, however, that diabolism was present in similar proportions in these sketchy cases as in those for which we possess witness testimonies or confessions, this still only accounts for about half of the cases.[20] During the mid-fifteenth century, in many parts of the German-speaking Alpine regions, banishment began to give way to execution as the standard punishment for sorcery and witchcraft. Yet the diabolism of the witch doctrine cannot explain this shift, because diabolism was not considered necessary to justify a death sentence.

This ambiguity over the definition of the capital crime of witchcraft also appeared in the normative realm of law. One ground for the execution of a witch was indeed heresy. The punishment for a non-repentant heretic was death and because of the extreme nature of the heresy of witchcraft, the death penalty was in theory extended to all witch-heretics.[21] Yet the death penalty was also firmly grounded in the crime of harmful magic, and sorcery had been punishable with death throughout the Middle Ages.[22] This continued to be the case during the early modern period, as demonstrated by the imperial law code of Charles V (*Carolina*) in 1532:

> 109. Item if anyone harms people or causes damages through sorcery, they shall be condemned to death and this punishment shall be executed with fire. Yet whoever uses sorcery but causes harm to no one should be punished differently.[23]

From the qualification in the second sentence, it is clear that the death sentence was grounded in the *harm* caused by the sorcery. Sorcery which did not cause harm, although criminal and subject to punishment, was not considered a capital crime in the *Carolina*. From a legal standpoint, heresy was not necessary to justify the death penalty for witchcraft, as long as harm was demonstrated to the satisfaction of the court.

Thus while many historians of early modern witchcraft have chosen to firmly maintain a definitional distinction between *witchcraft* and *sorcery* that hinges upon the role of diabolism in the former, I contend that this dichotomy is limiting. In this book I will be using a broader definition of witchcraft, one that encompasses trials that took place at both the beginning and the end of the fifteenth century. Following Wolfgang Behringer, the *witch* in this work is defined simply as *a person believed to accomplish evil through supernatural means*. It is not my intention to elide the crucial innovations that brought diabolism into cases of witchcraft, but to examine that transformation within broader continuities. The argument for using a broader definition of witchcraft is based on three main points.[24]

The first lies in the language itself. The German word for sorcerer (*Zauberer*) was frequently used in cases involving diabolism. Conversely, the word for witch (*Hexe*) predated the emergence of the diabolic stereotype of the witch doctrine, and was one of the primary terms used in the Swiss German of Basel and Lucerne. The other common term for witch in Swiss German, *Unholde*, does not appear in the early sources of Basel and Lucerne and may have been an import.

The word *Hexe* made its first known appearance in a judicial context in the Rhine-Alpine region when it appeared in Schaffhausen as an insult that resulted in slander cases during the late fourteenth century.[25] In Lucerne, *Hexe* first appeared in a slander case from 1419.[26] That *Hexe* was a potentially deadly insult even during this period is demonstrated by a case from Schaffhausen from 1402/3. The city expense books record a cost of five shillings "for dry wood for the witch burning."[27] In Basel, *Hexe* first appeared in the records in 1433, around the time that the witch doctrine was coalescing, but not only was the Devil absent from the case, the narrative it contains of a wolf-riding witch provides key evidence of the indigenous, pre-diabolic witch concept in the region.[28] Although sources prior to the early fifteenth century are extremely sparse, we have no reason to believe that the word *Hexe* did not have deep roots in the region. In his classic analysis of the history of the word, Johannes Franck included a passage from Heinrich Wittenwiler's fifteenth-century work *Der Ring*. There, witches appear in true Alpine form, riding on the backs of wolves; Wittenwiler's witches were *Häxen*.[29] Why should we refuse the name which contemporaries used for a particular phenomenon in favor of a cleaner, retrospectively imposed distinction between witch and sorcerer?

The second reason to expand the definition of witchcraft lies in the variability of the witch trials. The narrow definition of witchcraft currently used by scholars creates a formal distinction between trials in which diabolism played a role and those in which it was absent. In the fifteenth century, at least, this distinction did not always exist in judicial practice; it has been imposed retroactively by the historian. In so doing, we eclipse the continuities and commonalities that existed between magical crimes that were imagined in conjunction with diabolism and those that were not. In Lucerne, the charges against Dorothea Hindremstein in 1454 were similar to those levied against Else from Meersburg around 1450.[30] Both women were accused of using magic to harm people with whom they had come into conflict; while Dorothea was believed to cause people and livestock to fall ill, Else confessed to having used weather magic to accomplish her revenge. Their trials took place under the same jurisdiction around the same time, they were believed to have used magic for similar purposes and to similar end, and they were both condemned to be burned. Should we categorize their crimes as fundamentally different because of the addition of one element, Else's confessed relationship with the Devil?

It is quite possible that Dorothea did confess to diabolism, although the evidence is lost to us. Given the state of early modern sources in general, and of fifteenth-century sources in particular, the absence of Dorothea's confession raises serious problems for a historian seeking to classify her within the witch-sorcerer dichotomy. Should we assume that she confessed to diabolism because she was burned, ignoring the fact that this punishment was not reserved exclusively for magicians who confessed such? Or should we blithely assume that the extant evidence tells the whole story and call her a sorcerer? Aside from the methodological counterfactual, the problem is simply that the approach assigns overweening and distracting importance to a single issue – the role of the Devil – that appears to have played no role whatsoever in the origins of suspicion or the motives for formal accusation.

This leads to the third reason for expanding the definition of witchcraft beyond the witch/sorcerer dichotomy: to facilitate the analysis of the prosecution of maleficent magic during the fifteenth century without predetermining from the outset a search for the appearance of diabolism as the fundamental change. Diabolism certainly was important to the witch hunts in Europe. The fantasy of diabolic conspiracy gave interrogators a reason to seek denunciations; when present, the witches' sabbath provided the structure for these denunciations. It is because of this that in seeking the origins of the witch hunts in the fifteenth century, historians have searched for diabolism in particular. This has had the unfortunate side effect of eclipsing from view those magical crimes that preceded and ran parallel to diabolic witchcraft, especially in the fifteenth century. Restoring the various forms of maleficent magic to their shared context of judicial prosecution opens the question of the origins of witchcraft prosecution to new modes of inquiry and new interpretive insights.

Beneath the broad umbrella I have proposed for *witchcraft* were a number of distinct categories of persons. Several versions of the diabolic witch were among these, as were ritual magicians, village sorceresses, and various indigenous witches, such as the Alpine witch that encompassed the roles of storm caller, wolf rider, milk stealer, and child killer. Diabolism transformed local ideas of witchcraft over the course of many decades, grafting diabolic elements onto indigenous witch concepts, first in simple, then in increasingly complex forms. Throughout this transformation, however, local ideas of witchcraft persisted. They continued to dominate in accusations and to shape the confessions of the accused witches themselves.

Diabolic witchcraft grafted relatively easily onto indigenous witchcraft concepts for several reasons. First of all, the shift to diabolism did not require a substantial shift in the conceptualization of witches and their activities. It was the addition of a new character to an old narrative, and there were plenty of folk narrative models available to accommodate this addition.[31] Secondly, the narrative of diabolic evil that was being melded to local ideas of witchcraft was a very old narrative, one which described a chthonic nexus of evil and applied it definitionally to minority religious groups. Although our best sources for the history of this chthonic nexus are literary and legal, its very ancientness, combined with its presence in medieval trials against heretics and Jews, ensures that it had some currency, in some form, in the imagination of the broader populace by the fifteenth century. The third reason for the ease with which local witchcraft ideas accommodated the addition of diabolism was the recursive nature of the demonological discourse on witchcraft, by which indigenous ideas were first drawn into demonological discourse and then reflected back in demonology as it was applied to local trials. Because the material of the diabolic stereotype was drawn from local beliefs as well as from older literary traditions, it found easy confirmation, at least in part, in contemporary witchcraft accusations.

A fourth reason, and the one I will mainly concentrate on here, is that demonological and indigenous ideas of witchcraft shared a conceptual resonance. They made sense together.

The large witch hunts that had taken place during the second quarter of the fifteenth century represented the first massive actuation of the diabolic idea of witchcraft that was to change the European concept of witchcraft forever.[32] The first of these witch hunts was that which took place in the Dauphiné, beginning in 1424 and continuing well into the 1440s. This witch hunt encompassed some 258 trials and was conducted under the auspices of the secular government. As mentioned in the Introduction above, the head judge who oversaw these trials, Claude Tholosan, wrote a treatise justifying the active role of the secular government in the punishment of witches and describing their crimes. The first of these was apostasy:

> These people swear that those who enter their sect deny God [...] they raise their hands or some other thing and swear to renounce the laws of God and their faith, no longer believing in the articles of faith or the sacraments of the church.[33]

Having denied God, the witches in Tholosan's description worshipped the Devil instead, murdering children, creating evil potions and powders from human flesh, and at the Devil's command and with his assistance committing all manner of harmful magic.

Similar details also emerged during the witch hunt in the Savoy between 1434 and 1449. The anonymous *Errores Gazariorum* was written during the early years of this witch hunt, and in it the elements found in Tholosan's treatise appear again. Apostasy and Devil worship are followed by murder and cannibalistic concoctions:

> And mixing these drippings from the dead man on the gallows with the inner parts of dead children and those of poisonous animals, they make another ointment with the help of the Devil, of which the touch alone can kill people.[34]

This element of murder and cannibalism was taken further in other reports. Around 1436, Johannes Nider included such details in his descriptions of the new crime of diabolic witchcraft in his *Formicarius*. He wrote of having spoken with an inquisitor who told him "that in the duchy of Lausanne certain witches even devoured their own children."[35] Presumably Nider had been in direct conversation with the author of the *Errores*.

Apostasy, veneration of the Devil, and the completion of heinous and bizarre ritual abominations at his command all served to explain the power of witches to harm others. As they did later in the Dauphiné and Savoy, these elements of diabolic witchcraft may have appeared in a massive early witch hunt in the Valais between 1428 and 1434. Unfortunately, our only source testifying to diabolism in these trials is a report from the Lucerne chronicler Hans Fründ, who wrote a generation later. Andreas Blauert contends that the diabolism present in the report was an addition, a product of Fründ's understanding of witchcraft in the 1450s.[36] Fründ emphasized the role of the Devil, whom he referred to as the evil spirit, as the source of the witches' power:

> The evil spirit taught them this malice and murder, and gave them the power that those people with whom they had enmity or were angry, whom they threatened or cursed, might from that hour on suffer some trouble, that some become ill, others lame in their limbs, also that they might become mad, some blind, some lose their children.[37]

This was the essence of the new concept of witchcraft: the diabolic witch gained the power to commit harm through the veneration of the Devil, as sealed through heinous acts such as cannibalism.

The demonological concept of the witch wedded popular ideas not only to the Devil but to an entire collection of evils, an ancient conceptual association of murder and cannibalism, the worship of evil, deviant sex, and darkness. This conceptual nexus predated the Christian era and was part of the mental world of the Romans, who were deeply suspicious of secretive groups. The Romans suspected the early Christians of all those evils that the Christians would later ascribe to heretics and witches: that they secretly worshipped evil, engaged in orgies of deviant sex, and consumed the flesh of infants.[38] The conceptual nexus reappeared in the heresy trial of ten canons as Manichaeans in 1022 in Orléans, and recurred in accusations against heretics throughout the high and late Middle Ages.[39] These same elements reappeared in treatises on witchcraft in the early fifteenth century. In the *Errores Gazariorum*, ritual orgy figures prominently in the witches' sabbath:

> This most evil of banquets having been completed, the presiding devil cries out that the lights be extinguished and yells "Mestlet, Mestlet." After they have heard this command they join themselves carnally, a single man with a woman or a single man with another

man, sometimes father with daughter, some with mother, brother with sister, and the natural order is little observed.[40]

Despite the early date of the *Errores Gazariorum*, however, such a concept of the sexualized witches' sabbath was not widespread in the fifteenth century. Accused witches were occasionally brought to confess sexual indecencies, usually with their personal demons, and sometimes as a general condemnation of lifestyle. Ritual orgy as such did not appear outside the demonological descriptions and possibly the trials they directly describe.

Similarly, the gathering of witches mentioned in the literature of the early witch hunts, the synagogue or witches' sabbath, was largely absent from other fifteenth-century witch trials. The witches' sabbath appeared in the *Errores Gazariorum*, "when all are assembled at the synagogue,"[41] and is implied by the "sect" which Tholosan mentioned. The report of Hans Fründ regarding the events in the Valais included a staggering evaluation of the extent of the diabolic conspiracy: "They said [...] that altogether there were 700 of them in the sect."[42] In Martin le Franc's 1440 poem *Le Champion des dames*, the Adversary says:

> It's true. I've heard it. I believe it, that not just two or three old women, but more than three thousand, go together to seek out their familiar demons.[43]

Yet in witch trials throughout German-speaking Switzerland and north-ward into Upper Germany, such a vast conspiracy was rarely suspected. Instead, the accused confessed that they went individually or in twos and threes to meet with their personal devils. As with ritual orgy, the idea of a vast conspiracy was incompatible with the indigenous witch concept of these regions, and it would be over a century before its full effects were manifested in the great witch hunts of the late sixteenth century. If the diabolic witch stereotype had been rigorously applied in places like Basel and Lucerne, it might have failed. Since, however, both judges and the accused had an interest in creating a narrative that made sense, the elements drawn from the stereotype of the diabolic witch were those that were most compatible with the indigenous concept of witchcraft.

Indigenous ideas of witchcraft were highly local in early modern Europe, but there seems to have been a fairly cohesive, shared concept of witchcraft throughout much of the German Alps and down into the valley of the Upper Rhine and Lake Constance. Because certain aspects of this concept were strongly linked to the circumstances of the mountainous landscape, I use the term "Alpine witch" as a shorthand for the concept shared in this part of the Rhine-Alpine region. It would, however, be a mistake to assume that the same characteristics dominated throughout the Alps. The Franco-Germanic linguistic border, the contrasting political culture of the urban cantons and the Grey Leagues, and the different circumstances on the upper Alpine slopes as opposed to the valleys were all reflected in the cultural geography of witch beliefs. Even within the region, other concepts of evil magicians had currency, particularly in urban centers. The urban concerns with ritual black magic on the one hand and divinatory fraud on the other were shared by Basel and Nuremberg. It is not my intention to map out a full cultural geography here, but only to sketch out one broad element within it, the Alpine witch who dominated the fears of ordinary people in Basel and Lucerne and throughout the region from which most fifteenth-century demonologists were drawing their material.

The only near-universal element of witchcraft was harmful magic. Fear of supernatural harm was of crucial importance to the demonological concept of witchcraft as well as local witch concepts throughout Europe. Within this general rubric, however, some elements of *maleficia* appear more commonly in some regions than in others. Witchcraft was one possible explanation for all manner of domestic tragedies, from the sudden illness of a child to the death of a husband. In areas like the territory of Lucerne, where the husbandry of cattle was crucial to personal subsistence, sick and foundered livestock were often cited as a source of witchcraft suspicion. In particular, when a cow stopped giving milk or a suffered an infection and gave bloody milk, this might be interpreted as witchcraft. Like other aspects of the indigenous Alpine witch stereotype, this precipitated into demonological literature. Heinrich Kramer described witches stealing milk by means of sympathetic magic (milking a knife handle) with the aid of their demons.

In addition to being attributed with causing domestic ills such as bovine mastitis, the Alpine witch was strongly associated with the powerful dangers of the wild. A strong association existed between witches and wolves. Witches were believed to be wolf riders, and the mere association of a woman with wolves might mark her as a witch. In the late fifteenth century, wolves were regarded as a constant danger; the city of Basel, for example, offered a standing bounty on wolf pelts. The fear inspired by this real danger could also be activated with supernatural overtones. In 1433, a man provided the authorities in Basel with a harrowing tale of a close encounter with a witch. According to his testimony:

> He saw [...] Gerin Kolerin of Buckten riding toward him on a wolf. The wolf went its own way and she sat on its back holding its fur in her hand. [...] He was so frightened that he trembled [...] and wanted to hide. [...] When asked if he knew anyone [else] who could give testimony he said [...] there was a priest [who] said that a witch dwelt three houses down from the inn in Laufelfingen. [44]

Wolf riding and the rumor of being a witch reinforced each other; if a woman were seen with wolves this greatly strengthened the suspicion of witchcraft. Even in literary sources from the Lake Constance region the witch as wolf rider emerges clearly in the early fifteenth century, as seen in the example from Wittenwiler cited above. This comes out clearly in Wittenwiler's description of the leader of the witches in the climactic battle of his farce:

> Frau Hächel's wolf was so enchanted, that no one there could wound either [Hächel or her wolf] in any way. [...] No one could unseat her; this she had accomplished with her sorcery. [...] Later a dwarf named Trintsch came [...] and threw a net over both she and the wolf, I know not how, and then the others were upon them and strangled them both. [...] So the banner of the witches fell.[45]

As the story of the Laufelfingen witch demonstrates, however, the association of witches and wolves was not merely a narrative or literary trope. People claimed to have seen real witches on the backs of real wolves. In 1499, a witness in a Lucerne witch trial testified that one evening as he brought his cows in from pasture, he had seen the suspected witch "riding on a wolf across the long field."[46] Eye witness testimonies of wolf riding were fairly rare, but the association of witches and wolves was a recurring concern of witnesses and accusers.

When accusers lacked an eye witness to the complicity of witchcraft suspects and wolves, they found evidence in less obvious tales. In 1489, in Lucerne, a witness told of an encounter between a suspected witch and hunters. The hunters told how they had been on the trail of two wolves. They had just chased the wolves into a steep valley with a stream, hoping no doubt to trap them, when the wolves unexpectedly escaped. When some of the hunters went into the ravine to see how the wolves had escaped they found an old woman standing there. They asked her what she was doing "in that hole in the wilderness," and she began to curse at them. The hunters later identified the woman they had encountered with the suspect, Peter Kündig's mother, saying they were terribly afraid of her and wanted her to leave the country.[47]

The way in which this tale of a failed wolf hunt became charged with negative supernatural power indicates the importance of combating the Alpine wolves. The threat posed by real wolves in the mountainous terrain was certainly significant. In the French Jura, the presence and dangers of wolves seems to have contributed to werewolf beliefs.[48] It is possible that the story of Peter Kündig's mother was a werewolf tale, that it was she the hunters had chased into the valley in wolf shape. In the German-speaking Alps, however, the concept of the werewolf was rarely if ever explicit.[49] It is more likely that Peter's mother was suspected of being in league with the wolves, as were other wolf-riding witches.

Descriptions of wolf riding used the term "bluot schend," which was more commonly used for incest and was thus charged with all the horror of taboo violation. Willem de Blécourt argues accordingly that wolf riding may stand metaphorically for mother-son incest.[50] If this were so, however, and if the metaphor were transparent in the fifteenth century, this would certainly have stained Peter Kündig's honor. Although we do not know what became of his mother, Peter was later a member of the great council of Lucerne. There is no evidence that he ever had to defend his own reputation from charges of sexual impropriety. Although a reference to incest is clearly implied in the use of the same term for wolf riding, the main implication of this seems to have been that wolf riding was perverse and evil. The alliance of a woman with wolves was, like incest, a deep violation of the perceived natural order of things.

As Kieckhefer noted thirty years ago, the purpose of the wolf riding remains obscure in the sources. While demonologists would later interpret the presence of wolves as diabolic – a demon in the form of a wolf – there is no indication in the cases from Basel and Lucerne that the wolves who travelled with witches were anything but wolves. The indigenous association of the witch with the wolf mirrored the demonological association of the witch and the Devil, who was often imagined as a marginal man, a traveler, wanderer, or outlaw, a dweller in the spaces between the settled lands. This affinity between wolf and Devil may have contributed to the ease with which the diabolic concept of witchcraft was adopted and adapted in the region.

In 1532, three women were arrested as witches in the city of Basel. Their names were Dilge Glaserin, Agnes Salate, and Ita Lichtermut. There were few witch trials in Basel, and extensive confessions survive for only a small handful of them; the case of Dilge, Agnes, and Ita is one.[51] The case register begins with a record of Dilge's tale of her seduction by the Devil. As she related it, the trouble began twenty-four or twenty-five years earlier, around the time that her sister Ursula was drowned as a criminal and her first husband had died, leaving her destitute with six small children. No-one would help her, she said, not even her in-laws. At that time, she suffered so greatly from despair that she thought to kill herself but, through the grace of God, abstained from doing so. It was then that the Devil came to her in the form of a young man and said, "Dilge, how did it happen that you despise yourself, how can you do this? If you will turn to me, and do as I tell you, I will give you and your children enough to eat and drink."[52] When she asked him who he was, he answered her saying he was the Devil and his name was Frank. He spoke so kindly to her, and promised so much, that Dilge denied God and gave herself to the devil called Frank, taking him as her lover and serving him.

What a gentle Devil, and how ordinary his appearance! Dilge reported no sulfurous odors or goat's feet, no infamous kiss nor ornate rituals. Her devil looked more like an ordinary man who posed ordinary dangers. Although the Devil Frank offered what looked like a clandestine marriage (he would take care of her and provide for her if she gave herself to him) he ultimately abandoned her and failed in his promise to provide.

When Dilge and her two accomplices recounted their supposed witcheries, the tale became darker. The stories of all three converged under a cherry tree, where they said they met to plan some of their witchcraft. No longer were they ordinary, lonely, despairing women. Under the cherry tree they spoke of a supernaturally insatiable hunger, of wanting to eat all the birds in the land, drink all the wine and devour all the fruit. With the aid of their demon lovers they devastated the land with hailstorms, caused livestock to sicken and die, and injured their personal enemies.

Ita's confession adopts this darker vein in its entirety.[53] She was the third witch deposed, and the record contains no tale of her seduction. Indeed, the Devil, "her lover," is rarely mentioned. When she described a gathering of witches for hail raising, she was accompanied instead by a wolf, upon whose back she rode. She had met the wolf under a willow tree, and she said she always brought him food and stroked him on the back with her hand before she rode him. A postscript to Ita's confession (recorded in a different hand) explicitly mentions "her lover, the Devil," presumably in human form, who warned her not to speak to anyone of her witchcraft.[54] In the bulk of her narrative, however, the wolf appeared with her in situations in which the other two accused witches reported being accompanied by their demon lovers. Although in other times and places this wolf might easily have been interpreted as the Devil in animal form, this connection was never made. Ita's wolf was a direct reflection of the dominant indigenous witch concept.

Ita's relationship with her wolf was the older layer in the confession narratives of the three accused witches. The Devil had been grafted onto the local witch concept over the previous century. In Ita's tale he is still little more than an addendum, but in the confessions of the other two, the Devil-as-man figures prominently. In Dilge's tale the Devil appears as a seductive stranger, and this was the dominant mode of the integration of diabolism into witchcraft confessions in Basel and Lucerne.

In analyzing witchcraft seduction narratives, Lyndal Roper has noted that many are "cynically realistic about power between women and men." The Devil seduces, but he does not provide. His smooth words are soon revealed to have been in bad faith. As Roper puts it, "The Devil is a heartless young male seducer who seems to understand the woman's despair, but then leaves her in the lurch."[55] As such, the seducing Devil is modeled after the young men – from journeymen through soldiers and various more marginal rogues – whose occupations sent them travelling through the early modern world. Their mobility released them from the social constraints that would have bound them to the women they seduced if they had been settled in a single place and the seduction a matter of general rumor. At times there seems almost to be a plague of such young men.

In 1577 Verena Büttlerin was arrested in Lucerne on an accusation of having stolen money entrusted to her.[56] Tortured at least six times, she repeatedly insisted that she had stolen nothing, but had misunderstood about the money entrusted to her. After many rounds of questioning on the subject of the money, however, she began what reads like a witches' seduction narrative:

> Saturday the 14th of June, Verena Büttlerin was questioned again. She testified that approximately 20 years ago she spent the night in

an inn at Ebikon [...] a man came into her room and lay with her in the bed. She said, who is there? He answered, Herr Jakob of Luthern, saying, I will give you a fat penny if you let me lie with you. Then he [...] was about to have his way with her, but she felt that he was cold. This startled her so that she blessed herself and he disappeared. A few days later as she was on her way to Bern, she was weeping in the woods. A man approached her on a cream-colored horse saying, do not weep, I will give you enough money. She blessed herself and he disappeared. [Later] a man came to her in black clothes saying, I am the one who wanted to give you a fat penny. She did not acknowledge him but instead blessed herself. Thereafter, where ever she went she was always being accosted [by such men], but she never acquiesced, and she did not know whether it was Herr Jakob or another.[57]

In Verena's tale there was no escape from the Devil's attempts at seduction. No matter how often she refused him, he came again and again, insisting that she give in to him. Perhaps in this case the Devil was a reflection of Verena's experience with the interrogator. Later that day he questioned her again, and she confessed to having given in to the Devil and having asked him to cause a destructive frost; the following Monday she provided a classic witchcraft confession, complete with hailstorms and apostasy. Despite having resisted six rounds of torture, Verena Büttlerin died at the stake.

But what of her Devil? He appeared in so many guises that she said she never knew if it was him or not. The story gives us a sense of some of the dangers confronting a woman traveling alone, the many ways in which she might be victimized by well-seeming strangers. Verena's refusals indicated that she recognized such men for what they most likely were: regardless of their honor otherwise, they were simply there to take advantage of her. But a darker possibility lurked behind such tales as her encounter with the mounted stranger in the woods. Such strangers might be other travelers, or they might have been outlaws who lived in the wilderness and preyed on travelers passing through. A terrifying tale of such an encounter was told from the other side by convicted robber Durss Nagel in 1508:

He [..] confessed how he and [his companions] had raped a pregnant woman in a forest above Solothurn, and then beat her to death, cut her open, took the child out and tossed the head back and forth between them. The woman had been dressed in a blue cloak and a smock.[58]

It is impossible to know whether Durss and his companions actually committed the horrific crime he described, but in telling his tale he was reflecting and reinforcing the image of the outlaw as rapacious, bloodthirsty, and lawless. The spectrum between seductive strangers and bloody outlaws was fluid; some confessing criminals described lives in which they moved easily between such categories with simple tricks of presentation.

The Devil was an outlaw in the most fundamental and direct sense, of course, having been exiled from heaven in an act reflected in the banishment of outlaws from community. The connection between wolves and outlaws was similarly strong and direct. In Old English, "to cry a wolf's head" meant to declare someone an outlaw. The outlaw was literally to be hunted like the wolf, as a dangerous enemy of the community. Similarly, in German, the Grimm brothers noted that "wolf" was used as a term for outlaws, bandits, and predatory men generally.[59] In the early modern world, wolves and outlaws quite literally shared residence in the wild, uncultivated stretches between inhabited areas. Wolves and outlaws shared the same wild terrain, and threatened ordinary people with similarly destructive appetites. Conceptually, metaphorically, and analogically, the images of the two were interchangeable. Like the Devil, wolves and outlaws were embodiments of evil and, like the men that Verena and others described, they were solidly real embodiments of evil, within the experienced world. All three of these categories were mutually reinforcing conceptions of evil.

This analogical argument cannot explain why the diabolic concept of witchcraft was adopted into the local witchcraft ideas at the time and in the manner it was, but it does help explain the particular choice of the seducing Devil at the expense of other elements of the diabolic stereotype. It also demonstrates one reason that the indigenous witchcraft beliefs of the region were so easily accommodated into the developing narrative of diabolism. Local ideas made important contributions to the demonological understanding of witchcraft. The motif of wolf riding, apparently idiosyncratic to the small region under discussion here, fell out of the witch stereotype as it traveled to other regions, but another regional characteristic remained important: hail raising.

Wolves and outlaws were not the only dangers posed by the mountain landscape. The Alpine zone – or more accurately the sub-Alpine zone (the fertile valleys around the great Alpine lakes) – is particularly susceptible to hail. Several geological factors contribute to these meteorological conditions: Mountainous regions in general are prone to hail because the slopes produce strong updrafts, one of the necessary conditions for hailstorms. Moreover, mid-latitude regions with strong thunderstorms and pronounced seasons are more likely to suffer damaging hailstorms, due to the greater temperature differentials possible between the upper and lower atmosphere, a factor slightly but perhaps crucially exacerbated by the persistent warming effect of the lakes. Farther up in the Alpine reaches, witches were more likely to be accused of calling avalanches than hailstorms; in coastal areas of England and Scotland, for a greater contrast, witches were occasionally accused of raising storms at sea. The natural disasters of which witches were accused generally accorded with those most common in the region.

Hail making and weather magic in general appeared in the *Errores Gazariorum* and other early demonological texts as a particular power of the diabolic witch, and this has contributed to a tendency for scholars to discuss weather magic in conjunction with diabolism. Historians of the sixteenth- and seventeenth-century witch hunts often focus on the collective nature of storm raising, further linking it to the particular aspects of the diabolic witch stereotype that had the power to drive mass witch hunts. In describing weather magic in Swabian Austria and the Electorate of Trier, Johannes Dillinger has written that it was almost always imagined as a collective act of the witches, intensifying persecutions.[60] In some cases, this collective storm raising took place at the sabbath, and this image in particular seems to have caught hold of the scholarly imagination. Wolfgang Behringer has taken the link between weather magic and collective action one step further. Because the damage wrought by storms was collective, he asserts, disastrous weather events triggered mass persecutions of witches; the collective nature of storm raising is thus linked causally to the phenomenon of mass witch hunting.[61] Yet, as we shall see, the early Alpine weather witch was usually imagined as acting alone by those who feared her. Thus I would argue something closer to the reverse of Behringer's contention: that weather magic came to be imagined as a collective act in order to accommodate a regionally particular element of witchcraft to the context of mass witch hunting across diverse cultural geographies.

The original Alpine weather witch was a mainly solitary creature, a woman driven by anger to raise hail and smite her enemies. Such was Else of Meersburg, who was tried in Lucerne around 1450. In her confession, Else told of an encounter with a lecherous vagrant, apparently on an isolated road. Angered by the man's attempted sexual assault, she said, she cursed the beggar and called hail in hopes that it might strike him.[62]

Else's case is well known; hers was the first case in Lucerne to bear the unmistakable traces of the diabolical witch stereotype that had emerged during the preceding generation in the francophonic region of western Switzerland. It also came at the beginning of a long and unremitting history of witch trials in Lucerne, many of which included elements of diabolism.

Although most of Else's witchcraft was committed in solitude, we also find the beginnings of collective weather magic in her case. In her confession she mentions meeting other witches to discuss and commit harmful magic.

> These same women and she also raised a great hailstorm seven years ago, because their 13 companions complained saying the Confederation had ruined them, so they should also bring ruin. It happened in Menznau.[63]

At least one of Else's supposed accomplices, Margret Jägerin, was also arrested. As had Else, Margret reported gathering with a group of other witches on several occasions; each time they met together during the Ember Days. The number of witches varied from twelve to sixteen, but their purpose was always the same, to raise a hailstorm. "During the Christmas Ember Days, the 16 witches gathered together near Schaffhausen under a linden tree and discussed how to destroy the earth with hail and floods, but their numbers were insufficient." On another occasion they were more successful: "The 12 witches gathered and attempted to make a great hailstorm, but they did not wish to send it over the Confederation, and so directed the storm up the land over Basel, Strasbourg, and Wissenburg."[64] Although Margret reported that a demon was also present on at least one of these instances, he seems to have played no active role in the weather magic. The council of witches were the primary actors.

Even when the weather making of witches is framed as a collective act, however, in the details of the sorcery we find traces of the old solitary weather witch. Dillinger's Swabian-Austrian witches kicked over a urine-filled pot to stir up dangerous storms, a simple act of sympathetic magic that could have as easily been accomplished by one witch as by a diabolical convocation. The sixteenth-century French judge and demonologist Nicholas Remy opened his discussion of weather magic with the testimony of some two hundred witches, who asserted that "on certain set days it was their custom to meet together by the bank of some pool or river" to stir up hailstorms.[65] As Remy proceeded to give examples of weather magic, however, the details resolved into individual acts. One witch, for example, "went apart to a thickly wooded place where she dug a hole with her hands, filled it with water and kept stirring this with her finger until a thick cloud grew up and arose from it."[66] It would seem that although the collective nature of weather magic and storm damages became important both to the conceptualization of diabolic witchcraft and to the dynamics of persecution, the individual storm witch persisted. It is probable that in the original, indigenous understanding, the weather witch acted alone.

It would appear, moreover, that the belief in weather witches was particularly strong in mountainous regions. William Monter noted this in his study of the francophonic Jura. Examining mainly sixteenth-century cases, Monter describes the persistence of hail raising in witchcraft confessions across the region. Accusations of storm raising even appeared (though with less frequency) in Protestant states, where we would expect the negative stance of such Protestant figures as Tübingen theologian Johannes Brenz on the question of weather magic to have undermined the charge.[67] Monter's observation of the importance of storm raising to French Swiss witchcraft beliefs bears out for German-speaking Alpine regions as well. From the region of Basel we have evidence of a pre-diabolic, indigenous, popular association of witches and hailstorms. This evidence emerged during the 1450–51 trial of Gret Fröhlicherin in the city of Basel, which has been transcribed and analyzed at length by Dorothee Rippmann.[68] The significant mention of hailstorms appeared during Gret's first trial. One witness reported a conversation with another woman named Birine, after Gret and a number of other women had been arrested. In this third-hand context (the scribe recording in the third person the testimony of a woman reporting the words of another) we have Birine's comment on her role in denouncing or accusing the women under arrest. Opening with a common gutter oath, Birine exclaimed: "Anyone who I have turned in, or will turn in, they are all guiltier than I and are real witches ... she is one, she can make hail and frost, harm livestock and people."[69] The Devil is entirely absent here; the constitutive elements of witchcraft are harm to people and animals and weather magic, including specifically the power to raise hail.

In Lucerne, evidence that the belief in weather witches predates the diabolic stereotype is found in a case from 1419. In that early instance, hail making appears in the negative, but the manner of its mention simultaneously confirms both hail raising and milk theft as constitutive elements of the local witch stereotype. Conrad Glatz was banished for having said, among other things, "There is a witch here; she cannot make hail but she can certainly steal milk."[70] When witchcraft prosecution really began in the city, about thirty years later, questions about hail raising became standard in dealing with cases of suspected witchcraft. Confessions of hail making and storm raising can be traced through the entire history of witchcraft prosecution in Lucerne, from the case of Else of Meersburg in the mid-fifteenth century through the end of the trials in the eighteenth.

Although no standard list of questions survives from Lucerne, the fact that interrogators actively pursued questions about hailstorms can be traced in the responses they received. In some cases, a negative comment about hail seems to indicate the lost question, as in 1546 when Margaret Elsiner testified that she had never made hail (although she adds that on the day when a certain massive hailstorm struck she had cursed evilly).[71] Where the response was affirmative, it seems also to have been definitionally crucial. In the briefest synopses of diabolic witchcraft confessions, hail making stands in for *maleficia* in general. A note in the city council records on a 1490 execution reads:

> On this day Briden Schnider of Signau was burned on account of her testimony. She had confessed that she had raised some hail and given herself to the Devil.[72]

In the sixteenth century, hail making was strongly connected to diabolism, and as such it may have seemed particularly ominous to judges familiar with some of the narratives from demonological sources. There seems to have also been something particularly *evil* about hail making in the popular mind. This is demonstrated by a case in which the accused woman struggled to resist confessing to hail raising. Even after confessing to the theologically damning point of diabolism in 1577, Barbara Stenck struggled against admitting to the anonymous, mass destruction caused by storm raising.[73] Although she confessed to having raised a hailstorm by stomping in a brook, she later modified this confession, stipulating that the Devil had made her do it, and that no-one had been harmed by the storm that followed. Although Barbara was already damned by her confession, she actively undertook to revise it so as to avoid having admitted to causing storm damages. To have done so would have been to assume the identity of the weather witch, a figure who was older and more deeply feared and hated than the diabolic witch of the early modern period.

The Alpine witch was a frightening and destructive figure. She was the source, above all else, of otherwise inexplicable illness and harm to man and beast. She was associated with the destructive forces of nature, sudden crop-destroying hailstorms and ravenous wolves. Even in the hands of witches, the hailstorms and wolves were arbitrary and seemed to control the witches as much as the reverse. "The wolf went his own way," one frightened man had testified. Another explained that witches had to make hail whether they wished to or not.[74] Witches were perceived as spiteful and vengeful individuals, calling on the destructive power of storms for revenge. Prior to being associated with the Devil, the Alpine witch was already an embodiment of evil.

The demonological developments of the fifteenth century neither created nor introduced the idea of the weather witch to the Alpine region; in this regard they reflected indigenous witch fears. But until the introduction of diabolic witchcraft, the fear of the hail-raising weather witch was largely passive. The weather witch was a category distinct from the various hedge sorcerers who were occasionally persecuted during the period. She played a role in discursive uses of the witch concept (either as slander or insult) but did not appear in trials. The incipient shift to diabolism in the witch stereotype of the early fifteenth century activated the longstanding but largely latent indigenous fear of the weather witch. A strong resonance existed between storm raising and diabolism. Both were unequivocally evil and antisocial in the most fundamental sense. They worked to harm humanity *as a whole.* It was because of this strong affinity that the new rumors of diabolism could activate indigenous fears of the weather witch.

The chief defining characteristic of the witch was actually the most vague: evilness. Throughout Germany witches were referred to as "evil people" in much the same way that the Devil often appeared as the "evil enemy." In Latin, *maleficae* literally meant "evil doers" and the other frequently used Swiss German term for witches, *Unholden,* has as its etymological basis the simple but powerful construction "ungood."[75] The evilness of the Alpine *Hexe* was unambiguous prior to the introduction of the Devil. He, the evil enemy, was merely evil by another name: a new, personified way of understanding the powerful evil of the witch.[76]

Part I
Witch Trials in the Cities

This book undertakes an examination of witch trials in three cities: Basel, Lucerne, and Nuremberg. The urban subject of the book makes it unusual, if only because witch trials were more likely to originate in rural areas. Urban witch hunts such as those in Trier have been studied and scholars have noted patterns of suspicion different than those prevalent in rural areas. The specific dynamics of city governance could discourage witch trials. Alison Rowlands has provided an excellent example of this with her book on Rothenburg ob der Tauber. There, the city council was more concerned with maintaining the peace of the city and punishing slander than in pursuing accusations of witchcraft.[1] Yet most of the free cities of Germany held rural possessions, and the courts of those cities also had to handle witch trials originating in the countryside. Although some villages might claim old privileges of *Blutgericht* (the right to hear capital cases), as the cities engaged in early stages of the state-building processes of territorialization, they worked to monopolize the tasks of the high criminal court. Even rural witch trials were, as we shall see, an important concern for the urban lords. The period covered in this study, moreover, encompassed an urban phase in the history of European witch hunting. Many of the early trials, between the Council of Basel and the pause in witch hunting that followed the Reformation, were conducted under urban auspices. The witch hunting of Heinrich Kramer was mainly conducted in urban settings.[2] It is important, then, to analyze the particular urban contexts of these trials.

The three urban case studies that comprise the main material for this book offer a distinct contrast in their approaches to witchcraft accusations. The patterns followed in Basel, Lucerne, and Nuremberg fit the model laid out by Johannes Dillinger in his essay on witch hunting in cities. Dillinger notes that the smaller a city, the greater the likelihood that its ruling elite would see eye to eye with the populace on the subject of witchcraft.[3] With a close examination of the history of witch trials in each of these three cities, the following three chapters offer a nuanced description of how this simple yet powerful fact unfolded in these specific cases.

2
Basel: Territorialization and Rural Autonomy

The city of Basel sits on the bend of the Rhine where the river turns from the foothills of the Alps to flow north through Alsace and beyond. The oldest buildings in the city are remarkable to the visitor for their glittering and colorful glazed tile roofs. In 1356, Basel was leveled by an earthquake and what had not been destroyed by the temblor was consumed by the week-long fire which followed. With the assistance of neighboring cities the people of Basel rebuilt their city, the builders of the time favoring native sandstone and those remarkable glazed roofs. Amazingly, the city not only recovered from the earthquake, but by 1615 its walls enclosed a space three times that of 1356. The intervening centuries had been years of astounding growth for the city, territorially, economically, and culturally.[1] Around 10,000 residents lived within the city walls between 1429 and the beginning of the sixteenth century.[2] At times, the population of the city may have swelled to half again that many, as it surely did in the early 1430s, during the first seven years of the Council of Basel.

Basel had been controlled by prince bishops throughout the Middle Ages. Its emancipation from these overlords was effected primarily during the late fourteenth century through the gradual acquisition of rights and privileges. As part of this process, in 1386 the city council purchased the main organ of criminal justice, the *Schultheissengericht*, from the bishop. The city councilors became the lords of the city and its growing territories. The late fourteenth century also witnessed Basel's growing independence from the Holy Roman Empire, a process which was not formally completed until the mid-seventeenth century, although the city joined the Swiss Confederation in 1501.[3] The council that controlled the city between 1430 and 1530 also served as territorial ruler for an expanding rural hinterland, mostly to the south and east of the city. Thus as the council consolidated its autonomy, the power and authority of the urban lords was expanding.

Basel had been a center of humanism since the founding of its university in 1460 and underwent religious reform in 1529. Over the course of the late fifteenth and early sixteenth centuries, the city was host to a number of leading humanists. Among their ranks was Erasmus of Rotterdam, who visited and lived in Basel many times during his life. He returned for the last time as an old man and when he died in 1536 was laid to rest in the Basel cathedral.[4] Highly respected as one of the cultural centers of Europe, the city of Basel took on a special role in the Swiss Confederation. When the other members of the Confederation quarreled, so the agreement of 1501 went, Basel was not to take sides but to mediate the dispute.[5] The city of Basel was a flower of humanism and a light to the region.

A somewhat different view of the city emerged from the pen of Aeneas Silvius, later Pope Pius II, who spent several years in the city during the Council of Basel. "They are of unbending strictness," he wrote of the people of Basel, "and love justice."[6] He proceeded to describe the results of the city's criminal justice:

> Some end their existence bound to the wheel with crushed bones, others are drowned in the Rhine, others they burn, and still others they mutilate alive. Some they lock in cages, permitting them only a little bread and a few drops of water, until they expire of hunger or thirst. Also, to investigate crimes they use exceedingly cruel tortures, so that it seems preferable to die than to suffer such. Nonetheless, one hears that some would rather endure all of that than to confess, whether they have committed the crime or merely been accused.[7]

Such methods of criminal justice were widespread in the fifteenth century, and their use in Basel was not particularly unusual. Yet this description highlights a different side of the humanist city, reminding us that Basel was vulnerable to all the practices and beliefs of the time. The city that harbored Erasmus could, and indeed did, also burn witches.

In 1407 in Basel, more than a dozen well-born women were caught up in accusations of ritual magic ("zoufery").[8] At the center of the web was Ursula, wife of Arnold von Berenfeld. Her household servants, especially one rather suspicious housekeeper, noticed that she frequently spent time in a small chamber which was forbidden them. The housekeeper entered the room one day, after Ursula and one of her occasional guests had departed, and found what she took to be the remnants of ritual magic. When she tried to initiate an investigation, the housekeeper was scolded by a city official for disobeying her mistress. Frustrated in this attempt, the housekeeper spied on Ursula and began spreading rumors about her. When the rumors were investigated in 1407, most of the witnesses based their testimony on the housekeeper's words, including claims that she saw at least six women enter the chamber with Ursula at various times.

In all, eleven women were found guilty and banished from the city. Their crimes included love magic with occasionally harmful results. Worse, many of them were accused of conspiring to murder their husbands or other men with magic and poisons; in some cases actual deaths were attributed to the women's magic. Two of the women were convicted of possessing books of magic with illustrated catalogs of demons. One of these two, Grede Ennelin, wife of Henman von Leimen, was also accused of having invoked a demon on a rooftop as part of a spell. Grede escaped the city with two of her servants but was caught and banished later in the same year.[9] All of the women who were banished had to leave the city for life, despite their high birth and social connections.[10] Aeneas Silvius was not entirely unjustified in saying that the guilty in Basel were punished, even if they had many friends and relatives or great influence in the city.[11] When regarded as a witch hunt, this case from the early fifteenth century was the largest in the history of Basel, and even rivaled the chain trials that took place during a major witch hunt in Lucerne at the end of the sixteenth century. Yet it all took place before the introduction of diabolism and none of the women was executed. Although banishment was a harsh punishment, they escaped with their lives.

Fifty years later another trial of women for harmful magic turned out quite differently. Gret Frölicherin and Verena Symlin were burned to death in Pratteln in the territory of Basel in 1458.[12] The trial and execution took place outside the city of Basel but within its jurisdiction and in the presence of the city council's witchcraft expert, Peter zum Blech.[13] Gret had fallen afoul of witchcraft rumors eight years earlier in Basel in the course of a family quarrel, but had won a slander case against one of her accusers, Hans the *Hexenmeister* (witch master) from Fürenfeld.[14] Hans the *Hexenmeister* was a self-proclaimed expert on bewitchments. He was banished as a result of the slander case. Gret left the city herself and resettled in Pratteln, apparently leaving her husband behind in Basel. She was unable to hide from the rumors for long, however. The second time the charges emerged they were taken seriously by the authorities, and she and Verena Symlin were burned at the stake as witches. Gret and Verena were accused of harmful magic, sending an uncanny wind tearing through the houses of their victims at night, causing illness and injury. They were accused of a variety of crimes against small children, of frightening a pregnant woman so that she miscarried, causing the death of infants, and using the remains of dead children for their magic.[15] Both Verena and Gret confessed to having made a pact with a little demon, who aided them in their witchcraft. Verena's confession of the pact is typical for the period:

> Verena Symlin of Pratteln, [...] stood before an open country court, [...] on account of much evil and many misdeeds which she has practiced and committed in her days, especially that she denied almighty God and His worthy mother, and gave herself to the Devil and his spirit and therewith committed her evil with her companion Gret Frölicherin.[16]

This role of the Devil, although not nearly as developed as some which appeared in the sixteenth century, was quite different from that in the trial of 1407. When Gret and Verena were questioned about their crimes, their confessions focused on harmful magic, predominantly laming or killing livestock and children as revenge against their owners and parents. Yet in the midst of such details, Gret also confessed to having acquired the fingers of a stillborn infant to use for her witchcraft:

> She has also said that she was attending a woman in Basel, who was recovering from a stillbirth. She cut three fingers from the child [...] when they were preparing to bury it. She kept the fingers and injured people with them.[17]

Although these elements are unusual, some of magical crimes of which Verena and Gret were accused were identical to those of a half century earlier, namely misfired love magic and the attempted poisoning of Verena's husband.

Because of the similarities and differences between them, these two cases provide us with an opportunity to observe some of the crucial changes wrought in the intervening half century. They also provide evidence of the long-term continuities and the process by which the conceptual resonances between the diabolic witch stereotype and other, older ideas of maleficent magic facilitated those changes. The ritual magicians banished in 1407 were not referred to as *Hexen* in the sources, although as we have already seen the term did exist in the regional vocabulary. These women were not believed to ride wolves or raise hail. Their power derived not from an association with nature but from mysterious and chthonic forces firmly embedded in the social and religious world of the urban late Middle Ages: books, artifacts, demons, and the gallows. As such, though they were witches in the broad sense employed in this study, they were not *Hexen* in a regionally and historically specific sense. The ritual magician was a distinct category of person from the Alpine weather witch, but one that also shared important conceptual resonances with the diabolic witch. In creating the diabolic witch doctrine, demonologists had drawn on their knowledge of ritual magic as well as on indigenous witch stereotypes.

In examining the substance of the two cases, the differences initially appear quite substantial. The desecration of corpses and the overt, if limited, references to a demonic pact in 1458 had been absent fifty years earlier. The question is whether this is a difference of degree or of kind. In the tradition of Joseph Hansen, the tendency of historians has been to see this as a difference of kind and to argue that in the trial of 1458 we are witnessing the emergence of the diabolic witch. This is true, but it is not the only story that can or even should be told from the examination of these two trials. The difference could also be viewed as one of degree. Demons were present and important to the case of 1407, although an overt pact was not. Later writers such as Nider would have recognized an implicit diabolism in such ritual magic, even if the lay judges of Basel's secular court did not. In 1398 the University of Paris had condemned all magic, writing that it required an implicit pact with demons, as was evident in "every superstitious ritual, the effects of which cannot be reasonably traced to either God or nature."[18]

The disturbing and chthonic element of the desecration of corpses in 1458 also resonates with elements found in the earlier trial. While no explicit use of corpses appeared in 1407, the powers of the gallows and the graveyard were certainly invoked. One love spell involved a piece of gallows wood, held under the tongue as the words of binding were spoken. In the most extensive version of the spell, the executed dead themselves were invoked to perform the binding:

> On the earthen threshold I tread and reach in through the door. I wake all the dead, all the men the Devil Lucifer ever took. I conjure you all together, that you should rise up [...] and make P. Vischer my

love: twelve murdered men, twelve drowned, twelve hanged [...] they must cause Peter to love me.[19]

A new, explicitly diabolic concept of the crime of witchcraft was emerging in 1458. But while new aspects of the crime appeared, it was not systematically redefined, nor was diabolic witchcraft distinguished in practice as a separate crime from older forms of maleficent magic. Long after the appearance of the diabolic witch, in cases of witchcraft where the Devil and chthonic elements were largely or wholly absent, the accused often suffered the same harsh punishment as Verena and Gret. There was effectively no distinction synchronically in fifteenth-century judicial practice between the sorceress and the diabolic witch, but a substantial difference across the decades. In 1407, life-long banishment was the harshest punishment evidenced in cases of witchcraft. In 1458, although banishment remained an option in Basel, a new method of punishment had emerged: execution at the stake. This transition is reflective of a larger trend in the region. From the mid-fifteenth century onwards, accused witches in Basel were increasingly likely to be executed at the stake rather than being banished. If legal historians are correct in identifying the fifteenth century as a period of generally increasing judicial severity, this new, harsher punishment was part of that larger trend.

An examination of witch trials from the territory of Basel reveals that this transformation was not primarily motivated from the urban center, from an educated elite with access to new demonological ideas, but from the city's rural possessions, and the trials played out in a struggle between local and urban jurisdiction. Moreover, it is not clear that diabolism was even present in the mid-century witchcraft executions, although it is certainly possible. Before the first deadly trials in the 1440s, banishment had been the standard punishment for maleficent magic in Basel. Between 1405 and 1435, 22 people – most of them women – were tried in the city. Nearly all of them were banished as a result; in the few remaining cases the outcome remains unknown.[20] A typical example is found in the Basel banishment books from 1406:

> Item, Grede Gunnerin of Bern has committed sorcery with soft wax images and other things; therefore she shall remain five miles away from the city forever.[21]

Whether Grede suffered any other punishment is not stated, and neither time in the stocks nor corporal punishment was typically mentioned in conjunction with such banishments. That women suspected of witch-craft might have feared worse, either from the city or from their neigh-bors, seems clear from a case from 1416:

> Item [...] the furrier's evil wife, who limps on both sides, is reputed to have committed sorcery. Because of this she wanted to kill herself and had [tried to] hang herself. For this she shall remain five miles beyond the crosses forever. And in the case that she breaks her oath and returns, she will be executed by drowning.[22]

The furrier's wife may have been despondent at her damaged reputa-tion, or she may have tried to hang herself in prison under the pressure of torture. Whatever the reason, we have no evidence that she actually faced the possibility of execution. The threat of drowning was unlikely to be carried out even if she did break the banishment and return.[23]

Then, around 1444, the pattern of banishment was broken. Several women were burned as witches, first in neighboring territories and then in Waldenburg, one of the possessions of the city of Basel.[24] For these first trials we possess only traces, as from a case in 1446, mentioned briefly in the yearly income books for Basel:

> Waldenburg.
> Item, received from three witches who were burned there, 62£ 16s which we have shared with the men.[25]

Between 1444 and 1482, at least fourteen people – all women as far as we know – were burned as witches in the outlying territories of Basel. During this time, only two cases appear to have originated within the city of Basel itself; both of them followed the old pattern, ending in banishment.[26]

With the exception of Gret and Verena's trial from 1458, the surviv-ing records pertaining to these cases are all extremely brief. The only hints we have of the supposed crimes of the other executed women is the word used to describe them: *Hexen*. What kind of witches were they? As we have already seen, *Hexe* was a regional term with specific content that predated the introduction of diabolism. In 1450, in the city of Basel, Birine had used it to refer to women who could "make hail and frost, harm livestock and people."[27] What did the city scribes mean when they recorded expenses or income from "hechsen" burned in Waldenburg? From this one word it is impossible to know whether these cases contained diabolic elements. The more complete evidence from Lucerne indicates that while the introduction of diabolism and the practice of burning witches seem to have heightened the fear of the Alpine witch, the stereotype did not become imbued with diabolism in the popular mind. The question then becomes whether either the rural elite who conducted the trials or the urban officials sent to assist them chose to interrogate the witches about their relationships with demons.

The best hope we have of an answer may lie in the career of Peter zum Blech, which has been analyzed by Dorothee Rippmann. In 1444, the year of the first witch burning in Basel territory, witches were burned in Dornach, Gempen, and Büren in Solothurn territory. In the same year two witches had been burned in the territory of Birseck, in the lands of the bishop of Basel. The authorities in Birseck called in a consultant from Basel, Peter zum Blech. Peter became the Basel expert on witches; in 1446 he was sent as a witchcraft consultant to Heidelberg, and in 1458 he served in the trial of Gret Fröhlicherin and Verena Symlin.[28] In all of these trials, the only one for which we have clear evidence of diabolism from actual trial records is that of Gret and Verena. Despite being a tantalizing lead, Peter's career does not explain the introduction of diabolism in that case. What it does demonstrate, however, was a mechanism by which the city put its hand into the trials conducted by the rural *Bauerngerichte*. The judicial authority of the city was represented in the person of the *Oberste Ratsknecht*, the office held mid-century by Peter zum Blech.

In the instance of witch trials, at least, this changed in the last two decades of the fifteenth century. Beginning in 1482, the Basel authorities began bringing accused witches from the hinterlands into the city itself to stand trial. While this seems to have slightly increased the possibility that the accused would be banished or acquitted rather than executed, it also coincided with a transformation in the handling of cases which originated within the city. Between 1482 and 1530, nineteen cases of witchcraft were heard in Basel, involving at least 24 people. Nine of the accused were executed at the stake, two of them banished, and three released. The outcome of the other cases is unknown.[29] The details of the investigative process in these cases have not generally survived, but in at least some cases the investigation did prove the accused to be innocent. This is demonstrated by an expense entry from June of 1512:

> Item, 1£ 11s for food and other expenses for Margreth from Lupsingen who was imprisoned as a witch and found not guilty.[30]

The investigation of Margreth had not been gentle; the first evidence of her case came two weeks earlier, when Basel official Peter Ritter was sent to Waldenburg to question and torture the two witches imprisoned there.[31] Margreth's anonymous companion did not escape. An expense entry from mid-July "for wood to burn the witch" indicates her fate.[32]

The first witch burning within the city of Basel took place in the summer of 1487. An expense entry from late June of that year indicates costs to bind and torture two witches. Two weeks later, a witch expert called a *Hexenmeister* was summoned and sent into the tower to see the witches. The following entry makes their fate clear:

> Item 7s for wood to burn the witches [...] Item 6s to pass judgment in court, Item 9£ 2d for the witches' food, escort, binding, shaving, consumed by the servants, the friar, the priest to hear confession, arrest money, and the executioner.[33]

The practice of burning those convicted of crimes of magic was thus established in the city of Basel.

Is it possible that the witch burnings in Basel territory were the result of a split policy? Were they imposed on rural subjects by their urban lords? During the period in question, the territory of Basel was not a single, cohesive unit. The rural hinterland was a patchwork of jurisdictions and aristocratic holdings. We know that some early trials were conducted under the pressure of competing jurisdictions, as was the case in neighboring Büren in 1444. Jurisdictional and territorial concerns also played a minor role in the trial of Gret Frölicherin and Verena Symlin in 1458. Furthermore, although we do not know the nature of all the trials in question, it is clear that some of the early rural trials were initiated *ex officio*.[34] Were the witch trials in the Basel possessions imposed by the city as part of the process of territorialization? Juliane Kümmell contends that they were, given that waves of witch trials in the 1450s and the 1480s coincided with attempts by the city to establish financial claims in the rural district of Waldenburg.[35]

I disagree with Kümmell on the basis of my own investigations into the autonomy of the rural deputies of the city. I found that the impulse for witch trials came from the rural territories, during an effort to shore up rural claims to autonomous jurisdiction, and that the urban lords co-opted the trials in their own efforts to consolidate jurisdiction. Rippmann has presented a more thorough criticism of Kümmell's general thesis, arguing first that Kümmell assumes characterizations of the process of territorialization in Basel that properly belong to the early modern, and secondly, that Rippmann's research, like my own, supports a contrary conclusion.[36] As it is one of the aims of this study to challenge the rigidity of the category "early modern," particularly with regards to the German cities, I am open to the possibility that some aspects of territorialization may have appeared earlier than expected. That said, Rippmann's assessment is based on her thorough familiarity with the history of Basel in particular, rather than on general models of territorialization. The discussion that follows wades into this complex debate with a single snapshot of the tensions between urban and rural authority in the early sixteenth century. I am not engaging models of territorialization nor embarking on a thorough analysis of factors of administration and rural life, but merely adding evidence from the material of my own investigations into the criminal and financial records. From these I find that while the urban authorities sought to extend and consolidate their administrative and judicial control over their rural possessions, they were cautious in the face of the risk of being directly thwarted by the rural elites on whom they depended to execute their authority.

In order to better understand the significance of the Basel territories in the development of witchcraft prosecution within the city, we turn to events from 1530, the last year of this study and the first following the official adoption of the Reformation in Basel. During that year, the city of Basel struggled to gain control over the widespread practice of Anabaptism. Following its entry into the Swiss Confederation in 1501, the city of Basel had begun keeping substantially more extensive records. With these better sources, the contours of the city's struggle with Anabaptism are quite clear.[37] Anabaptism had a strong following, mostly outside of the city of Basel in the same territories which had earlier given rise to witchcraft prosecution. The Basel authorities initially responded by arresting known or suspected Anabaptists and imprisoning them until they confessed, recanted, and swore loyalty to the city.

This response, however, failed to curb the problem. Many recanted Anabaptists lapsed shortly after being released and were brought before the Basel authorities twice or even three times within one year. Furthermore, rural deputies of the city often simply refused to carry out an arrest warrant. While claiming not to be Anabaptists themselves, these men, often in violation of their oaths of office, contended with the city's authority in local matters. In a particularly noteworthy case in February of 1530, forty-nine men in the territory of Farnsburg refused to carry out orders to arrest Anabaptists. Of these, six had sworn oaths of office binding them to obey the authorities of Basel. At least three of the forty-nine refused to carry out arrest orders again on a later occasion, and two of them later appeared facing charges of Anabaptism themselves.[38] It was only when the city began to employ the death penalty for the most infamous Anabaptist leaders and to banish some of the lapsed Anabaptists that they slowly began to get a handle on the situation. This story demonstrates that the people living in the rural territories of Basel were not docile subjects. They felt empowered to actively resist the city when they deemed it necessary.

In light of this contested local autonomy and in the absence of any signs of conflict between the city and the rural areas during the earlier persecution of witchcraft, it becomes impossible to argue that witchcraft persecution was imposed by the city. In fact, while concerns over territorial control played an important role in Basel's involvement in those witch trials, the trials themselves were initiated and largely conducted by local, rural authorities. The goals of territorial and jurisdictional consolidation that motivated the Basel authorities to become involved in witch trials and even to oversee witch burnings were essentially the aims of territorialization, if only in a larval form. Anything less than active involvement in witchcraft trials could well have served as an invitation to local authorities to turn elsewhere for justice. This would have been highly problematic for the urban authorities. As the Nuremberg humanist and jurist Christoph Scheurl wrote in the early sixteenth century, "One follows to war the lord who serves his justice."[39] This is the insight we gain from examining the struggle of the Basel authorities with Anabaptists in 1530; the city's control over its territories was imperfect and required give and take.

Indeed, given what we know of witch trials in the early 1440s, it is quite likely that the practice of witch burning was introduced to the city from the surrounding area. The origin of witchcraft prosecution in Basel was popular, not imposed by urban elites. The earliest witch burnings took place in the rural hinterlands, but under the auspices of the urban government. As control over those territories tightened and competing jurisdictions were closed out, the immediate display of justice became less important. Rather than sending a representative to the territories to oversee trials, the Basel council began fetching accused witches to the city itself and conducting the trials there. In so doing, the urban authorities gained greater control over the witch trials, but after the practice of witch burning was already well established. The pattern of deadly witchcraft prosecution was not ended, but rather incorporated into the city itself. This took place at a time when, following the Council of Basel, demonological concepts of witchcraft were more easily available in Basel than in most of the rest of Europe. Yet the practice of burning appeared first in the territories of Basel, outside the context of literate discourse within the city. The evil fear came from the hinterlands, where it had quite likely crossed invisible and shifting territorial boundaries as a rumor shared between neighbors.

The immediate result of importing witch trials into the city seems to have been the importation of the witch fear, as well. There were more witchcraft executions in Basel between 1480 and 1500 than at any other time in the city's history. But if we are to read the history of the witch trials in the city and its territories as a struggle between urban control and rural autonomy, we must add that this adoption of witch trials was a short-lived trend. After the turn of the sixteenth century, things changed in Basel. Witch burnings first became rare, then disappeared altogether. The course of judicial practice in Basel after 1500 represented a return to earlier practice. There may have been many reasons for this, and the paucity of the sources makes some of them utterly inaccessible. One crucial event, however, cannot be overlooked. In 1501, Basel joined the Swiss Confederation. While the Confederation was still technically part of the Empire, its members had long worked for their *de facto* independence, limiting the authority of the emperor wherever possible. Even before the city became part of the Confederation, the council of Basel had worked to curtail the imperial right of judicial review. The lords of Basel disliked the implicit subjugation of their high court.

After 1501, we know of only two women executed as witches in the city of Basel. A number of other women were also accused as witches. Some of them were released, others were banished, which had been the traditional punishment for witchcraft in Basel prior to the introduction of diabolism in the mid-fifteenth century. After the Reformation in Basel, the judges went even further. After 1537, they apparently ceased to punish witchcraft altogether. Following Gary Waite, it may be that post-Reformation Basel's cessation of witchcraft prosecution was due in part to the distraction of battling the heresy of Anabaptism.[40] This cannot be a complete explanation, however. The Anabaptist threat in Basel was eventually bested, but the few witchcraft cases the city heard over the following sixty years all ended in acquittal and Basel never returned to executing witches. In light of this, we can read the brief flurry of executions in Basel as a concession to rural demands, and perhaps also a genuine response to the influence of rural fears. In their Reformation social disciplining, the city fathers of Basel used powerfully providential language, warning transgressors that their sins would anger God, who might make the grain and grapes less fruitful in response.[41] Here we have not only evidence of the theology behind a secular government's responsibility to control sin, but also a providential attitude toward agrarian suffering that may well help to explain why Basel ceased trying witches after the Reformation.[42]

The history of witch hunting in Basel was thus relatively brief and restrained. Between 1440 and 1540, sixteen women were executed as witches in the territory of Basel. The motivation for witch hunting appears to have been largely rural. Although we have almost no details from those cases, enough indications exist that the peasants living in the territory of Basel shared the fear of the Alpine weather witch with their neighbors. The urban lords of Basel succumbed for a time to this pressure and accommodated the rural demands for trials. In our next case study, Nuremberg, we observe the choices of an urban elite far more independent of subaltern pressures during the fifteenth and early sixteenth centuries.

3
Nuremberg: The *Malleus* that Never Struck

The old city of Nuremberg is built on the banks of the Pegnitz river, surrounded by thick, high walls. The cityscape, now as then, is dominated by the *Kaiserburg*, the imperial fortress at the apex of the hill that rises on the left bank. Nuremberg straddles the usually sleepy river, covering it with many bridges. At the beginning of the fifteenth century these bridges were wooden, and when the Pegnitz flooded during the spring thaw they were sometimes damaged or even destroyed by the rushing water. The late fifteenth century witnessed a transformation of the bridges of Nuremberg. By the end of the century many of the city's main bridges were solid and stately structures, with stone arches resting on pillars in the river.[1] The rebuilding of the bridges of Nuremberg was only a small part of the creative and constructive energy of the city on the threshold of the early modern era. This was the golden age of Nuremberg, which was one of the preeminent cities in the empire. The city was presented as a model by the men of letters who lived within its strong walls, and with success. Nuremberg was widely admired and praised for its laws and good governance, and the institutions of the city were copied by other urban polities.[2] Aeneas Silvius, who had commented on justice in Basel, lavished praise on Nuremberg, writing:

> What a splendid appearance this city presents! What a beauty of location, what learning there, what culture, what a superb government! Nothing is missing to make a perfect civic community. How clean the streets, how elegant the houses![3]

Elegant houses and clean streets reflected the substantial wealth of the city. Nuremberg was a center of long-distance trade at the turn of the sixteenth century. Production within the city, which was controlled by patrician merchants in the city council, provided a substantial basis for this trading success. Through careful control, high quality work was ensured in the trades, and Nuremberg was especially renowned for fine metalwork in iron, gold and copper.[4] This vibrant economy supported one of the larger urban populations in Germany. Calculated from a tally made during a war with the Margrave of Brandenburg-Ansbach, the population of Nuremberg around 1450 was close to 30,000. As many as a third of these people were normally residents of the rural possessions of the city, who were taking shelter inside the city walls due to war. The normal population must have been closer to 20,000. Emil Reicke has refined this number even further, counting around 17,600 citizens, 446 clerics and their company, 150 Jews, and around 2,000 non-citizens, mercenaries and foreign servants.[5] As such, Nuremberg ranked among the largest of the imperial cities. Of the cities examined in this study, Nuremberg was by far the largest, being twice the size of Basel and four times that of Lucerne.

Nuremberg was also the most powerful of the three, one of the unofficial capitals of the old empire. It was the epitome of an imperial city, with its fortunes bound to imperial privileges. Although Nuremberg remained a powerful player in the diplomacy of the empire, the political position of the city at the beginning of the early modern period was one of progressive decay, due in large part to the erosion of the German cities' power to the advantage of the princes after the Cities' War of 1388.[6] Meanwhile, the city expanded its territory considerably during the fifteenth century, acquiring one of the largest rural hinterlands of any imperial city. The lands of the city were surrounded on three sides by the possessions of the Margrave of Brandenburg-Ansbach. The clash of the city's territorial ambitions with those of the Margrave and other neighbors led the city into a series of wars during the fifteenth century.[7]

The councilors of Nuremberg were the rulers of both city and territory, appointers of captains for war and watchmen to keep the peace. The city's institutions of justice ranged from the peasants' court, which adjudicated quarrels for the city's rural subjects, to the Five Lords, who mediated conflicts between the greatest potentates of the city and punished excesses of luxury.[8] The criminal court of the city was composed of the city judge and thirteen juror-investigators who were, according to the Nuremberg jurist Christoph Scheurl, "required to be present during torture, to confirm the aberrations of the tortured, and to pass judgment over blood guilt."[9]

This was the court which held jurisdiction over witchcraft. Between 1430 and 1530, 46 people were accused of maleficent magic in

Nuremberg, in 31 separate trials.[10] Of these individuals, over half were simply released or were released with a reprimand. In the remaining cases, one third of the outcomes are unknown. The other fifteen individuals received punishments varying from penance to execution. This means that the only general statement which can be made about the Nuremberg council's propensity to punish witchcraft during the period was that in most cases it chose not to. It does seem that any association with the Devil increased the likelihood of more severe treatment, but did not guarantee it. In six cases involving eight women in which some reference to the Devil appears, only one woman was released. One, Els Gernoltin, was executed. She is the only person known to have been executed for witchcraft during the period in Nuremberg. The other six suffered variously humiliation, physical punishment, and banishment.

Yet in Nuremberg the element of the Devil was neither a late addition, having appeared already in 1434, nor one with any depth of detail. Whereas cases from Basel include detailed confessions of a relationship between Devil and witch, such specificity is absent in fifteenth- and early sixteenth-century Nuremberg. Instead, it seems that magic and witchcraft were merely associated with the Devil in the minds of the magistrates. Thus sorceresses were placed in the stocks with the image of the Devil in both 1434 and 1489. A chronicler's account of the punishment in 1489 reads:

> This year, on the Saturday following St. George, Margreth Salchingerin was placed on the ladders, with a paper sign on which the Devil was painted, and banished from the city; she had used sorcery.[11]

Even in cases where the association with the Devil was somewhat more explicit, the references were quite brief. In 1468 Els Kramerin was placed in the stocks and branded for sorcery and because she had taken "the goat" as a lover.[12] In 1487, Els Rutzscherin was banished from the city for sorcery and because she had promised the "evil spirit" that she would violate Christian law.[13]

In two cases from the early sixteenth century, including that of Els Gernoltin who was drowned in 1520, the Devil only appears in the legal opinions of jurists. The jurists, in assessing the severity of the crime of witchcraft, referred to it as "the Devil's work." These two cases involved four women, of whom only Els suffered execution. Yet Els's crime went beyond simple magic in another way. She confessed to attempting love magic, for which she killed small fish in her vagina and then fed them to eligible bachelors.[14] After torture, she admitted that her attempt at binding had resulted in the physical poisoning and death of at least one man. The confession of murder stands out as unique among witchcraft trials in Nuremberg during the period, and it was the reason for Els's unusually harsh punishment. Her confessed teacher, Anna Sewrin, was released upon the intercession of her family; the council considered her sufficiently punished by her imprisonment, torture, and interrogation. Although one jurist consulted in the case, Johann Protzer, explicitly based his justification of Els's execution on the religiously heinous nature of the crime of sorcery, he also argued for lesser punishment of Anna because her attempts at love magic had resulted in no harm. Christoph Scheurl, who was also consulted in the case, explicitly justified executing Els on account of the man's death.[15]

Full-blown diabolism remained absent from sorcery trials in Nuremberg not only throughout the fifteenth century, but even after the publication of the *Malleus Maleficarum*. In 1491, Heinrich Kramer had sent advice to the Nuremberg council on handling witchcraft cases, based on the *Malleus*.[16] Yet this *Nürnberger Hexenhammer* does not appear to have had any impact in Nuremberg. In the decade following its arrival in the hands of the city council, four witch trials took place in the city. In the first, in 1497, Barbara Schlitzin was tortured on accusations of "misdeeds and sorcery."[17] Although the outcome of this trial is unknown, it does not seem that Barbara was accused of diabolism or made to denounce accomplices. Two other trials ended with the release of the accused and in the fourth a woman was banished from the city.[18] Even when the council took charges of sorcery seriously, it did not search for evidence of a diabolic conspiracy like that which Kramer had described.

During this same period, the *Malleus* appears to have had an impact in the neighboring Margraviate. In 1505 a day-laborer's wife named Barbara Schwab was burned as a witch in Schwabach, south-west of Nuremberg.[19] The local chaplain possessed a copy of the *Malleus Maleficarum*. Perhaps this chaplain had an influence on the questions asked when Barbara was questioned under torture administered by the Nuremberg *Henkerknecht* Hans Rosenzweig, on loan from the city. Barbara confessed to sorcery and diabolism, and denounced not only her own daughter but several other women. For the history of witch hunts in the Margraviate, Barbara's trial is notable for its failure to produce a witch hunt. The daughter was pardoned and sent away, the other denounced women were released on an oath of peace and were not prosecuted. In Nuremberg, also, the absence of any emulation of this trial is notable. Hans Rosenzweig returned to his duties in the city, where torture was being given the upper hand in prosecutions at that time.[20] Yet diabolism did not appear in any witch trials in Nuremberg until 1536.

Barbara's trial is also notable for the impact it did have in Nuremberg. Heinrich Deichsler included a long description of the events in Schwabach in his Nuremberg chronicle. It is a conflicted report, which never clearly questions the woman's guilt, yet is highly sympathetic in description:

> As the letter and confession were read in the court, [the accused] sat nearby bound to a cart by her neck, her waist, and her feet. She clenched her teeth and spoke thus: No, I do not confess any of it; I confessed it all because of terrible torture; I have done nothing to you. Then two were brought [...] who testified under oath that she had confessed the matter without any torture.[21] And in the meantime all the while the executioner laid wood on the place for the fire [...] and the woman on the cart bit her lip, smiling although she trembled, and looked to the heavens with a prayerful gesture as if she desired that fire should come from heaven and burn him [the executioner] first.[22]

Barbara was placed on the pyre and the executioner began to sprinkle her head and body with ashes. "She was a pretty woman, with a beautiful body and white bosom," Deichsler wrote.[23] Then he described the execution itself:

> Before she was set in the fire, a priest spoke [...] Dear woman, stand firm in Christian belief and die as a Christian. She said: I wish to die as a Christian. [The priests] said: When they ignite the fire, cry with us in prayer and with a loud voice: Jesus Nazarenus Rex Judeorum, Lord have mercy on me. This she did as long as she could [until] she could no longer cry out for the smoke and heat. She gave powerful evidence that she was a good Christian.[24]

Deichsler seems to have felt that something was wrong with the pitiful scene of Barbara's demise. Although this was his opinion alone, it reflected a growing trend toward skepticism in the ruling elite of the city. The position of Deichsler himself was, at most, on the margins of that elite; he was a brewer, from a respectable family but not one with the hereditary right to sit on the city council.[25] It would seem that empathy with the victims of witch trials had some currency in Nuremberg. This may have made it easier for real skepticism to make inroads within the closed discussions of the urban lords and their advisors.

In the early sixteenth century, the council frequently consulted with the city jurists in cases that touched on witchcraft, as they did in the case of Els Gernoltin. The Nuremberg jurists were not of one mind; some recommended handling the cases seriously, employing torture, and in case of conviction imposing punishment up to and including the death penalty.[26] Others dismissed the problem altogether, as did the jurist Johann Hepstein in 1533, writing that he "had never believed in such matters and sorceries, and therefore had nothing in particular to recommend."[27]

This surprising expression of skepticism came during the greatest concentrations of witch trials in the entire history of Nuremberg. Between 1521 and 1550, the council of Nuremberg heard 24 cases. In only five of these cases, however, do we know of any judicial sanction imposed on the accused. The patrician lords of Nuremberg were not concerned with the dangers of witchcraft as a real crime, but instead with the possibility that self-styled sorcerers would prey on the superstitious tendencies of the ordinary people.

An extraordinary case from 1536 reveals the strength of the court's reluctance to pursue diabolic magic as a real crime and the constellation of skepticism about diabolism and concern over magic as fraud.[28] In March of 1536, the council decided to arrest Adelheit Schneiderin. Adelheit was accused of having magically harmed some cows. The story as it unfolded over the course of the investigation began with a farmer named Cunz Erhardt. Cunz had a sickness among his herd, and he turned to Adelheit for help since she had a reputation for magical knowledge. She demanded a high price for her work: Cunz paid her five florins to cure his cows. She prepared magical medicine for the beasts, using polytrichum moss as her chief ingredient. The medicine did not help the animals, however, and Cunz watched as one after another of his cows died. Angered, he believed that Adelheit had mixed magical poison instead of medicine, and that she was responsible for his heavy losses. Cunz's suspicions were echoed by other farmers in the area; many had lost livestock over the years, and all seemed to find the expensive magic worker Adelheit a reasonable suspect.

When Adelheit was arrested, she initially denied all charges. During a second round of questioning under the threat of torture she named two other women – Els Schneiderin and Katharina Maylin – as the true witches, both of whom lived in the district of Cadolzburg in the neighboring Margraviate. Els Schneiderin was Adelheit's mother, although why Adelheit chose to accuse Els and Katharina remains unclear. But the council immediately issued orders for their arrest, should they set foot in the territory of the city. They then ordered Adelheit to be tortured and questioned again. Under torture Adelheit confessed everything of which she was accused. She described the actions of her supposed accomplices, saying she had seen them using polytrichum moss. In light of this confession, the council had her tortured again and questioned yet further. During this fourth round of questioning and second round of torture, Adelheit descended into descriptions of diabolism. She confessed having sealed a pact with the Devil with sexual intercourse, and having flown with him to the witches' sabbath. The other two, moreover, were also in league with the Devil and had flown to the witches' sabbath. Adelheit even claimed that Katharina had become the Devil's bride.

Around this time the council managed to arrest Els Schneiderin. Els not only denied everything in the first round of questioning, but maintained her innocence under torture. This made the council uncertain of Adelheit's testimony as well as Els's guilt, and they sought more actively to arrest Katharina, hoping that she might clarify the truth of the situation. When they succeeded, Katharina also insisted on her innocence. Although rumor confirmed that both Els and Katharina were suspected of witchcraft, their success in maintaining their innocence threw the case into doubt. The council turned to their juriconsultants for advice. The response they received was no purely skeptical document; although the consultants noted that they did not put much confidence in tales of sorcery, they went on to say that witchcraft was clearly a real possibility and danger, and that plenty of examples existed of such bizarre details as the night flight of the witches. The use of polytrichum moss, widely believed to have magical properties, was alone sufficient evidence of sorcery in the eyes of jurist Christoph Gugel. Christoph Scheurl argued that as Adelheit had confessed to witchcraft, which was a capital offense, she should be told that she would be executed and then questioned further.

The list of investigations Scheurl proposed included further interviews of neighbors and others who had accused the women, as well as specific questions for Adelheit and her husband, aimed at ferreting out the truth about her relationship with the Devil. It is here, Hartmut Kunstmann argues, that we finally see the impact of the *Malleus*. Yet this was fifty years after the publication of the infamous "hammer of witches" and over forty years after the Nuremberg council was given a manuscript version by Kramer himself. And while Scheurl proposed investigating the full truth behind Adelheit's confessions of diabolism, jurist Johann Hepstein argued that witchcraft was merely "fantasy and self-delusion." He insisted that Els and Katharina should be released for lack of evidence, "for it would be better to release 100 guilty persons than to condemn one innocent."[29] A few days later the council minutes indicate that the two were in fact released.

Adelheit remained in the dungeon, however, and her confessions put the council in a difficult position. As Scheurl pointed out, she had confessed to a capital crime and her life was accordingly forfeit. But the councilors appear to have been more persuaded by Hepstein's argument that Adelheit's chief crime was having defrauded farmers such as Cunz Erhardt. This was further strengthened by the opinions of the theologians that the council then consulted on the case, who likewise accounted the witchcraft to be pure fantasy. These Lutheran theologians did not fundamentally discount the reality of diabolic witchcraft; they add that if indeed she had done what she confessed, Adelheit undoubtedly deserved to die. Despite accepting the reality of witchcraft, however, the theologians felt as Hepstein did that Adelheit's chief crime was fraud. Kunstmann concludes in the face of silent sources that the council probably followed Hepstein's advice, since it had been confirmed by the theologians.

Two years later the Nuremberg council sent an opinion on witchcraft to their peers in Ulm. The notation in the council records from 1538 reveals the skeptical position they had embraced:

> Write back to those in Ulm, [saying] that my lords regard witches and Devil's work as nothing and have had the same [sorts of] case[s] but have learned from their scholars and theologians and jurists that it had no basis but rather was pure madness. For this reason they were not further punished, but merely banished from the land.[30]

Not only had the *Malleus* failed to make an impact on the practice of prosecuting witches in Nuremberg; when diabolism did appear it was actively rejected. Although Nuremberg's reputation of having never burned a single witch is undeserved,[31] there were no witch hunts in the imperial free city. This fact must be attributed primarily to the restrained stance of the city council and the advisors they chose to consult.

It was not because they were unwilling to believe theories about evil conspiracies that the Nuremberg authorities were reluctant to prosecute witchcraft. The tragic history of the Jews of Nuremberg makes this abundantly clear. The Black Death sparked a pogrom against Jews in Nuremberg in 1349. Not only were over a third of the Nuremberg Jews killed in that year, but royal protection was temporarily withdrawn and the survivors were driven from their homes and their possessions plundered. Three years later, in 1352, Jews were allowed to return to Nuremberg under the renewed protection of a royal edict. From then until the end of the fifteenth century, the Jews lived in Nuremberg under the protection of their status as the king's personal subjects, paying an extraordinarily high special tax directly into the royal coffers for this privilege.[32]

By the mid-fifteenth century, there was once again a Jewish community in Nuremberg, although according to Emil Reicke's estimate, the Jewish population of the city in 1450 was 150 people, only one tenth of its pre-1349 strength.[33] This small community was tolerated largely for financial reasons. Not only did Jews pay special taxes, but fines levied against individual Jews were extraordinarily high. In 1430, several young Jewish men appear in the city budget paying fines for having sexual relations with Christian women and gambling.[34] During this period, simple fornication was not generally handled by the Nuremberg council at all and gambling was usually punished with a one pound fine in local currency.[35] These six young men, however, paid between 100 and 1,000 gulden each, totaling over 2,500 gulden. Such heavy fines may be understood in part as a reflection of the strength of the taboo against miscegenation. Yet the practice of extracting the maximum cash from the Jewish community, through fines as well as taxes, was standard. When a Jewish woman named Mossin lost her temper in court, she was fined 25 gulden. Around the same time, when Christian Bertholt Vierhall did the same, he was fined five pounds in local currency.[36] The differential made clear in these fines was present also in criminal justice. In 1449 a Jewish woman and two Christian men were arrested on criminal charges. The woman was tortured; her supposed accomplices were not.[37]

Thus the Jews in Nuremberg were barely tolerated, and lived in the context of a massive, city-run extortion racket. They paid staggering taxes and fees to guarantee their safety, but that guarantee was of questionable value. By 1473, the Nuremberg council was petitioning the king to allow it to expel the Jews once again. The legal reform drafted in Nuremberg in 1479 and enacted in 1484 was so hostile to the Jews in the city that it is said that they actively refused to acknowledge the new law.[38] It was in this context, in 1483, that the council of Nuremberg received an ominous gift:

> Item 1£ and 10s to the Lantzendorf book binder, for the book containing the evil deeds and murder committed by the Jews of Trent against a young Christian boy, which Count Eberhard of Württemberg gave to the honorable council here.[39]

It was the story of Simon of Trent, a Christian boy found murdered on Easter morning in 1475. The Jews of Trent had been charged with ritually murdering him, and many of them were burned.[40]

The case from Trent was an example of the application of the same conceptual nexus of evil which had been applied to the early Christians and medieval heretics. The Jews, like these other outsiders who worshipped differently and separately, were suspected of horrible, anti-human crimes, of killing Christian children to drink their blood and desecrating the host as a repetition of the torments of Christ. As with medieval heretics and the imagined society of diabolic witches, it was suspected that the Jews actually worshipped the Devil. Ronnie Hsia writes that in the two generations preceding the Reformation, blood libel cases reached a climax in the Holy Roman Empire, having built momentum during the late fifteenth century as each new trial furnished more evidence for the supposed historical reality of ritual murder.[41] The gift received by the council of Nuremberg in 1483 probably confirmed and refreshed the longstanding suspicion against the Jews at a time when the position of the Jews in that city was already slipping from bad to worse.

The results of this dangerous situation were nearly fifteen years in the making. In the meantime, while the council members and other powerful Christians in Nuremberg were stewing over the continued presence of the Jews in the city, the council received the abridged *Malleus Maleficarum* from Kramer. The *Malleus* presented such a virulently misogynistic image of witchcraft and such heinous procedural suggestions that it could have well proved quite dangerous in the hands of a powerfully placed sympathetic reader. Yet as we have seen, the council largely chose to ignore the advice of the *Malleus*. Kramer's suggestions about the nature of witchcraft and his proposals for procedure were not adopted by the Nuremberg elite.

If we can judge the councilors' responses to these two texts from their judicial actions, then they proved a much more sympathetic audience for the story of Simon of Trent than for the *Malleus*. A chronicle of executions in Nuremberg laconically relates the tragedy that followed:

> Anno 1497. Eighteen Jews, who had murdered four Christian boys in their cellar, as was brought to light by a Jewish girl, were burned here on the Jew hill.[42]

The story behind these few lines may be lost, but it likely mirrored that from Trent. The collective, secretive crime, the specification of Christian boys, and the chosen punishment all suggest the accusation of ritual murder. Within two years, the remaining Jews in the city were driven out. The emperor had given his permission for this step in 1498, writing:

> The Jews in question have in their malice and malicious will and intent [...] secretly given shelter and aid to some lost and aberrant persons, from which has resulted theft and other unchristian, improper and evil deeds, which is most difficult to suffer.[43]

Thus the Jews of Nuremberg were expelled twice in 150 years, with the accompaniment of bloodshed and fantastic charges of anti-Christian conspiracies each time. This history demonstrates that the city council of Nuremberg was not entirely reluctant to see truth in stories of a secret, cannibalistic, Devil-worshipping cult. In the case of witchcraft, however, they suspected instead that confidence artists were at work, defrauding the simple people.

Perhaps the best example of this is the story of the sorceress of Dormitz, which occupied the Nuremberg city council's attention from 1531 until at least 1538.[44] In October of 1531, the council arrested Kunigunde Hirtin of Dormitz and questioned her several times under torture and the threat of torture about her "soothsaying and sorcery" and her "diabolical prayers."[45] Yet somehow, Kunigunde was out of prison and being sought by the Nuremberg authorities in November. The problem, however, was not merely that a suspected criminal had escaped. The council expressed concern over the number of "simple" farmers, and even some citizens, who were apparently traveling to Dormitz to consult with Kunigunde. The council took measures to prevent this, with an open warrant for her arrest should she ever enter their territory, but also with reminders to the city ministers to preach against consulting soothsayers. In 1536, frustrated by the continued popular patronage of the sorceress of Dormitz and other magical practitioners, the council issued a mandate against sorcery and divination. At times the ordinance sounds like a sermon, at others it warns explicitly that sorcery is fraud; the council sought to educate the public about the religious and financial dangers posed by people who claimed to have magical powers. In ordering the execution of the mandate, the council minutes included specific mention of the sorceress of Dormitz. As a successful and well-known local practitioner, Kunigunde Hirtin stood in for fraudulent magicians generally.

The paternalistic attitude of the Nuremberg elite toward the beliefs of the uneducated masses built up a bulwark of resistance to the learned concept of the diabolic witch; it was in reforming the erring beliefs of their subjects that the urban lords largely avoided one of the greatest persecutory impulses of zealous early modern criminal justice. It is a sad irony of the story of this skepticism that it was paired with deadly credulity when the city council was faced with accusations of ritual murder levied against the Jewish residents of the city.

4
Lucerne: Urban Witch Hunters

Lucerne is a lake town, built on the shores of the Reuss river where it enters Lake Lucerne beneath the snowy peak of Mt. Pilatus. In the fifteenth century, as today, images of the city frequently depicted the Kapellbrücke – the covered wooden bridge which stretches across the river near its mouth – and the tower, the Wasserturm, which anchors it midstream. The Wasserturm served double duty as a watchtower to guard the mouth of the Reuss and as an interrogation and torture chamber. Around the same time that the Kapellbrücke was built, during the wars of the late fourteenth century, the citizens of Lucerne built an outer wall, fortifying the steep hill called the Musegg that rises behind the city. Beyond the wall, the steep descending slope of the hill was pasture. With their high vantage, the towers on the Musegg wall made excellent lookout points for fire in the city or for enemies without.[1]

The city's situation beneath the Gotthard pass made Lucerne a natural anchor for transalpine traffic. Although the usual routes from Nuremberg over the Alps ran to the east of Lucerne, traffic between Basel and northern Italy often passed through the city.[2] Because of its position on the road to the Gotthard pass, Lucerne was host to many pilgrims and merchants. By the sixteenth century, this favorable location had facilitated Lucerne's development into a financial center for the region and beyond.[3] The city was small, however, with an average of 3,200 souls during the fifteenth century. This figure represents a peak in Lucerne's population, and the city had dwindled to as few as 1,300 people by the early seventeenth century.[4]

Lucerne bound her fate early to the Swiss Confederation, with the eternal oath of the *Vierwaldstätterbund* in 1332. This alliance soon led to conflict with the Habsburg overlords of the region, but after the battle of Sempach in 1386 Lucerne was effectively independent of Austrian control. Despite this, Lucerne and the rest of the Swiss Confederation remained a restless part of the Holy Roman Empire. The fifteenth century was the golden age of the Swiss Confederation, when it enjoyed the height of its power. It was also a century of wars, including the war against Burgundy in the 1470s, which brought the Confederation into clear conflict with the empire. In 1495, the Swiss refused to adopt the decrees of the Diet of Worms, rejecting the introduction of the imperial appeals court, the *Reichskammergericht*, and refusing to swear the Perpetual Peace. This led to the Swabian war in 1499, in which the Swiss won their independence from the empire.[5] This *de facto* independence was finally formalized in the Peace of Westphalia in 1648.

The city of Lucerne took a substantial part in the Swiss wars of the fifteenth century, but those wars never reached its walls. Surrounded by allies and protected by mountainous terrain, Lucerne enjoyed significant local power. In 1383, shortly before the battle of Sempach, the city had established itself as ruler of a rural territory around the city and stretching up the Entlebuch valley to the southwest. By 1415, this territory had nearly doubled in size and reached its outer limits on the border with the territory of Bern. Around that time, Lucerne also established control over some of the areas to its east, close to the lake. The rural territories immediately surrounding the city, however, did not become subject to Lucerne until the latter half of the fifteenth century, and their incorporation marked a small but significant final expansion of urban control over the rural countryside.[6]

As a small city with a large rural territory, deeply embedded in the forested mountains, Lucerne developed early into a city that hunted witches. Beginning around 1450 and continuing almost without pause into the mid-seventeenth century, the urban lords actively prosecuted witches, executing over 200 people in the process.[7] Unlike Basel and Nuremberg, Lucerne was a city where the danger of witches and the need to combat them were as real to the ruling elite as to their subjects. The first witch burning within the territory of Lucerne took place in 1423, in the subject town of Sursee. At the time, Sursee possessed the privilege of a high criminal court, which allowed the town a symbolically important degree of autonomy. The 1423 trial and execution there of Verena Rehagin remains somewhat obscure: we do not even know for certain if she was actually executed as a witch.[8] Meanwhile, accusations of witchcraft were being handled as slander within the city of Lucerne itself.

Beginning around the turn of the fifteenth century, sorcery (*Zauberei*) appeared in a number of slander cases in Lucerne. It was usually an insult flung by one woman at another, often coupled with the insinuation of being a thief or the daughter of a thief. The city council of Lucerne, in its capacity as high court, continued to act on accusations of sorcery and witchcraft mainly as slander throughout the first half of the fifteenth century. In 1419 the word *Hexerei* appeared for the first time in the sources from the city, again in a case handled as slander; Conrad Glatz was banished for spreading rumors that certain people were witches.[9] In 1432 witchcraft resurfaces in the council records from Lucerne, in a brief note of two matters to be heard before the full council: a case of suspected bigamy and another of five people rumored to be witches.[10] This may be a sign that the tendency of the Lucerne council to regard rumors of witchcraft exclusively as slander was fading. The referral of the case from the small ruling council to the full "council and hundred" may be an indication that it was being pursued as a criminal matter. The full council held jurisdiction over capital cases and oversaw criminal justice generally.

Our first definite evidence of a shift in the city's treatment of witchcraft comes from the late 1440s, and a radical shift it was indeed. Witchcraft accusations became quite suddenly a matter that demanded thorough investigation, interrogation, and deposing of witnesses. Beginning around this time, convicted witches regularly suffered the danger of death at the stake. This shift was precipitated, it seems, by a witch trial in a neighboring jurisdiction. In 1447, the city council in Lucerne received from Solothurn a summary of the witch trial of Anna Vögtlin, a native of Lucerne territory. Anna had confessed a long history of witchcraft to the authorities in Büren. According to the report sent by Hermann of Russegg in Büren, much of Anna's witchcraft had taken place within Lucerne territory, and she had even been arrested there.[11] While the report was sent as an acknowledgement of Lucerne's natural interest in a case that had partially played out in their territory, we might see the trial itself as a usurpation of Lucerne's authority, and the council of Lucerne may well have viewed it as an insult. A similar incident had taken place in 1444 within Basel's circle of influence, when the authorities of Büren brought a witch from the territory of Sisgau, which later became a part of the territory of Basel.[12] Such witch trials presented challenges to the jurisdictional control of the territorial lords of Sisgau and Lucerne. In Lucerne, the response seems to have been the beginnings of active witchcraft prosecution in that canton.

Shortly after the letter about Anna's trial reached Lucerne, the trial of Else of Meersburg began. The dating of Else's trial is not certain: E. Hoffmann-Krayer and Joseph Hansen both dated the surviving document to circa 1450, based on the handwriting and internal textual references.[13] The exact date of the trial, however, remains unknown. One possibility is that Else was tried in the summer of 1448. An entry in the Lucerne expense books from June of that year mentions costs for the imprisonment of a certain "black Else."[14] If this was indeed Else of Meersburg, no trace of her probable execution remains. We do, however, have the record of a full confession.[15]

Else's confession is rich in detail, and allows us to pick out quite easily the melded elements of the Alpine storm witch and diabolism. The two elements are bound together when she first mentions them:

> On the Monday on which the most recent hail took place, she has confessed, she was between Malters and the city. There a beggar approached her and tried to rape her so that she would marry him and have relations with him. She became angry and went from him to a brook and threw [water] into the air with both hands behind her back in the names of all the devils and especially of Beelzebub and Krütli, who was her chief master among the devils, and to whom she had given herself. And she cursed the beggar with the falling sickness[16] and if he should be struck by hail and lightening it would have pleased her. And the hail came that she had made.[17]

Else's ability to make hail was bound up with her relations with her personal devils. In this way the old, indigenous idea of witchcraft was integrally tied to the emerging stereotype of the diabolic witch. Yet in Else's confession, the old witch concept predominated. Weather magic was the red thread running through the entire narrative of her life as a witch, beginning with her instruction in storm raising as a child. When she described working together with other witches, they were raising storms together.

Alongside Else's confessions of weather magic, the motif of wolf riding also appears, completing the image of the Alpine witch. Else's confession of wolf riding, however, goes beyond the usual mode of the Alpine witch, incorporating elements of a ritual battle reminiscent of Ginzburg's *Night Battles*. Ginzburg notes this case, specifically the confession of Else's accomplice Margret Jägerin, writing, "It probably was not accidental that in the first witchcraft trials held in the Canton of Lucerne…the defendants stated that they went to the sabbath on Thursdays in the Ember Days."[18] Ginzburg's source was not Hoffmann-Krayer's transcription of the confessions of Else and Margret, but Joseph Schacher's 1947 work on Lucerne witch trials. Schacher quotes only a brief except from Margret's confession that indicates the tantalizing timing of the witches' convocations.[19] A close examination of Else's confession, however, reveals more details that support a link between the gatherings described in these confessions and the ritual battles of Ginzburg's *benandanti*.

Else's confession mentions gatherings during the Ember Days twice. The first was in a description of a gathering of storm witches "in Menznau during the Ember Days" where, she said, "they rode on dogs and wolves." Else had to go to this gathering, she explained, "or they would hurt her." There is little to go on here, but in addition to the timing of the gatherings, both the element of good and evil (here in the form of dogs and wolves) and the element of compulsion were also present in the confessions of the *benandanti*. Whether we ought to interpret the "dogs and wolves" as evidence of good and evil is an open question, but this interpretation is at least partially supported by more explicit details that appear later. The second time Else mentioned the Ember Days, more elements of ritualistic battle emerged:

> Note regarding Thann [in Alsace]. The twelve were together in a grove in the monastery and whenever they were together hay became more costly. [It] was on a Thursday in the Ember Days, [and they were] jousting and holding tourney with hemp stalks. Some of them rode on dogs, she [does not] know whether they were dogs or wolves.[20]

Else's protestation that she did not know whether, in fact, some witches rode on dogs or if they all rode wolves reads like the response to a lost query from the interrogator. The interrogator does not seem to have expected this mention of dogs, which did not fit with the stereotype of the weather witch that haunted the fears of Alpine dwellers. Given the arc of Else's confession, we can assume that the interrogator also had at least passing familiarity with the concept of diabolic witchcraft, but in this passage we gain glimpses of a third narrative that seems to have been alien to the interrogator: a gathering during the Ember Days to do battle with hemp stalks, some people mounted on good beasts, some on evil. The outcome of their tournament, if indeed anything hung on their jousting, seems to have fallen without fail to evil. Whenever Else told of witches gathering, the result of their convocation was a hailstorm.

If these were indeed the traces of the fertility cult that Ginzburg identifies behind the story of the *benandanti*, there are two important observations that should be made. First, this tradition was far from the dominant strain of popular beliefs in the Lucerne witch trials. Indigenous ideas of evil witchcraft dominated both witness testimonies and confessions. It was the deeply feared Alpine witch that defined the common understanding of *Hexen*. Secondly, the story of the introduction of diabolism in Lucerne cannot be written as a theologically sophisticated process of the demonization of a fertility ritual, as can the history of the *benandanti*. Aside from the general absence of theological sophistication, this was the only case from Lucerne in which such elements emerged – in the confessions of Else and of Margret Jägerin, whom Else had denounced as her accomplice. In the confessions of both Else and Margret, the concern of the interrogators appears to have been to establish the witches' apostasy and the Devil as the source of her power. The tantalizing descriptions of witches' gatherings were often left free of the Devil entirely, and they rarely appear in later trials. The witches' sabbath did not become an important theme in early witch trials in Lucerne.

It is highly unlikely that either Else or Margret Jägerin escaped with their lives, although another woman denounced by Else of Meersburg, Gret Kunigin, was banished in 1450. Five years later the Lucerne council condemned Dorothea Hindremstein to be burned as well, and for that case we possess only witness testimonies that make no mention of the Devil at all. We lack positive proof that Else and Margret were executed, and only a note on the back of witness testimonies in Dorothea's case suggests that she had been burned. A woman was burned in 1456, and although the laconic expense record details only the cost of the execution and not her crime, it is likely that she was executed as a witch.[21] Incomplete as they are in details, together these cases mark the beginnings of a new approach to witchcraft by the Lucerne authorities, a suspicion that the Alpine witch was the Devil's servant and a readiness to prosecute based on the witchcraft suspicions emanating from the populace. The immediate effect of this change during the following generation was a jump in the number of witch trials heard by the council. Eight witchcraft cases were heard in Lucerne during the 1460s; there had been none in the decade preceding Else's confession.

Although the precedent of prosecution had clearly been set, the practice of burning witches at the stake was not unequivocally established in the city. Only three of the nine cases between 1460 and 1469 ended in execution. In 1460 and 1461 witches were burned in the city and in Willisau; in September of 1460 another woman was burned in Rothenburg. As the decade progressed, however, the trend shifted and the witches were banished instead. In more than one case where the oath of banishment survives we find explicit language of mercy. In 1469 Gret of Russwil was arrested after she had broken a previous oath of banishment sworn on account of witchcraft. Her new oath of banishment reads formulaically: "My merciful lords could well have judged harshly and severely over my life, limb, and property, [sentencing me] from life to death [...] I was a condemned person." Yet the authorities chose clemency: "They showed me mildness and mercy."[22] Gret's second banishment, and probably also her first, fell within a generation of mildness in Lucerne criminal justice. Between 1470 and 1482, there were no witch trials in the city; during the same period executions in general were extremely rare.[23] It seems that at least in that generation, collective sentiment among the urban authorities had shifted against judicial severity.

The absence of witch trials in Lucerne during the 1470s is a bit of a puzzle. On the one hand, external factors would lead us to expect fewer trials. Over the course of the 1460s, an increasing reluctance to execute witches and a growing emphasis on mercy seem to indicate dissatisfaction with witch burnings on the part of the city council. Moreover, the 1470s were a decade of remarkably good weather and plentiful crops. Good growing weather dominated the summers and the winters were mild, few late frosts were reported in the springtime and the autumn weather, though cool, was not too wet.[24] Not only did this reduce the general social stress that might lead to witchcraft accusations, it also meant that fewer specific events took place that might serve to trigger the accusation of weather magic so closely linked to witchcraft in the region. Although the entire fifteenth century was part of the climatic minimum of the Little Ice Age, contemporaries lacked a concept of climate change that might have equipped them to analyze larger trends. Their attention was drawn and their fear inspired by individual weather anomalies: storms, floods, droughts, bitter cold, and early frosts.[25] In the general absence of such disasters, combined with the apparent reluctance of authorities to prosecute witches, it is no surprise to find no executions, indeed no witch trials at all, during the decade.[26]

But here we encounter the perennial uncertainty of fifteenth-century history: lost and incomplete sources. There are multiple sources on witch trials from Lucerne, but none of them is reliable. The best details come from a handful of *Akten*, case files containing either witness depositions or confessions, many of which were transcribed and published by Hoffmann-Krayer. Although they are the richest sources, these *Akten* are scattered across the years and simply do not exist for many trials. Then there are *Urfehde*, which in this case were oaths taken at the time of banishment, although the term was also used for the oaths of peace taken when anyone was released from prison.[27] Highly formulaic, these *Urfehde* contain at best a summary of the crimes of which the exile was accused and usually convicted. Not only would written *Urfehde* only exist for cases of banishment, they survive only for a small portion of such cases. A third, potentially rich source is the city council minutes. These exist both for the privy council and for the council and hundred, usually intermingled in the same books but sometimes recorded separately. Although council records exist for the entire period, it seems that during some years one or the other strain has been lost or omitted. Even during periods of consistent council records, not every trial or execution appears in their pages. When such events do appear, the quality of the source can vary greatly, from a few lines of summary to multi-page records of confessions. The last major source for witch trials in Lucerne during the period is the city's expense record, the *Umgeldrödel*. Although these expense books should in theory contain notes of every execution that took place within the city, comparison with the council minutes quickly reveals that they do not. Certainly some trials are lost to history altogether. During the 1470s, however, this problem is more acute: the expense records are missing and for part of the decade only the privy council minutes appear in the council records. As the full council usually decided capital cases, we are left with significant cause to doubt the total absence of witch trials between 1470 and 1482. These caveats notwithstanding, it is unlikely that there were many trials during the period. This clearly and drastically changed, beginning in 1482.

In the spring and early summer of 1482, at least four women were burned as witches. We have no details from their cases, only the notation in the expense records of the city.[28] Just two days after the first of these trials, the delegates of the Swiss Confederation met in Lucerne. The testimony of the recently burned witch was discussed at the meeting. Here we get a hint as to the content of her confession. Apparently she had not only confessed to weather magic, but had also testified that many other storm witches were still at large.[29] In November of the same year, several women were arrested as witches in the city. At least two of them were banished, a remarkable display of mercy, given that they had both confessed to witchcraft.

The trials of 1482 launched a wave of persecution that lasted until 1496, encompassing 34 trials, including at least nine executions. Again, these trials appear when we might reasonably expect them. The benign climate of the 1470s was followed by a pronounced and persistent shift for the worse in the 1480s. Although the winters were mild, too warm even, the weather during the summer growing periods was wet and cold. These poor growing conditions persisted well into the 1490s, ending with a beautiful summer in 1497.[30] When we examine the details of the cases from the wave of trials that coincided exactly with this period, we find reports of the kinds of disease and devastating weather that accompanied climatic distress and served as focal points for witch fears and as triggering events for witchcraft accusations. This is not to say that bad weather was the cause of witch trials, but rather that it presented a facilitating condition for longstanding fears and suspicions to emerge in specific accusations.

In order to examine the witch fears that were being pursued in this wave of trials, it is helpful to look closely at the testimony of those who brought accusations. In the early 1480s a woman called the Rüschellerin came to be suspected of witchcraft by her neighbors in the village of Reiden, out near the northern edge of Lucerne territory.[31] Nine men volunteered testimony against the Rüschellerin and their depositions were sent in writing to Lucerne with a request to send "Klaus, the big bailiff" out to arrest her. It seems that the city complied, but the outcome of the case did not match the expectations of those who denounced her. They had hoped she would be burned at the stake, but the Rüschellerin was banished. The Lucerne council minutes read:

> Since the woman who was in our prison as a witch had hefty testimony against her but she would not confess, she shall swear [to go] beyond the Rhine and Aare and never return to our territory without our permission.[32]

It is interesting to note that the Rüschellerin was able to escape execution during a witch panic, even with so many witnesses against her. This indicates that the authorities felt bound to certain rules of evidence, even if they did not rigorously follow them in every case or every generation. The essential principle followed in the Rüschellerin's case was that even fairly substantial circumstantial evidence was insufficient to condemn a person of a secret crime. A confession was needed, and in the absence of a confession, an execution was not likely. Such principles were widespread in the fifteenth century, but were largely uncodified and were not strictly followed.[33]

The peasants of Reiden, however, had different evidentiary standards for establishing the guilt of a suspected witch. The nine who testified against the Rüschellerin clearly believed her to be a witch, and they expected that denouncing her to the authorities would result in her execution. One of the men, Niklaus Meiger, called Kleiwi, had made this expectation explicit. He told how one of his horses had fallen gruesomely ill, "so that it sweat blood through its whole hide."[34] Kleiwi immediately suspected witchcraft and believed that the Rüschellerin was the witch responsible. He found her and confronted her, using a thinly disguised threat in the place of direct confrontation. "Great God's blood!" he cried out upon meeting her at a well, "One of my horses has been bewitched, and if it dies, I am going to turn [the witch] in, so she has to burn."[35] In this brief utterance the constellation emerges clearly: a woman was feared and despised as a witch and her neighbor expected that escalating the matter by denouncing her to the authorities would result in her death. Official justice became the hammer used by ordinary people to control the witch in their midst. Kleiwi wanted his horse to recover, and he was satisfied when it did. The rest of his testimony reveals the limits to his capacity to compel the witch. Like a tragic hero, he made a crucial error born of pride. Having twice forced the Rüschellerin to cure ailing horses (or so he believed), Kleiwi began to brag to his friends of how he had healed his horses by threatening the witch. After this, one of his horses took ill again and died, despite all his efforts.

Kleiwi's actions were based on the assumption that the Rüschellerin was a witch, and this assumption underlay all of the testimony against her. As confirmation of its truth, several of the witnesses cited conversations with a former miller of Reiden, who had died some time earlier. The miller, who claimed that he could "recognize all witches when he first laid eyes on them,"[36] had openly believed the Rüschellerin to be a witch. Two witnesses cited his words as evidence of her guilt, saying they had gone to him once and asked him what he thought of the Rüschellerin. The miller had replied:

> She is a witch and a truly evil [woman]. I once encountered her in a field near Reiden, and she hitched up her skirts and ran at [me], fell on [my] neck and put her arms around [me], saying: My godfather, [surely] you are not afraid of me? And [I] said: Get away! I know full well who you are.[37]

The miller's belief that the Rüschellerin was a witch not only supported the general suspicion, it also kept him out of the village. Another witness described how the miller had purchased a house in Reiden, hoping to move up from the mill near the stream to the village proper. Then the Rüschellerin moved into a house on the same street and the miller began to delay his own move. Asked by the witness when he was going to move to his new house, the miller grumbled that he never would, because then he would have to see a witch every day, a witch who knew that he recognized her true nature.

In a number of stories offered in the witness depositions against the Rüschellerin, we catch a glimpse of the dynamics that gave rise to the suspicion against her. The bundle of depositions began with that of a man named Reider, formerly of the village Reiden. At the time of the deposition, Reider lived in Langnau, just across the mill stream. Reider testified that while he had lived in Reiden, he had fallen into a quarrel with the Rüschellerin, "and his cow gave nothing but blood."[38] The situation went on for so long, he said, that he left the village and moved to Langnau because of it. Beginning with Reider's tale of conflict avoidance and closing with Kleiwi's story of confrontation, the collection of depositions is thus framed by cases that tie the Rüschellerin's story to patterns of witchcraft suspicion throughout Europe. She was suspected, at least in part, because she was a quarrelsome woman and a difficult neighbor. Her behavior threatened the community itself. At least two men, the miller and Reider, were driven from the village by her presence.

While stories of direct interpersonal conflict are key to understanding how suspicion of the Rüschellerin arose, the depositions are also replete with tales of eerie encounters with the witch, tales that provide evidence of the hair-raising substance of local witch beliefs. Heini Fuchs set the tone with this story:

> One morning just as the day had begun to break, he encountered [the Rüschellerin] coming out of a forest, some distance from Reiden. [She] ran toward the village with her [skirts] hitched up high. She came in such a dreadful manner, her mouth nearly blue, that he became so terrified of her that his hair stood on end[39] and from that day onward his mouth was covered in sores. But what she had done [in the wood] or what her business had been, he knew not.[40]

A man named Gassenrumer offered another eerie tale that made clear at least one thing she might have been doing in the forest: raising a storm.

Gassenrumer testified that about ten years earlier he had been working for the governor. One morning, he said, he saw the Rüschellerin heading toward a wood in which there lay a pond. Again he described her running with her skirts hitched up, a frequent motif in descriptions of the woman in suspicious circumstances. She was running so fast, he added, that he would not have been able to recognize her but that he was mounted on horseback. He spurred his horse after her, and when he saw who she was he rode straight away to the governor and reported the matter. He went on:

> The whole day there was a cloud over the pond; many people saw that cloud. And the whole day they had to ring the bells against storms, but toward evening a powerful storm came with rain but no hail. If they had not been so quick to ring the bells, it would have been worse.[41]

Clearly, the Rüschellerin was believed to be a storm witch.

Several of the eerie narratives that were told of the Rüschellerin's behavior centered on her coming out of the woods at dawn. Storm raising was not the only possible interpretation of her presence there: that was just part of her frightening weirdness. She was frequently described as running in a terrifying, even predatory fashion. This bestial behavior was clearly associated with the darker forces of nature. The Rüschellerin was believed to be in league with dangerous and hated predators:

> [Rudi Metziner] testified that his child once sat with the Rüschellerin's child. There were a number of other children [there], also Metziner's. And the children said: We have baby birds. And some children said: We have baby geese. Then the Rüschellerin's child said: But we have baby foxes and baby wolves, and when my father is away, my mother feeds them on the barn floor.[42]

Not only does an eerie note here enter a scene of childish conversation, but the Rüschellerin's child described a direct subversion of patriarchal authority. The unholy alliance between the witch and the wild, savage beasts seems to be undermining the family.

The Rüschellerin's supposed alliance with wolves went further. She was said to have been seen riding wolves. Three of the witnesses against the Rüschellerin – Metziner, Fuchs and Gassenrumer – told of a time they had been fishing together. A man from Reitnau (some 8 km distant from Reiden) approached them. The man was known to them: the witnesses described him as a trustworthy man. He told them that he had seen a woman of Reiden astride a wolf on the equinox, adding that she had not seen him. The three men from Reiden questioned him, hoping to discover the identity of the wolf rider. In the customary manner, the man from Reitnau described her by the clothes she had been wearing, saying she wore green sleeves with distinctive buckles. The description matched the Rüschellerin. Upon hearing this tale, Gassenrumer rushed to the village of Reiden and confronted the women there as a collective, crying, "You shed God's blood, you women of Reiden! Why do you not ride horses instead of wolves?"[43] The shame of having a witch in the village touched them all, and with his words Gassenrumer painted them all with the taint of witchcraft.

An element of horror ran through the stories about the Rüschellerin, and we find the aspects of the Alpine witch bound up with this element. But the terrifying aspect of the witch was part of her domestic powers as well. She caused sores to cover Fuchs's mouth, onions to wither at her touch, a horse to sweat out its blood in such quantities that it "flowed down." Whether the witnesses truly feared their neighbor or simply hated her cannot be divined across the temporal divide, but their narratives were drenched in fear and hatred in equal parts. The witch as they described her was an ally of wolves, a summoner of storms, an unholy terror, a source of domestic woes, and a destroyer of their community.

The Rüschellerin's case demonstrates quite clearly that the concerns of ordinary people remained focused on the Alpine witch as the fifteenth century waned. They knew that execution at the stake was a likely outcome of a witchcraft accusation, and they would at least have heard tales of the witch burnings of the preceding few years. Yet although diabolism would have been present in many of the confessions customarily read aloud at those executions, none of these witnesses instrumentalized suggestions of diabolism as a means to rid themselves of an unpleasant neighbor.

Johannes Dillinger has argued that once a person came to be seen as an "evil person," others noticed the attributes of a witch even in the most seemingly harmless interactions.[44] It was not being encountered in questionable circumstances that gave rise to witchcraft suspicions, but witchcraft suspicions that made the circumstances suspect. People came to be seen as "evil" due to conflict that breached the conventions of community. Although the details of these conflicts are lost to us in most cases, their fault lines can be seen in the social profile of the accused.

The Rüschellerin was not a "classic" witchcraft suspect. From the testimonies, we know that she was neither impoverished nor widowed. In fact the typical accused witch in the Lucerne territory was a peasant woman of means sufficient to support herself and perhaps even to evoke some envy among her neighbors. Her vulnerability to accusations lay not primarily in that envy, however, but in her quarrelsome nature and, intriguingly, her likely status as an immigrant to the local area. It seems that when such women failed to integrate well into their new communities, this disrupted social equilibrium, resulting at times in witchcraft suspicions and even accusations.[45] Such was the case in 1500, in the village of Kriens, within the territory of Lucerne, which has been analyzed by Andreas Blauert. Blauert notes that the witchcraft accusations raised against the central figure in the trials, the Oberhuserin, arose from the tensions that had developed between her family and their neighbors after the family's arrival in the area. The Oberhusers were relative newcomers without affinal ties to the long-standing residents. This left little to counterbalance the envy those neighbors felt of the slightly better-off Oberhuser family. When interpersonal conflict sparked suspicions, the social distance between the Oberhusers and their neighbors hindered a peaceful resolution. The Oberhuserin became the central suspect in a witch trial involving at least four other women.[46]

There is one aspect of the profile of accused witches that was nearly iron-clad in Lucerne around 1500: they were all women. In fact, one of the most striking characteristics of the indigenous witch stereotype in the region between the Alps and the Rhine is that the witch was strongly gendered female. The strength of this gendering is sufficient to allow us some confidence in interpreting the execution of any woman by fire in Basel or Lucerne as evidence that she was convicted of witchcraft. The logic for this can be demonstrated with a comparison of witchcraft and sodomy executions in Basel. We have evidence of 52 fiery executions in Basel between 1453 and 1532. Of these, only ten were explicitly cases of witchcraft. Twice as many involved accusations of sodomy or bestiality. Of the remaining 22 victims, six were women and sixteen were men. An examination of burnings in the city by crime and gender reveals several things. Firstly, no male witches are found, and no female sodomites. Of female victims for whom a crime is known, all of them were burned as witches. Of the men who met their end at the stake, only one is known to have been convicted for a crime other than sodomy. Conrad in der Gassen was burned in 1530 after a detailed confession of atheism.[47] Conrad appears to have been a man for whom the turmoil and doubts brought on by the Reformation ruptured his faith altogether. The case also appears to have been a complete anomaly. It is not unreasonable to assume that in Basel during this period, the burnings of women and men for unspecified causes were almost always for the gender-related crimes of witchcraft and sodomy respectively.

As Suzanne Burghartz has rightly pointed out, even in the case of the Germanic Alps, it is a mistake to refer to witchcraft as a gender-specific crime.[48] There were exceptions to the rule, though in places like Basel and Lucerne they were quite few in number. Although there were men accused of witchcraft in Lucerne, almost all known executions of men by fire involved accusations of sodomy and all known cases of women being executed by fire involved accusations of witchcraft. There is only one exception to this rule: In 1511, Rudolph Erenbolder was burned for theft and diabolism.[49] Although he confessed to no magic and the sources imply none, his case stands in closer relation to cases of witchcraft than to those of sodomy. Several cases are found in Lucerne which complicate the gender model by mixing accusations of sodomy and witchcraft. These cases all took place in 1519, and in two of them, as in Erenbolder's case, the primary charge appears to have been theft. Three suspects, two women and one man, confessed to both sodomy and witchcraft; a fourth man confessed to sodomy. An examination of the details of their cases reveals how they diverge from the strict gendering of witchcraft and sodomy, but confirm it in principle.

The first three were executed together, in July of 1519.[50] This was the case of Andreas from Tschafel, whom we have met before, and his two apparent accomplices, Hans Stächli and Barbel Vermeggerin. The confessions of the three began in the usual style of theft confessions in Lucerne, with a list of items and the circumstances in which they were stolen. In addition, Hans confessed to habitual bestiality. Andreas also confessed to bestiality and to having sodomized six boys. Andreas's confession goes on to include both diabolism and attempted storm raising, several murders and more theft. The third member of this gang of thieves was a woman, Barbel Vermeggerin. Barbel's confession also begins with a litany of thefts, a purse containing three pounds in coins, four shillings from her brother-in-law, and so forth. Then her confession shifts abruptly to diabolism and witchcraft:

> Also she has confessed how the Devil came to her in the shape of a man with goat's feet, and won her over with good words, [saying] that he would teach her to make hail.[51]

Barbel confessed to trying to raise hail many times, but succeeding only twice. Although briefer than many witches' confessions, hers contained the essence of diabolic witchcraft: the local stereotype of the witch as storm raiser and the newly important detail of the Devil. She went on to confess that Andreas, whom she had been with for the last twelve years, had sodomized her twice.

The fourth case is that of Madlena Graffheinrichin of Urach who was burned the following month. Her confession was recorded briefly, without much detail:

> She has confessed that she denied God and all the saints. Also she has confessed that she made hail three times, and she has confessed that she had sex with a dog many times. [Based] on such confessions, my lords have had her burned.[52]

Despite the succinctness of the scribe, the essence of diabolic witchcraft is also contained in this confession. The additional detail of bestiality is unique and likely to have been her own invention (or experience) rather than a response to pointed questioning.

A significant trend emerges from the details of these cases. The confessions of the women place more emphasis than that of Andreas on the supposed witchcraft. Conversely, his case contains more detail pertaining to his supposed sodomy than do theirs. Furthermore, in the confession of Barbel Vermeggerin, Andreas is the agent of her being sodomized. These exceptions thus seem to confirm the general rule: sodomites in Lucerne were male, witches were female. This general rule facilitates such important assumptions as those that appeared earlier in this chapter: that Verena Rehagin and the anonymous victim of 1456 were burned as witches. It also makes clear that a significant change took place in Lucerne after 1519. Although most witchcraft suspects continued to be women, a small number of men began to appear among the accused. As I will argue in more detail later,[53] I think the triple trial of 1519 was crucial to this change and indicative of a general demonization of ordinary criminals in Lucerne. In order to see how this was the case, however, we need to first examine the broader context of criminal justice in particular and social control in general in these late medieval cities.

Part II
A Revolution in Criminal Justice

During the same century that the concept of the diabolic witch developed and was merged with indigenous witchcraft beliefs to produce deadly trials, the basic procedures of criminal justice were changing. Although this transformation was already underway in the fourteenth century, criminal procedures were in flux throughout the fifteenth, as accuser-driven prosecution gave way to inquisitorial process with official prosecution. Inquisitorial prosecution relied heavily on torture and was a key factor in facilitating the mass witch hunts of the late sixteenth and early seventeenth centuries. For this reason alone it makes good sense to examine the early witch trials within the context of these procedural changes.

There is another aspect of criminal justice that provides crucial context for this analysis: patterns of actual prosecution. Patterns of witchcraft prosecution have been analyzed for many times and places, often with complete disregard for how that prosecution fits into criminal prosecution generally. The forces that drove witchcraft prosecution are often assumed to be fundamentally different from those that drove ordinary criminal justice. In the case of mass witch hunts, this might be confirmed by a comparison with regular criminal prosecution. Many witch trials, however, took place by ones and twos, fully integrated into the ordinary procedures of criminal justice. Most of the trials examined for this study were relatively isolated from other witch trials; the cases that were being heard at the same time by the same men were instances of theft and violence. Before we can draw conclusions about the patterns they manifest, we should examine them in the context of daily criminal prosecution.

5

Between Two Worlds: Fifteenth-Century Justice at the Threshold of the Early Modern

The late Middle Ages in Germany were the locus of a massive transformation in criminal justice. The revolutionary changes wrought during the period were long and slow, and they remained incomplete even after the codification of the new mode of criminal justice in the imperial penal code of 1532 (the *Carolina*). Assumptions that had characterized medieval justice enjoyed enduring currency throughout the early modern period, and traces of procedural forms usually identified with the early modern can be found well before the fifteenth century. Nevertheless, the differences between the usual modes of criminal justice in the two eras were profound. Fifteenth-century criminal justice existed between two worlds, and the long procedural transformation that took place across that century was characterized by borrowing and experimentation.

While medieval criminal justice could be harsh, it paled in comparison to that of the early modern era. According to legal historians, the former operated in a compensatory and restorative mode, the latter in a punitive and deterrent mode. In medieval jurisprudence, a crime damaged the peace, which then had to be restored. One of the primary instruments of this process was the oath of peace (*Urfehde*). The *Urfehde* had its initial purpose in the resolution of feuds. To the medieval mind, it was a greater crime to break one's oath than it was to lose one's temper and kill another man. By requiring that the feuding parties swear to keep the peace between them, the *Urfehde* brought the possibility of the death penalty to bear if that peace were broken. The oath of peace came to be an instrument of criminal justice more generally. By the fifteenth century, the most common use of the *Urfehde* came at the end of the criminal process. Upon release, the individual who had been tried, whether found guilty or innocent, was required to take an oath of peace with the men who had imprisoned and interrogated him.[1]

The legal concepts of the peace of the land (*Landesfriede*) and later the peace of the city (*Stadtfriede*) had also developed during the Middle Ages. The theoretical counterparts of the practical *Urfehde*, they were initially intended to quell and resolve feuding. The oldest *Landesfriede* laws, from the time of the Peace of God in the late eleventh century, threaten death for acts of robbery, murder, arson, and kidnapping committed during feuds. In practice, and in some written codes, mutilations and banishment replaced execution. Furthermore, other crimes such as theft came to be considered violations of the peace, even though they were not associated with feuding. It was from this kernel that medieval procedures pertaining to the death penalty derived.[2]

Within the medieval compensatory system, a key means of resolving conflict was financial reparations. Generally paid to the injured party, fines came gradually to accrue also to the adjudicating court. Of course, not everyone could pay fines, and those who could not were usually subjected to either banishment or corporal punishment. Banishment was not only reserved for those who could not pay financial penalties, however. In medieval cities, it was an effective means of maintaining the *Stadtfriede*. Even for potentially capital crimes, such as oath breaking, theft, and sodomy, banishment was commonly employed. In a city with walled boundaries and a relatively small population, a secret return into the city itself rarely remained hidden for long. Banishment functioned well in late medieval cities and was widely used.[3] Basel, Lucerne, and Nuremberg all followed this general trend. In each of these cities, banishment was the preferred mode of punishment for many criminal transgressions before the mid-fifteenth century. In both Nuremberg and Basel, lists of banishments are the best archival source for the investigation of fourteenth-century criminal history.[4]

Already in the fourteenth century, however, the death penalty was advancing. As the cities established greater judicial autonomy and struggled with the criminal elements of an increasingly mobile population, they turned more and more to the ultimate punishment to maintain the peace. By the late fifteenth and early sixteenth centuries, even crimes usually treated with banishment were increasingly falling subject to the death penalty. Thus the late Middle Ages witnessed the beginnings of a modernizing revolution in criminal justice. The compensatory system, known among legal historians as *composition*, began to give way to the punitive, the state (here the city state) began to function as accuser and prosecutor as well as judge. Rather than restoring the peace by banishing the offending person from the city, the peace was ensured by destroying that person altogether.

This transformation in punishment was based on the replacement of the restorative justice of the composition system with the criminal justice of the inquisitorial process.[5] Within the composition system, the essence of public justice was the restoration of the peace. Medieval criminal justice, moreover, was a personal confrontation between adversaries in which the accuser was potentially subject to harsh penalties for failing to prove the case. Under inquisitorial process, the function of public justice was the discovery and punishment of crime and cases were pursued by officials who enjoyed a high degree of immunity to reprisals. It is no accident that the term "inquisitorial process" immediately conjures images of the Inquisition of the medieval church against heresy. The medieval Inquisition practiced inquisitorial process *par excellence*. Yet the history of the development of inquisitorial process in German law is not that of the direct adoption of Inquisition practice into secular law. Rather, it is the story of an indigenous development, influenced by such examples of inquisitorial process as the Inquisition, and culminating during the period of this study with the reception of an Italian version of the same process.[6]

When speaking of the fifteenth century, it is important to emphasize that the transition was gradual, and elements of the old system remained long after inquisitorial process was established. To present a simple dichotomy between inquisitorial process and accusatory process would be to eclipse the great variety which existed in early modern legal practice.[7] Indeed, one of the main thrusts of recent work in German criminal history has been to complicate and even fundamentally challenge the legal-historical narrative of transformation that I have sketched out here.[8] Nonetheless, the old grand narrative of the advent of inquisitorial process certainly applies to the cities examined here, and it is quite helpful in understanding the transformations within fifteenth-century judicial procedure.

Inquisitorial process consists of two elements: the official responsibility for prosecution and the duty to investigate. During the early Middle Ages, the responsibility for prosecution rested with the individual. Most justice was private, in the form of revenge and the feud. The function of state power was to control feuding and limit its excesses.[9] It was from this peacekeeping duty of government, the maintenance of the *Landesfriede*, that the earliest precursors of inquisitorial process developed. The *Landesfriede* was essentially a renunciation of force by

participants. But what of individuals who did not join in this renunciation of force, those who circulated in a predatory manner, using theft
and force to maintain their existence? It was against such persons,
called *schädliche Leute*, that the state acquired its earliest responsibility
to prosecute in the absence of an accuser. As public justice developed in
the Middle Ages, the accuser was central to the proceedings. Not only
did the accuser bring charges, but he also played a central role in the
prosecution, participating in the modes of proof – ordeal, oath, and
ritual battle – which might be brought to bear. Against the *schädliche
Leute*, however, a new process was developed, procedure upon reputation (*Verfahren auf Leumund*).

Procedure upon reputation was developed as a tool against harmful
outsiders. Citizens of urban communes had the right to clear themselves
with an oath of innocence.[10] Within this limitation, the cities exercised
the right to prosecute and punish persons of ill repute. In a Nuremberg
ordinance of the fourteenth century the procedure is explained:

> If a person is imprisoned who has a reputation that puts him in dan-
> ger of physical punishment, then the judge and investigators and
> the council should come together regarding this matter during the
> council. The judge [...] should ask every man on his oath what he
> knows of the reputation. If they cannot agree about the reputation,
> they may investigate the matter for a week, or until the next council,
> and when the reputation has been investigated as well as it may be
> [...] the judge should ask, if he is better alive or dead.[11]

Such procedure upon reputation also developed in Lucerne and Basel,
and even after inquisitorial process became more elaborate in these cities the language of reputation remained.[12] If the reputation were substantial, it alone was enough to warrant punishment. As procedure upon
reputation was introduced, the oath also suffered erosion as a means of
proof. Initially, this was because such proceedings were used against
strangers, the *schädliche Leute*. As outsiders whose honor was already
suspect, such persons could not clear themselves with an oath of innocence and were unlikely to find a sufficient number of oath-helpers.[13]
Different means of evidence were needed.

Nevertheless, oath-based legal culture was not eliminated. Although
such cases were increasingly rare, local residents and citizens were
still able to clear their names with an oath from time to time. In most
fifteenth-century cases, however, the accused was unable to do so. Where
oath-helpers had once supported the accused with sworn statements of

faith in his innocence, positive proof of guilt was now sought, through eyewitness testimony and confession. The judge and his investigators undertook the task of uncovering the truth, by questioning witnesses and the accused. In rare instances, though, oaths continued to appear in Lucerne as proof of innocence. For example, when a shoemaker was accused of rape in 1524 he was allowed to swear to his innocence:

> It is decided that the shoemaker may swear an oath to God and the saints that [...] he has not forced nor raped her [...] If he will swear, he should be free of this woman's accusation, but if he will not take the oath, my Lords will act [...] and let justice be done.[14]

Yet such instances were the exception, rather than the rule. The right of the accused, should he be a man of honor, to clear his name with an oath only appeared occasionally in Basel during the fifteenth and early sixteenth centuries.[15] Even when the possibility of the oath of innocence existed, the injured party possessed the right to demand an examination of evidence and testimony instead, as for example in the case of Fridlin Ring from 1507:

> When, however, the accuser demanded of the court that his opponent should acknowledge the accusation without reservation or else suffer investigation, it was declared that Fridlin Ring should [do so].[16]

Thus we can see that where the old modes of proof continued to exist they were relegated to secondary status next to the newer, investigative means of evidence. As in Basel and Lucerne, the oath of innocence appeared in rare instances in Nuremberg during the period. The circumstances in which such an oath might be used were clearly limited, however. The right to swear to one's innocence was generally reserved for citizens. It was left up to the council to decide on a case-by-case basis if the oath were admissible.[17] The oath of innocence was, in other words, no longer a right but a privilege.

As the new procedural standards took hold, honor and status remained important, but they were not the only determining factors. Indeed some historians have located the beginnings of the modern rejection of status-specific justice in the late Middle Ages. In his analysis of late medieval crime as evidenced in the Nuremberg chronicles, Helmut Martin has argued that the punishments he found cannot be spoken of as status-specific justice. I think that Martin's view is rather too optimistic. It is certainly true, as Schuster has found for Constance, that poverty and lack of social connection left individuals vulnerable before the law. As Martin points out, economic class and status are different qualities, but the effects of different standards relating to status can also be seen in criminal justice.[18] The effect of status can be clearly seen when parallel cases are examined in which the relative status of perpetrator and victim are reversed. There was a clear difference of power and status between a husband and his wife, and as in every other age, matrimony occasionally turned to violent dispute. When wives killed their husbands it appears to have been invariably handled as murder, but when husbands killed their wives they stood a fair chance of having their case handled as accidental and excusable.

There was no suitable context for near-deadly violence by a wife against her husband. If the method is mentioned at all it was usually poison, a particularly despised means of murder. Such was the case in Nuremberg in 1486:

> Anno 1486, the 26th of March, Margaretha Haasin, who poisoned her husband Hans Haas, who was a mercenary here, [...] was torn with red-hot tongs and buried alive under the gallows.[19]

If a man killed his wife, however, he might successfully argue that it had been an accident. In 1508, in Lucerne, Jacob Ferrer was charged with having killed his wife, a fact that he did not contest. Rather, he argued that for years his wife had scolded and cursed him, so he had taken the matter to the local magistrate. The magistrate had given him free rein to punish his wife should she not desist, which he did. Apparently the woman died from a powerful blow to the head. Jacob's defense was sufficient; he was acquitted of any wrongdoing in the case.[20] That a deadly blow to the head was considered a reasonable response to a sharp-tongued wife is indicative of the deep power differential between husbands and wives in the fifteenth-century. Nonetheless, unrestrained wife beating was usually frowned upon by the urban authorities.[21] It is significant that Jacob received permission to discipline his wife. Even in the absence of such permission, however, wife killing as a result of a beating was not handled as murder.

One case in which a dead wife was regarded as a murder victim is the exception that proves the rule. In 1525, Thomas Spring-in-Clee was executed on the wheel in Basel, for murdering his wife Barbara.[22] Thomas confessed that he had attacked his wife on the bank of the Rhine, strangled her, stabbed her, and thus murdered her. Moreover, he made efforts to hide his crime. He said he threw Barbara's body in the Rhine and discarded some of her clothes, presumably because they were bloody. Having committed the killing in secret, Thomas attempted to keep it a secret. No mention was made of a quarrel which might have led him to kill her in a rage, or of misbehavior on her part which might have induced him to justify his actions as punishment. Thomas's actions, at least as he confessed to them, framed his crime quite clearly as murder. In this light, Helmut Martin seems correct when he that says the key to punishment in the late Middle Ages was not the status of the accused, but the definition of the crime. Yet we can also see that status was an intrinsic factor in how certain actions were defined.

There is, however, a real difference between status-specific justice and justice that, while theoretically applying the same law to everyone, remains sensitive to status. The transition from the former to the latter was not complete until after the French Revolution, but it took place in stages across the centuries. Ironically, the process of integrating torture into ordinary criminal justice was a step on the road to the modern rule of law, but it was not only present when inquisitorial process was used. In the seventeenth century torture was readily employed in cases handled under customary law, and Jerouschek argues that torture had deep roots within German traditional law.[23] Over the course of the long fifteenth century – beginning with the pogroms that followed the Black Death and ending with the promulgation of the *Carolina* in 1532 – torture became a regular part of German jurisprudence, reaching up through the social scale and into the protected ranks of citizens.

Throughout most of the Middle Ages, torture was not a part of ordinary judicial practice in Germany. Early uses of torture, such as during the interrogation of suspected sorcerers and heretics in the eleventh century, were irregular, extra-judicial measures even if they were not expressly forbidden.[24] From the thirteenth century onward torture was used increasingly, even appearing in some statutes. The struggle of urban communes to establish and defend a degree of sovereignty resulted in some of the earliest German legal documents referring explicitly to torture, fourteenth-century imperial privileges granted to the cities that testify to their right to use torture in criminal trials.[25] This development was bundled with directives from the emperor to the imperial sheriffs ordering them to pursue the *schädliche Leute* as well as the creation of a simplified trial form in the cities for roughly the same purpose. This early expansion of torture remained limited to a small number of persons, those not integrated into or connected with a community.[26] The use of torture in extraordinary circumstances appears to have helped pave the way for its use more generally. In 1349, in the wake of the Black Death, a wave of trials against Jews took place, as a rumor spread that the pestilence had been caused by poisoning. Accused of causing the plague, the Jewish community in Nuremberg was attacked in a pogrom, and over five hundred people were killed.[27] In Basel, many Jews were also killed in a pogrom; they were driven into a wooden house which was then set ablaze. Others were condemned in a formal trial, confessing "without torture and also after torture" that they had poisoned fountains and thus spread the plague.[28] The use of torture in the attack on the Jews in 1349 may well have provided a model for the more widespread introduction of torture in the generation that followed. In 1356, the Golden Bull of Charles IV that laid out the constitutional structure for the empire, included a provision for the use of torture in cases of high treason.[29] Between 1350 and 1400, torture was essentially normalized in German criminal judicial practice.[30]

The early history of torture in Basel is difficult to trace, as the evidence is scant. We do know that torture was used in the trial of the Basel Jews for poisoning in 1349. After that we have no clear indication of its use until the first weekly expense records, which begin at the turn of the fifteenth century. At that time, torture was a part of the most common of capital cases, theft. Thus we read in an expense entry from 1403: "To the judge, 2s on account of the man who was hanged in lesser Basel. Also 2s to torture the same."[31] It is impossible to know exactly when torture became a normal part of the judicial process, but we do know that it was an established method of obtaining evidence before the sorcery trial in 1407 and long before the first witch burnings in the 1440s. In surveying the Basel expense records from 1428 to 1432, I found frequent mention of the use of torture.

In 1430, money for torturing, called "tumgelt," appears twelve times in the expense records. Given that such expenses in consecutive weeks might have been repeated torture for a given suspect, we can estimate that the number of cases which involved torture was between nine and twelve. Three people were executed that year in Basel, of whom two were tortured. Who were the other seven to ten? The entries for "tumgelt" are anonymous. Given the relatively low caseload of the criminal court in Basel, however, we can establish some of the identities through guesswork. It seems that three of the individuals who were tortured were thieves. Of them, only one was executed (on the wheel, so he was presumably condemned also for murder); the other two were punished and banished.[32] A fourth was also executed, possibly for theft as well.[33]

A fifth may have been Agnes of Wissenburg, who was banished for sorcery in September of that year.[34] A sixth man, who was probably tortured twice, was released on the tenth of June. He was given two pounds to go to the baths, as compensation for his suffering.[35] The others remain unknown.

The pattern which emerges from the evidence for 1430 is generally reflected in the sources for the next century. Torture was employed in capital cases in Basel, but its application does not seem to have necessarily resulted in a harsher penalty for the accused. Indeed, from time to time suspects were acquitted after torture. When this happened, the city council generally compensated them for their suffering. As in 1430, so in 1453: "Also, 2£ to the prisoner from Liestal, given in compensation for his suffering."[36] There is no evidence that torture was used in Basel for non-capital offenses. In light of this, one might ask what to make of the probable torture of Agnes of Wissenburg, during the period before the introduction of the death penalty for witchcraft. It pays to remember, however, that although in practice the city of Basel did not apply the death penalty in such cases until the middle of the fifteenth century, witchcraft was in theory a capital crime throughout the Middle Ages. After the practice of witch burning appeared in the territory of Basel, torture seems to have been used frequently in cases of witchcraft.

Between 1433 and 1452, the expense records that provide traces of torture in Basel are lost, and the evidence becomes shakier for the years after this record gap. While in the early period specific expense entries for torture were the rule, after 1452 entries pertaining to "tumgelt" disappear altogether. Instead, numerous entries list expenses for prisoners in the Eselturm. The Eselturm contained the city's torture chamber but it also housed prisoners, and the expenses probably reflect both torture and prison costs indiscriminately. Thus torture within the city walls becomes all but invisible after the mid-century. A series of cases from the 1470s to 1490s, however, do mention the use of torture. In those years, twelve expense entries detail the cost of sending an officer of the city to one of the outlying territories to "gichtigen," or interrogate a prisoner under torture.[37] From 1478 to 1484 Ulrich Ringler served as the city's traveling investigator, from 1485 to 1489 a man called Durch-den-Wind. Most of the entries pertaining to their work contain no information about the supposed crime of the accused. Some entries are more specific: "19s to Ulrich Ringler for his pay and board, to go to Farnsburg and Liestal to torture two witches."[38] Four of the twelve entries specified that the task was the interrogation of witches. Of the rest, all but one offer no details. That one was a case from 1478 in which a man was burned:

> 1£ to Ulrich Ringler to go to Liestal and torture a poor man twice. Also 7½s for his horse. Also 1£ to the executioner to burn the same.[39]

It is probable that this man was executed for sodomy or bestiality, in the course of a persecution which paralleled the persecution of witches in Basel.[40] It is impossible to know if the other cases of torture were also witchcraft or sodomy cases, but it is likely that they were more common capital cases, such as theft. The unusual costs which a burning entailed made it far more likely that specifics of such cases would find their way into the expense records. Anonymous cases were more likely to have been those which did not entail unusual expenses.

It is difficult to speak of any application of torture as mild, but protections appear to have been in place in Basel which were not widespread in the fifteenth century. No prisoner appears to have been tortured more than twice, although we cannot say with certainty that this never occurred. Furthermore, in cases where torture failed to prove the guilt of the accused, the city council took on a responsibility to compensate the victim of its justice. These are the kinds of safeguards which were introduced more broadly in legal reforms at the end of the fifteenth and beginning of the sixteenth century, most notably in the *Carolina*. In Basel, where torture was adopted early and used regularly, such safeguards appear to have developed indigenously.

The city of Nuremberg is seen by some as a model of the influence of Italian law schools on German judicial practice.[41] This process, known as the reception of Roman law, profoundly influenced criminal trials by emphasizing the official duty to investigate crimes even in the absence of an accuser, and by requiring positive proof of guilt. Because of the importance of judicial confession to Roman law, torture was often employed in areas where Roman law was followed. This narrative of the reception of Roman law in Germany quickly becomes complicated once we begin to examine the actual practice of criminal justice in a city like Nuremberg.

During the fifteenth century, the city of Nuremberg employed a staff of jurists as regular consultants, which is one reason the city serves as an exemplar of the reception. As Nuremberg jurist Christoph Scheurl wrote in his 1516 description of the city's constitution:

> The [city] fathers do not admit the doctors into the council. Whenever they are in disagreement or require an opinion in a legal case, they order two of their members to go to the doctors after breakfast and take council with them and report back the next day with their advice.[42]

But these jurists offered consultations primarily on the judgments to be reached. While they certainly demanded particular kinds of evidence, the methods used in obtaining that evidence were left to the city council, which in turn increasingly delegated part of that responsibility to some of its youngest members.

By the mid-fifteenth century, torture was being used regularly in criminal proceedings in Nuremberg. As investigations were undertaken in capital criminal cases, the city council received regular reports from the *Schöffen*, the men assigned as juror-investigators. These investigators were usually junior members of the city government, generally from the powerful patrician families who dominated the council. After each round of interrogation, the investigators reported back to the city council and received orders on how to proceed. The origins of this process date back as far as the late fourteenth century. An ordinance from 1371 reads:

> When *schädliche Leute* arrive in [Nuremberg's] prison, and the greater part of the council decides they should be tortured, it shall be done.[43]

Thus the best archival sources on torture in Nuremberg are the *Ratsverlässe*, the daily minutes of the city council.[44] In succinct entries, these books contain details of a wide range of council business, including decisions pertaining to ongoing criminal investigations. Although the council minutes rarely contain any information on what the investigators reported about their investigations, the orders they received are included in terse but specific notations.

The earliest surviving *Ratsverlässe* come from the council year running from the spring of 1449 to the spring of 1450. Beginning in the 1470s, a consistent run of the *Ratsverlässe* exists into the eighteenth century. As the sheer volume of these records made a complete survey impossible, I have undertaken instead to examine particular years closely. For the purposes of investigating the use of torture in Nuremberg, the years chosen were 1449–50, 1471–2, 1483–4, 1506 (January through December), and 1520–1. An examination of these years reveals that the use of torture in the city became extreme in the late fifteenth century and was being reined in by the early sixteenth century, even before the introduction of the *Carolina*.

In the council minutes from 1449, torture was mentioned about fifty times in over thirty cases dealing with a variety of crimes from theft to counterfeiting and treason. The notations are usually specific about whether the suspect was only to be questioned, to be threatened, or actually to be subjected to torture. For example, a man named Hieronimus Stadler was arrested for theft in the spring of 1449. The council minutes from April 4th read: "Interrogate Stadler in the dungeon and torture him." On the next day the orders were less severe: "After lunch, go to Stadler and threaten him."[45] Of course, the usual practice of questioning suspects in the torture chamber was itself tantamount to a threat. In a few cases torture was permitted under one condition: the suspect was to be tortured only if he refused to talk. An entry in March read: "Interrogate the Limping Man and show him the one who denounced him. If he still will not talk after that, torture him."[46]

As we might expect, many of those tortured confessed and were executed. As in Basel, however, although the use of torture was reserved for capital crimes, its appearance did not predetermine execution. In April of 1449, a woman named Kathrin Halmhawerin was imprisoned in Nuremberg, suspected of theft. First, the council ordered witnesses questioned about her case. A few days later, on the strength of this testimony, they ordered that Kathrin be tortured and interrogated. Within a week of the initial investigations, Kathrin's case was decided. She was released with an oath of peace and banished from the city for five years.[47] From the relative mildness of her punishment, we can guess that either Kathrin's theft was minor, or the evidence against her was not strong enough to warrant a full conviction. The practice of banishing those suspected of capital crimes, even when the evidence against them was not sufficient for a conviction, was widespread in the fifteenth century.[48]

If we use 1449 as a model of mid-century practice in Nuremberg, we find that the city council kept fairly tight control over the use of torture. Torture was a regular part of criminal investigations, and its use fell into a fairly close pattern. If a suspect in a capital case did not confess when presented with the possibility of torture, torment would be alternated with questions, twice if necessary. If torture failed to elicit a confession, as in Kathrin's case, guilt was considered improvable and the suspect was released, although this could be coupled with banishment if suspicion remained strong. The council minutes do not always record the final verdicts of capital cases, but it is clear that the decision to proceed to torture did not constitute a death sentence as it could in other times and places. The council expressed caution in the use of torture, declaring that excesses in the matter were as criminal as murder.[49]

Over the following generation, this pattern changed substantially. The fact that anyone suspected of a serious crime could be tortured was burned into the public consciousness in 1469 by the notorious and unforgettable case of Nicolas Muffel.[50] A high-ranking city official from one of the most powerful patrician families, Muffel was accused by his peers of treason and embezzlement. He was arrested and tortured, and confessed to the crimes. Although he later protested that he had only confessed to stop the torment, and although in theory he should have been able to claim the privilege of substituting lifelong imprisonment for execution, Muffel was hanged ignominiously like a common thief.[51] Muffel's case became the subject of continuing controversy. Over forty years later, Christoph Scheurl criticized the council's condemnation of Muffel, writing, "They did him violence and injustice thereby."[52] With Muffel's execution, the social barriers that protected certain people from torture were breached. Although status would continue to serve as protection against prosecution and particularly torture, it was no longer a guarantee of immunity. Muffel's trial demonstrates that the practice of torture in Nuremberg had completed the transition from a medieval mode in which it was reserved for outsiders to an early modern mode in which it was theoretically applicable to anyone suspected of a crime of sufficient gravity.[53]

Muffel's claim that torture had forced a false confession from him may well have brought to mind an infamous case from a generation earlier, in which suspicion against a servant led to torture and a false confession. The greatest difference between the two cases, of course, lay in the social status of the accused. In 1446, after a ball in the city council chambers in Nuremberg, the wife of patrician Hans Waldstromer misplaced her jewelry. The whole house was searched, but to no avail. Suspicion fell upon an old man who had served in the household for many years.

> As he in his simplicity, however, could not provide a sufficient alibi, he was arrested and, being greatly tortured, confessed that he had committed the theft.[54]

The old servant was executed, proclaiming his innocence at the gallows. Some time later, when Waldstromer had his house thoroughly cleaned, the lost jewelry was found. The story appears as a sad tale in a chronicle of executions, without mention of any repercussions for Waldstromer. It is no surprise to find that the word of a council member carried more weight than that of his household servant. The tragic case of the old servant did not undermine the use of torture in Nuremberg, despite its clear injustice. Even more surprising, perhaps, is the fact that Muffel's case did not convince the council of Nuremberg (among whom the Muffel family continued to be prominent figures) that torture was a fundamentally flawed technique. Indeed, the opposite appears to have taken place: interrogators were given freer rein.

In the 1470s and 80s, the practice of criminal investigations was far more abusive than it had been at mid-century. Multiple orders for torture became frequent, as in the case of Claus Kumiagell, called "the Polack," who was tortured at least eight times. Claus first appeared in the Nuremberg prison in April of 1470, suspected of theft. Within ten days he had been tortured six times. When the usual means of torture (the strappado) failed to produce results, Claus was tortured first with fire and then with water. Still frustrated in the attempt to extract a confession from Claus, the council ordered that he be allowed to "rest" for a week. Time alone in the dank, dark dungeon to contemplate the horrors he had recently experienced might soften his resolve. In mid-May, Claus was tortured again. His resolve not to confess does not seem to have weakened, but perhaps in the solitude he attempted to end his life before the torment could be resumed. At any rate, an order was given to watch him night and day. In June, Claus was still in prison, and the council deliberated his case. Since Claus had not confessed, the council could not decide what to do with him. Further deliberation was ordered. On July 6 of 1471, the council ordered one last attempt to squeeze a confession from Claus, "[In the case of] the Polack who will not talk, torture is to be undertaken as [the investigators] see fit, in order to draw a confession from him."[55] Presumably this last torment did not induce Claus to confess, and the councilors seem to have been satisfied that nothing was left to be done. In a step unusual for the time, the council ordered that a record be made of how his case had progressed. Claus Kumiagell was then released.[56] Although Claus's case was extreme, it was indicative of a shift in principle. It was no longer the case, as it had been around 1450, that if a suspect refused to confess after two rounds of torture he would most likely be released. In 1471–2, torture was ordered more than twice in seven cases. In the meanwhile, the legal proceedings of the city were being examined and overhauled.[57]

The formal legal reforms of the 1470s appear to have had no immediate impact on the practice of torture in the city. The trend toward the repeated use of torture continued in the 1480s, as evidenced in the *Ratsverlässe* from 1483–4. Investigators were allowed greater discretion in deciding if torture should be applied. The language used in most of the conditional torture orders, "if he won't talk, torture him again," makes it likely that torture was being applied nearly as often as it was allowed. Moreover, torture was being used to gain details of the supposed crime, independently of the confession. In April of 1483, a man named Fritz Diemen was interrogated under suspicion of theft. Within six days, torture was ordered four times in Fritz's case. By the beginning of May, torment had produced results, and Fritz's testimony was read aloud before the council. This confession was not sufficient to end the investigation, however. In the second week of May, Fritz was interrogated twice about further instances of theft, and both times investigators were permitted to use torture if they deemed it necessary. On May 30 of 1483, Fritz Diemen was beheaded.[58] Altogether in 1483–4, torture was ordered more than twice in eight cases.

The logic implicit in Fritz's continued torture is directly related to the belief that pain could draw out the truth. Historians have offered various explications of the logic behind this belief. In her analysis of torture in Toulouse Lisa Silverman roots it in both religious beliefs about redemption and medical understandings of the purpose of pain.[59] According to other interpretations, torturers felt they were overcoming the flawed will of the criminal. Pain was a tool to compel criminals to tell the truth about their crimes, the judicial act of confession which, it was hoped, would be followed by a voluntary religious confession. Hans Fehr argued that the logic which lay behind torture was explicitly demonized, that torture was imagined as a struggle between the righteous torturers and demons who held the criminal in thrall. To early modern people, demons were active and pervasive. They not only played a role in the crimes of witches and the afflictions of the possessed, but were also understood to play an active and direct role in all manner of evil. This understanding of demons permeated everything from meteorology to political philosophy and criminal justice.[60] Such demonized understandings of the criminal will accord well with the prevalence of demons in early modern thought generally, but torturers and investigators were no theorists. Demons are absent from the traces of torture examined here; what remains is evidence of a clear interest in the pragmatic functionality of pain. Properly handled, pain was believed to function *ad eruendam veritatem*.[61] The reasonable corollaries of this axiomatic relationship of truth and pain were, first, that torture was a reliable means to establish guilt and, second, that additional torture was a reliable means to gather details of the crimes and names of accomplices. Neither having an iron will like Claus Kumiagell nor confessing like Fritz Diemen was sufficient to end the torment. Torture had come to serve as the chief tool of the interrogations that were the primary mode of investigation; unrestrained, its use became even more extreme.

Of the years surveyed, 1506 represents the height of judicial torture in Nuremberg. The number of cases in which torture was used varied between 32 and 38 for each of the other years, but in 1506, torture orders appear in 64 cases. In 1483 we observe a tendency to order torture conditionally, leaving its application to the discretion of the investigators, and this was the case in 1506 as well. Yet in twenty cases, torture was ordered more than twice, and in eight cases it was ordered five or more times. In November of 1506, a man called Lazy Peter was arrested after being denounced by Hans Popp, who was already in prison. Peter was accused of theft and was promptly tortured and interrogated. It seems that Peter confessed the first time he was tortured, but the investigators sought further details of his crimes. In all, torture was ordered six times in Peter's interrogation, one of the orders specified:

> Lazy Peter is to be interrogated about the parts where Popp has accused him, and if he does not wish to talk without torture, he is to be tortured twice as before.[62]

Although this is the only time when multiple rounds of torture are explicitly mentioned in Peter's case, it is clear that this was no exception. Peter was executed together with Hans Popp and a third man named Jorg Stretz. Each of them had been tortured at least seven times in the course of a week, with multiple rounds of torture on a single day.[63] In ordering multiple rounds of torture, the council was most explicit in Jorg's case. On November 12th, it declared:

> Jorg Stretz shall be questioned now before lunch and again after, and tomorrow in the morning. And if he does not wish to talk without torture, he is to be tortured twice each time.[64]

In the face of such excesses, it is hardly surprising that all three confessed and were executed.

Why did the use of torture become so much more extreme as the century waned? It was, for one thing, part of a general intensification of criminal justice in the city that peaked in the early sixteenth century, as a study of the city's employment of *Stadtknechten* for policing has shown.[65] The extremity of torture around the turn of the century may also be in part because the council of Nuremberg increasingly left discretion over whether to use torture up to the investigators. This does not mean that the council had relinquished its voice in the process – indeed the very evidence that remains to us is the council's orders to the investigators. Thus Hermann Knapp concluded that the city fathers of Nuremberg were very strict in deciding when to permit torture, not allowing the legally uneducated investigators to take a single step without specific instruction.[66] Yet by the late fifteenth century, instead of positively ordering torture as it had around 1450, the council most often simply declared that torture was permitted. Whether or not it was actually employed was left to the investigators. In his letter on the constitution of Nuremberg, Scheurl described their responsibilities:

> [The investigators] are required to be present during torture, to confirm the aberrations of the tortured, and to pass judgment over blood guilt – although they do not judge anything unless the fathers have already so decided.[67]

These investigators, as I have mentioned, were generally pairs of relatively young men, assigned to the work for a year at a time, in order that they might gain experience and be groomed for higher positions. The trust accorded these men in judging the appropriateness of torture in the process of investigation fits with the social context of their appointment to the task. It is also indicative of the fact that torture was not considered too volatile a tool to be entrusted to the judgment of any honorable layman. It is likely that some councilors were reflecting on their own experience in the interrogation chamber earlier in their careers when they decided to allow the young investigators to use their discretion in the matter of torture.

Yet the excesses of the late fifteenth century also seem to have inspired some skepticism among the powerful men of Nuremberg, and perhaps for some of them this skepticism also grew out of personal experience with interrogations. From the 1470s through the early sixteenth century, torture was ordered in about twice as many cases each year as it had been in the mid-fifteenth century. Compounding this, in individual cases the number of times that torture was ordered was far greater. By 1520, the trend toward the extreme and repeated application of torture had begun to reverse itself. The number of cases involving torture returned in 1520 to the level of the mid-fifteenth century. In nearly half of these cases, torture was only to be threatened (the process formally called *territion*). In the rest, conditional permission to employ torture was typically preceded by an order to use *territion*. In only one case was torture ordered explicitly. It seems from this that the city was developing a practice of regulating torture through its application in stages, a practice that would soon be codified in the *Carolina*. Although the abuse of repeated torture was less marked than in 1506, there is no clear evidence of a limitation in 1520 on the number of times torture might be applied in a given case; torture was ordered more than twice in seven cases.

One of the most extreme cases of torture from 1520 reveals the potential for scandal posed by the use of unchecked torture in interrogations. This was the case of Hieronimus Fogel, in which torture was ordered conditionally thirteen times. Once, interrogations were ordered for "both before and after lunch," as they had been for Jorg Stretz. Hieronimus's case appears to have caused some controversy. Accused of theft and murder, he seems to have confessed to at least some part, and in February of 1521 an order was given to arrest his accomplices. After two weeks of interrogation, a date was set for Hieronimus to be executed, but the execution was stayed. It seems that Hieronimus protested that his confession was false, and the council reconsidered whether his punishment should be carried out. As the council year drew to a close in March, Hieronimus's case still lingered, the confession he had made under torture still in doubt despite renewed attempts at interrogation.[68] Whatever resolution was found in Hieronimus's case, the change in personnel with the new council year allowed it to slip beneath the surface of the records remaining to us; no mention was made of his case thereafter. The possibility that Hieronimus's confession was false introduced a potential crisis for the assumption that pain elicits the truth. While it is clear that the council struggled with Hieronimus's case, however, the edifice of torture as a rational process did not crumble under the weight. The near-crisis may have given further weight to the argument that torture had to be limited in order to maximize its efficacy and reduce the likelihood of false confessions. The fundamental assumption that torture produced truth could be protected by limiting torture just enough to prevent the occurrence of scandalous spectacles to the contrary.

The reforms in the application of torture that were beginning in Nuremberg in the 1520s took place within the realm of practice, not theory. They were largely modifications of the unwritten procedural law handled by the investigators rather than an innovation within legal theory.[69] The council's legal consultants, including Christoph Scheurl, were not in the habit of commenting on interrogation techniques. When suggesting further investigations, they might go so far as to include a list of points for interrogation, as Scheurl did in the witchcraft trial of Adelheit Schneiderin, but the method of interrogation was left up to the council.[70] The limitation of torture shifted to a formal legal context after the promulgation of the imperial criminal code, the *Carolina*. Shortly after the *Carolina* was issued in 1532, the city council of Nuremberg voluntarily accepted it as a firm guide to its policy in criminal justice.[71] Among other reforms, the *Carolina* included specific limitations on the use of torture. In this carefully controlled and regulated form, torture continued to be a part of criminal justice in Nuremberg. The excesses of the late fifteenth century were reined in before they could precipitate a complete crisis of confidence in torture as a reliable means of obtaining a confession.

The restraints on torture that developed in both Basel and Nuremberg also appeared in Lucerne by the latter half of the sixteenth century.[72] We have no evidence that this process was underway in the fifteenth and early sixteenth centuries, however. Torture was adopted fairly late in Lucerne, and the city appears to have had little experience with it as an investigative tool during the early fifteenth century. In his seminal work on the legal history of Lucerne, Philipp Anton von Segesser made this clear in his brief comment on the use of torture there in the fifteenth century.[73] The regular mode of criminal trial, Segesser believed, was a contest between two persons, the accuser and the accused: classic medieval German accusatory trial procedure. Only occasionally in the fifteenth century did a new kind of trial appear in Lucerne, a trial initiated by officials against persons of evil reputation: inquisitorial procedure. It was to gather evidence for these unusual trials that torture was brought to bear. "This is the role that torture played in the criminal procedure of the fifteenth century: it was a component of a rare proceeding."[74] Segesser's analysis fits well with the old reception-oriented view of German legal history, in which Lucerne may serve as an example of a slower and later reception of Roman law. It fits less well with an examination of actual criminal proceedings in Lucerne. Accusers did not play a large role in fifteenth-century criminal procedure there; even when accusers did exist, the city officials took over the proceedings entirely. Accusers do not seem to have risked the danger inherent in accusatory process, that they might be themselves subjected to the punishment for a crime of which they falsely accused another. Only rarely were they even charged with slander, generally suffering lighter penalties. A hundred and fifty years after Segesser wrote, it is clear that the dichotomy between accusatory and inquisitorial proceedings is a false one, and that reality was (as it so often is) a much more mixed and muddled thing.[75]

While he was too certain of the distinction between two modes of criminal procedure, Segesser seems to have been right about the rarity of torture, although the evidence for this is thin. Unlike Nuremberg, there is no regular record of torture from fifteenth-century Lucerne. We can find traces of the use of judicial torture, but before the mid-sixteenth century these are relatively rare. If we examine these traces we can gain a rough picture of the development of torture in Lucerne, but the frequency of its application must remain a matter of speculation. The best indication we have of the frequency of torture is the incidence of capital criminal cases in the city, which increased drastically over the fifteenth century. From this we may speculate that torture was indeed rather rare in Lucerne during the early fifteenth century, but that by the end of that century it had become a regular part of criminal justice in the city.

The earliest hint I have found of torture in Lucerne comes from 1416.[76] A man had been convicted of murdering his wife and was condemned to be broken on the wheel. In investigating the matter, the authorities began to suspect that his maid Elsi Zimmerman and her friend Metzi Schellin had been involved in the murder, possibly even that they had used love magic on the married man. The two were arrested and questioned "greatly" but confessed nothing. They were released with an oath of peace.[77] Much more explicit was a case three years later in which a man was tortured on rumors of witchcraft. He was also not proved guilty, but was made to swear not only to take no vengeance, but also to leave the city and never return.[78] Two references to torture from the following decade follow the same pattern – men tortured under suspicion of theft and released on an oath of peace when they did not confess.[79] It seems that torture only surfaces in the fifteenth-century sources when it was not vindicated by a confession, from which we can reasonably surmise that torture was being used considerably more often than it was being mentioned. Even if torture were used in every potentially capital case in Lucerne in the early fifteenth century, however, it was a rare occurrence. The execution rate in Lucerne prior to 1450 was, so far as it can be determined at all, something less than one execution every two years. Of course capital crimes did not always result in execution. The most ubiquitous of these was usually theft. Between 1430 and 1460 in Lucerne, there were only about ten theft cases reported in the *Ratsprotokolle*.[80] Prosecution of capital crimes was low across the board.

Although we know of cases in which the tortured individual was proved innocent in early fifteenth-century Lucerne, the council appears to have taken minimal responsibility for the well-being of the tortured person. Unlike in Basel, the Lucerne authorities do not appear to have accepted a responsibility themselves to compensate persons found innocent after torture. In 1429, the council did require compensation to be paid by a third party to an innocent man who had been tortured.[81] That man, Hans Höfling, was accused by Claus im Bach's son of having stolen a suit of armor. Hans was thrown into the tower and tortured, but his friends came to his aid with the truth. When it became clear that Claus's son was the guilty party, Hans was released with a letter attesting to his innocence. Claus was required to pay the expenses of Hans's imprisonment and to compensate Hans with four pounds for his suffering. Claus's liability in the case is a classic example of the dynamic of accusatory process, in which the accuser bore personal responsibility for the truth of his charges. Although the council of Basel appears to have taken over some part of this personal responsibility in pursuing charges collectively *ex officio*, the council of Lucerne did not.

In general the use of torture remained quite rare in Lucerne before 1485. There are some indications that this was changing already in the 1450s, during the first small witch panic of the century. Although it is certainly impossible to prove, it may be that the concern over witches motivated the authorities to ramp up their instruments of prosecution. In 1454 and 1456, the weekly expense records include the costs of constructing torture devices, a "torture barrel" and a "torture basin."[82] Although the records do not make clear in what cases these devices were employed, it is probable that they were used in the witch trials of the late fifties and early sixties. In 1482, in the course of another witch panic, we have a clear indication of the use of torture. In early September, costs are listed which were incurred "as the poor woman from Weggis was tortured."[83] A few weeks later similar costs are listed for torture in the tower, probably during the interrogation of a man named Meiger, who was subsequently broken on the wheel.[84]

By the last two decades of the fifteenth century, the city of Lucerne was conducting an average of four executions per year, a number including but not determined by a growing number of witch trials. Probably in response to the rising expense of importing an executioner from

Zurich while executions were on the rise over the mid-century decades, the city of Lucerne hired a full-time executioner of its own in 1485. During that year, the council specified the pay rate for the work of torturing, setting it at fifteen shillings' worth of provisions.[85] In August of the next year, another ordinance detailed the duty of council members to take turns being present at interrogations:

> Council and hundred have established that two [members] of the new council and a judge shall [be present during] torture, beginning with whomever is the first in the new council and after him proceeding through, such that everyone carries the same burden, except that my lords the new and old mayor shall be exempt.[86]

Thereafter, expenses for the work of the executioner and the judge in the tower, usually paid in the form of a provision of wine, form a regular part of the weekly expenses of the city. Torture had become part of the ordinary process of criminal justice in Lucerne.

Although it is difficult to say exactly what effect the use of torture had on the decisions of the judge, it is significant that the decades of the 1480s and 90s saw the highest execution rate of the century. Execution rates dropped again in the late 1490s, around the same time that an embarrassing case emerged in which false accusations were made under torture. In 1498, while he was being interrogated, Franz Eggli denounced a shoemaker. The council decided:

> Between the parties justice is decided following accusation and answer, that Franz should swear that what he said of the shoemaker he said only [...] because he hung on the torture rope, and otherwise knows nothing of him [the shoemaker] and that he should pay my lords 1£ as a peace fine.[87]

The case of Franz and the shoemaker does not seem to have slowed the use of torture in Lucerne, which continued unabated. It is more likely that the skepticism shown towards Franz's accusations was a product of the relative calm between periods of prosecutorial zeal in Lucerne.

Overall, the city of Lucerne does not appear to have developed as sophisticated a response to the use of torture as did Basel and Nuremberg. It appears likely that torture was introduced later and more slowly in Lucerne, which prior to the mid-fifteenth century had only a handful of capital cases. The use of torture only seems to have become normal in judicial proceedings in Lucerne in the late fifteenth century, during a period of intense judicial severity. Perhaps this is why the city does not seem to have developed safeguards against its abuses prior to 1530. When such safeguards were developed, they appear to have been the product of long experience, a process we can see most clearly in the case of Nuremberg.

Practical experience dominated the development of torture as a judicial tool in fifteenth-century cities, as lay prosecutors and lay judges made the long transition between two worlds of criminal justice by way of experiment, using trial and error. The practical experience they accrued ultimately led to the limitation and regulation of torture. Those limits, even when codified in the *Carolina*, remained open and flexible. They functioned to prevent spectacular abuses that might undermine the legitimacy of torture in ordinary circumstances but held out the possibility of just such extreme use of torture in extraordinary cases. Because these flexible restraints developed locally, through the accumulation of experience across generations, they appear at different times in different places. The fact that Lucerne, in particular, was still beginning its experiments with torture when the witch trials began in that city was to drive a massive acceleration in criminal prosecution there over the course of the late fifteenth century.

6

The Advancing Death Penalty and the Re-imagining of Magical Crimes

The practice of criminal justice as it developed over the fifteenth century on the long threshold between the medieval and the early modern was increasingly severe. Legal and social historians have recognized that both levels of prosecution and degrees of punishment were generally on the rise during the period. A close examination of this increasing judicial severity for Basel, Lucerne, and Nuremberg reveals for each city a unique periodic pattern within the overall escalation of prosecution and punishment. These periodic waves of persecution were common in late medieval cities and seem to be the means by which city governments sought to master criminal behavior.[1] By analyzing the details of this pattern of criminal justice decade by decade we can identify the relationship between ordinary criminal prosecution and the origins and development of witchcraft prosecution. As the death penalty advanced in the late medieval urban communes, the re-imagining of magical crimes proceeded apace.

It is difficult at best to establish reliable criminal statistics for the late Middle Ages. Where archival sources exist, they are rarely consistent in recording practices over the years. Throughout the fifteenth century in Basel scribes often failed to note the mode of execution for a given case. The brief expense entries in the city ledgers, often the only evidence which remains to us, are laconic in the extreme, although they are reliable enough to permit the compilation of a list of executions. Then, after the city became part of the Swiss Confederation in 1501 and continuing at least until 1531, every single expense entry pertaining to an execution specifies the style of that execution.[2] This tiny revolution in record-keeping is certainly a boon to historians, but it makes any comparison of fifteenth- and sixteenth-century trends in modes of executions quite difficult. In Lucerne, the problem is more substantial. In 1485, when the city hired its own executioner, he was given a weekly salary.[3] This meant that the previously dependable entries listing pay for each execution disappeared. The traces of particular executions in the Lucerne expense books after 1485 are less dependable, although payments for supplies and various personnel appear with fair regularity. Fortunately, this loss is compensated in the Lucerne archive with well-maintained and thoroughly indexed city council records. By surveying the two sources, we can compile a fairly complete list of executions. In Nuremberg, the fifteenth-century expense records exist only for a handful of years. A compilation of execution statistics might be possible for the years after 1470 by means of a complete survey of the daily council records, but this would be a task of truly epic proportions and has not been possible for this project.

What do we find when we examine execution rates in Basel and Lucerne? The expense records that provide the record of executions for Basel have been lost for the 18 years from 1434 through 1451. My survey of these records for executions begins in 1428 and continues through 1532.[4] For the entire period taken together, Basel averaged just under four executions per year. The earliest period, from 1428 to 1433, had substantially fewer executions, averaging only around two per year. When this period is compared to that immediately after the records gap, the difference is considerable. The decade following 1452 averaged over six executions per year in Basel. Because the weekly expense records for the intervening years are lost, we cannot date this change in judicial severity with any precision. Another significant change took place during the same interim: the first evidence of witch burnings in the area dates from 1444. In that year, four witch burnings took place in the territories of the city of Basel, and around 1446 three more witches were burned in the Basel territory of Waldenburg. It is impossible to say whether the general burst in judicial severity preceded or followed the witch burnings of the 1440s, but it is clear that it roughly coincided with them.

The severity of the years immediately following 1452 did not continue unabated. Between 1462 and 1532, executions in Basel averaged about four per year, while a closer analysis by half-decade reveals a fluctuating pattern. The execution rate in the latter half of the fifteenth century represents a substantial and sustained increase in execution rates as compared to the earlier years, but the decades in the middle of

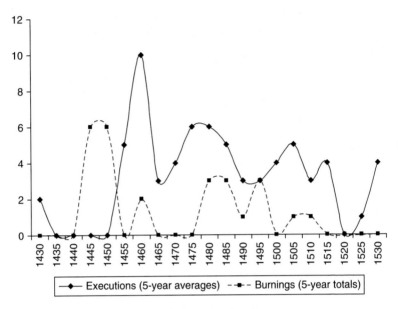

Figure 6.1   Executions and witch burnings in Basel

the fifteenth century, around the time that the practice of witch burning appeared in Basel, were clearly unusual.

An examination of execution statistics for Lucerne reveals a similar trend.[5] Although the weekly expense records are missing for the
1470s, fairly reliable execution rates can be established for the rest of
the period. Between 1430 and 1449, the city of Lucerne averaged one
execution every two years. In the 1450s and early 1460s, this rate more
than tripled. Beginning around 1450, Lucerne had been experiencing a
small flurry of witchcraft cases, the first being Else of Meersburg's trial.
Because the records are incomplete, we do not know how many of these
women were executed, but the evidence points to a small but deadly
cluster of witch trials.[6] As in Basel, a mid-century jump in the execution
rate coincided with the appearance of the practice of witch burning.

The following decades, however, did not follow the pattern evidenced
in Basel, where execution rates established a stable norm above that of
the earlier part of the century. During the 1470s, we know of only three
executions in Lucerne, all from 1472. No weekly expense records remain
from that decade, and only partial city council minutes, and a defini-
tive statement is impossible due to the missing records. After the record
gap of the 1470s, a second even more substantial jump is evidenced in

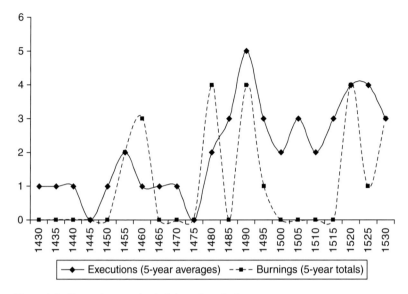

Figure 6.2 Executions and witch burnings in Lucerne

execution rates in Lucerne. Between 1481 and 1494, the executions in the city averaged over four per year, eight times the rate from 1430 to 1440. Interestingly, this second jump in execution rates also coincided with a concentration of witch burnings. The same years saw the greatest intensity of deadly witch trials between 1430 and 1530. Thereafter, execution rates did subside in Lucerne, although not by much. Between 1495 and 1511, we find an average of 2.5 executions per year; between 1512 and 1530, an average of just under four.

When measured by execution rates, judicial severity intensified most substantially in Lucerne, but a modest yet sustained intensification is evidenced also in Basel. The spikes in execution rates in these cities correspond with the onset of witch burnings. It is conceivable that the sudden addition of witch burnings accounted for the jump in execution rates, but on closer examination this turns out not to be the case.[7] In neither Basel nor Lucerne do the additional burnings fully account for the change. In Lucerne, burnings represent a substantial percentage of the upsurge in executions after 1450. It should be noted that sodomy executions represent a significant portion of these burnings, a factor which will be discussed at length in the final chapter. I have included all burnings together in the discussion here.

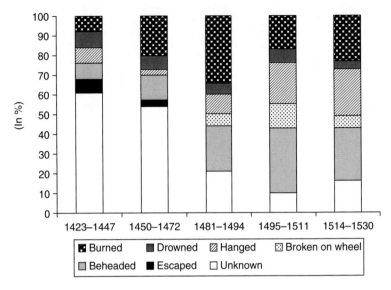

Figure 6.3   Modes of execution in Lucerne

Between 1450 and 1472, burnings accounted for 20% of all known executions, 34% between 1481 and 1494, 17% between 1495 and 1511, and 23% between 1514 and 1530. These periods represent the execution trend as far as it can be discerned; the intervals between them had no known executions. Overall, in the period from 1450 through 1530, burnings accounted for just over 20% of all executions in the city of Lucerne. Before 1450, such executions had been exceedingly rare.

The advent of fiery executions in Lucerne does not account for the city's swelling execution rate. If all executions by fire are removed from the tally of Lucerne executions, we are left with the same basic trend. Before 1450, about one execution took place every two years. During the 1450s and 60s, that rate doubles to one execution per year. After 1480, the execution rate without burnings is relatively stable at nearly six times that of the 1430s, with approximately three executions per year. Insofar as it exceeded the years which followed, the surge of the 1480s appears to have been the result of an upsurge in executions by fire. The general trend of increasing judicial severity, however, was not.

In Basel, conversely, when burnings are removed from the calculation of execution rates, the relative severity of 1452–61 becomes more pronounced. This is largely because there were only two burnings in Basel territory in that decade, while there were more in the decades which followed. Thus the analysis of executions other than burnings confirms the trend previously noted for Basel. The advent of witch burnings in the territory of the city corresponded roughly to a modest but sustained increase in execution rates, marked particularly by a surge of executions in the 1450s. Although there were few witch burnings in the 1450s in Basel, the two that did take place were those of Verena Symlin and Gret Frölicherin, whose dossiers contain the earliest local confessions of a demonic pact.

In Basel and Lucerne, the beginnings of witchcraft prosecution clearly had an impact on local execution rates. However, since we know that burnings alone do not account for the increasing number of executions, other crimes must also have been handled more severely or prosecuted more heavily in the late fifteenth century. Where fairly reliable data exist on a single crime with a variety of possible punishments, it is possible to analyze trends in sentencing. As the most common capital crime of the era, and one with a wide range of possible judicial responses, theft is suited to such an inquiry as few other crimes are. Theft was a crime with many shades and even more possible punishments. Leaving aside the sort of theft such as wood theft which was actually a misuse of public resources usually punished with a fine, the punishment of theft ranged from forgiveness coupled with a warning to execution. Although there were degrees of theft, based on the kinds of goods stolen and the frequency of the transgression, they were not strictly codified. This, combined with the many mitigating or exacerbating factors that could be considered at the judges' discretion, makes theft a perfect case for examining trends in punishment.

In Lucerne, between 1430 and 1530, we find 118 cases of simple theft, that is, theft without the combination of other capital crimes. In order to map out the punishment trends for theft, I assigned each possible outcome a number on an eight-point scale and plotted them on a graph.

For someone accused of theft, the best possible outcome was that the accuser would be charged with slander (–4 on the graph). If the case were taken seriously as theft, the accused might still hope for acquittal (–3) or to be forgiven and released with a warning (–2). Failing that, he might be fined or required to repay the value of the stolen goods (–1). Real punishment began with banishments (+1), to which corporal punishment might be added for extra severity (+2). Worst, clearly, was to be executed. Although the outcome was the same for the convicted man, to be beheaded (+3) was considered a mitigation of the usual punishment

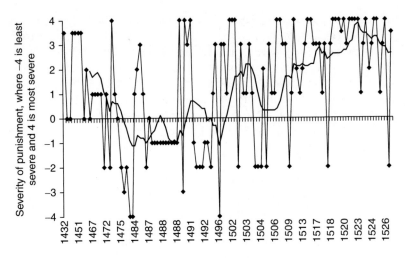

Figure 6.4   Punishments for theft in Lucerne

for theft – execution with the noose, regarded as extremely dishonorable (+4). In weighting these various outcomes for the purposes of establishing the punishment trend for theft in Lucerne, I have accordingly weighted beheading as less severe than hanging. Cases for which the outcome is unknown have been plotted on the zero line. As the great variability of outcomes over the years makes any trend impossible to discern at first glance, a trend line of the ten-case average has been added to chart the general tendency of the data. From this trend line we can discern a distinct upsurge in the severity with which theft cases were handled in Lucerne. Notably, the surge does not coincide with the rise in execution rates in the 1480s, but instead follows it.

This observed increased severity in handling theft might be the result of improved record-keeping in the later part of the century. Given the overall trend in Lucerne of increasing reliance on the death penalty, however, it is likely that these data represent a real change. Over the entire period, an average of about 45% of theft cases resulted in execution. Execution rates from 1430 through the 1460s averaged around 45%. Then in the 1470s and 1480s, only 10% of known theft cases resulted in execution. By the 1490s, the execution rate again returned to around 45%. What happened during the 1470s and 80s? The absence of executions for theft in the 1470s is perhaps best explained by the gap in weekly expense records for those years, as the expense records are the most reliable source of information regarding executions. In the 1480s there were a number of executions for theft, but also an unusually high number of individuals were fined and released.

This anomaly can be traced to a single case from 1487. Eight men who had served as soldiers in a recent campaign in the Valais were charged with having robbed a church during the fighting. In the course of the investigation, the eight testified that they had looted a house in which they found some clerical vestments and a number of other valuable items. The booty that was clearly clerical they had dropped off at a church nearby, but they had kept the rest, not realizing that it was also church property. The men were required to ship the items back to the church in the Valais at their own expense and each had to pay a fine of five pounds. Although the case was handled as theft it was not truly punished as such, as it was seen instead as a case of improper looting. The low execution rate in the 1480s was exaggerated by this event. Without that case, the execution rate for theft in the 1480s was closer to 20%. Thus, although it is impossible to know with certainty what percentage of theft cases in these two decades resulted in execution, it is fair to guess that the true figure is substantially higher than 10%.

The clearest and most verifiable deviation from the average execution rates for theft in Lucerne is observed in the first twenty years of the sixteenth century. During those years, the death sentence dominated in cases of theft. Execution was the outcome in 68% of theft cases in the first decade after the turn of the century and rose to 77% in the decade which followed. It is, of course, problematic to assume that the preference for the death penalty continued unabated across the sixteenth century. In Cologne and Augsburg the use of banishment as an alternative to execution appears to have increased in the late sixteenth century.[8]

These data pertaining to executions for theft are important because they cannot be explained away as merely reflective of rising crime rates. This is because while overall execution rates are absolute figures that were probably driven by some combination of prosecutorial zeal and actual crime rates, I have reduced punishments for theft to relative figures. Each possible punishment for theft has been examined here in proportion, thus isolating it from some of the unknowable factors that drove prosecution directly. We cannot ascertain actual crime rates for the century under examination, although it would be imprudent to assume that an increase in prosecution bears no relation to the immeasurable factor of crime. The analysis of these theft cases from Lucerne has been made as independent of the crime rate as possible, through the examination of how similar cases were handled at different times. What we find is a clear increase in judicial severity, but well after the practice of witch burning had been established in the city. Here again we are encouraged in the speculation that the prosecution of witchcraft was determining and driving the transformation of criminal justice in Lucerne. This analysis of theft punishments points in particular to the early sixteenth century as a moment of intense judicial severity. This moment turns out to have been significant beyond the history of theft: indeed it marked a convulsion of prosecutorial zeal that coalesced into a demonization of crime in general and a crucial transformation of witchcraft prosecution in Lucerne.[9]

In order to see why theft came to be treated more harshly in Lucerne in the early sixteenth century, we need to examine the crime of robbery. Both theft and robbery are essentially property crimes, the taking of material possessions from their rightful owner. But whereas theft is a secretive crime, robbery is a violent crime. To a fifteenth-century mindset, this meant that theft was substantially more dishonorable than robbery. Robbery, however, posed a much greater threat to the *Landesfriede* and especially to trade. While only remarkable cases of theft made their way into chroniclers' reports, the ever-presence of robbery is unmistakable.

Chronicles are one of the best sources for the city of Nuremberg, which otherwise largely falls out of this discussion of judicial severity for lack of data. Reports of widespread robbery appear in nearly every year of Müllner's *Annalen*, a seventeenth-century history of Nuremberg based on chronicles and archival sources:

> [1441] Not only did the council of Nuremberg often touch on the problem of wide-spread highway robbery this year, but [the council] has also written to Count Wilhelm of Kassel, [asking him] to provide escort through his territory to the merchants, for whom the thieves lurk, as they travel to the Frankfurt Fair. If he should desire it, the council will send him 30 or 40 guards with muskets and crossbows for this purpose.[10]

Because of its broad trade network and proximity to the castles of numerous lesser nobles who provided protection for some robbers, Nuremberg was especially hard pressed by the problem in the fifteenth century. Robbery was rarer in Lucerne; in fact no cases are found during the period of this study until the middle of the 1480s.

Unlike in Nuremberg, where *Placker* (highwaymen) and *Räuber* (robbers) are frequently mentioned, the city council in Lucerne does not appear to have clearly distinguished robbery from its component elements, theft, violence and murder. The distinction between robbery and theft becomes clear only from the mode of execution. Robbers were not hanged in Lucerne, but beheaded or broken on the wheel as murderers. Take for example the first such execution, from 1486:

> On this day a foreign pilgrim named Hansen of Gesteinen was dragged out as a murderer and executed with the wheel, because he killed a poor, sick man in our city and took from him five gulden or more and that, moreover, in order to hide this act he shamefully killed an honorable man.[11]

What is interesting is that murder only began to appear in conjunction with theft in Lucerne after 1480. In all, only fifteen cases of robbery appear in the city council records of Lucerne from 1486 through 1523 – fewer than one every two years. While these few cases cannot account for the substantial upsurge in executions during those years, they do represent what must have been a disturbing new element in crime. Prior to 1470, murder was very rare in Lucerne; between 1430 and 1450 there is no evidence of even a single case. After 1470, however, murder appears in the city council records with much greater frequency. Thirty-one cases of murder and four cases of aggravated *Todschlag* (manslaughter[12]) are evidenced between 1470 and 1530. Moreover, after 1486, murder charges were 50% more likely to turn up in combination with other charges than alone, whereas before 1486, murder charges appeared only in isolation.

Two noteworthy trends are evidenced here. The first is that extreme personal violence, outside of the honorable rubric of *Todschlag*, was a substantial and largely new element of crime in Lucerne after 1470. The other is that murder and theft often appeared in conjunction with other crimes. They appear not only together but also in combination with charges such as oath breaking, blasphemy, bestiality, witchcraft, and arson. Further investigation reveals that, even more than the appearance of murder, the mixture of various crimes together characterized capital criminal cases of the late fifteenth and early sixteenth centuries in Lucerne. In over a third of the executions for which a crime is known, multiple crimes are listed. Of these mixed capital cases, all but three appear after 1480. To varying degrees, any of these crimes in isolation might be punished without the death penalty. In combination, however, the chance of a death sentence was substantially increased. Such was the case for "bad Heini" in 1502:

> On the abovementioned day, said bad Heini of Hochdorf was condemned from life to death and his head cut from his shoulders,

because he said "God's wounds," "God's strength," "God's sex," and other such oaths, [also because he stole], and he bought some bread and charged it to the innkeeper of Reid, and other such crimes which he committed in Reid according to the testimony.[13]

Bad Heini's oaths were fairly common ones, which had come under increasing attention from the city council over the second half of the fifteenth century. Others who used such oaths were frequently punished, but rarely with execution. His thefts were petty and few, and his fraud relatively minor. Had any of these crimes stood alone, he might have escaped the executioner's sword. As it was, his transgressions taken together convinced the judge that Heini was a bad man, better dead than alive.

It is possible that this appearance of multiple crimes in capital cases is at least in part a product of better records. The details in the city council records do become more complete later in the century. As record-keeping in Lucerne was becoming more thorough, so too was the interrogation of prisoners, drawing out additional confessions where previously none might have been sought. Moreover, some of the additions would have resulted in a changed punishment. A career thief who had also murdered one of his victims was usually broken on the wheel. Likewise, the appearance of bestiality confessions in such litanies of thefts usually resulted in burning.[14] In such cases, the records still refer to the convicted man primarily as a thief, but from his execution it is clear that theft was not his only crime. Such executions were intended to signal the crime of the executed, and if necessary as many of his crimes as possible. A good illustration of this is found in the case of a beggar named Peter Vitztum from 1491. He had confessed to being one of twenty-four men who had sworn to set fire to the Swiss Confederation, for which they would be paid four gulden apiece by the duke of Württemberg.[15] Peter further confessed to having helped murder a beggar and set fire to a mill in Sursee. For his confessed crimes, Peter was broken on the wheel and the sign of a fire was placed on the wheel.[16] Through the wheel, his status as murderer was conveyed, whereas fire was the traditional punishment for *Mordbrennen*, deadly arson.

The multiplicity of charges in capital cases also resonated with the developing crime of witchcraft. Witchcraft was a crime with many aspects, and where full confessions exist they are almost always a list of discrete and often separate supernatural criminal acts. In addition to "victimless" crimes such as night flight and attending the witches' sabbath, witchcraft confessions stretched from anti-religious crimes such as blasphemy, apostasy, and diabolism, to personal violence such as murder, infanticide, and physical harm of all sorts, to crimes against the common good, such as storm raising. Much of the harm believed to be caused by witchcraft corresponded to the crimes which were being punished more frequently in the latter part of the fifteenth century. Indeed, as Ed Bever has recently pointed out, a significant portion of the accusations against witches had a physical, criminal element such as assault or trespassing.[17]

We have established with a fair degree of certainty that execution rates rose substantially in Lucerne and modestly in Basel in the late fifteenth century. The utility of quantitative analysis is limited, however, when examining a century poor in verifiable statistics. Although the analysis of theft punishments circumvents some of the problems created by inconsistent records, it would be useful to have some other way to gauge judicial severity for this period, to confirm that this surge in executions was not merely reflective of a surge in crime. In order to gain a more detailed and nuanced window on judicial severity, we can examine the rituals of execution.

In the late Middle Ages, modes of execution were matched to each crime. Witches, sodomites, arsonists, and counterfeiters were burned. Thieves were hanged with the noose, traitors drawn and quartered, murderers set on the wheel.[18] Female thieves were drowned and murderesses were usually buried alive; both of these were sex-based mitigations of the usual mode of execution. Similarly minors were drowned; doubt existed regarding the full culpability of women and minors and the punishment of drowning was slightly more survivable than other modes of execution. As such, it contained an element of ordeal, leaving the final verdict up to God.[19] When confronted with Anabaptists in the early sixteenth century, the authorities in Lucerne found it appropriate to drown them, while those in Basel chose to be more merciful and had them swum, a punishment which might well drown the person but was not intended as an execution. As the Anabaptists had transgressed in a matter pertaining to water, it seemed fitting that their crime should be purged by water. Such crime-specific punishment cannot be used to measure independent severity on the part of the court. In every case, however, alternative modes of execution existed. Beheading, the most honorable form of execution, was frequently substituted to honor the request of the family or city of the convict. Should the court decide to show mercy, a thief might be beheaded rather than hanged, a witch drowned instead of burned.

In Lucerne, the style of executions does not appear to have changed much in the period under consideration. After 1501 the city of Basel began beheading many criminals, rather than staging more symbolically laden forms of execution.[20] A shift toward more honorable and merciful executions can also be observed in Nuremberg. Between 1472 and 1483 the standard execution for theft in Nuremberg appears to have changed from hanging to beheading.[21] Similarly, in 1502, the executioner in Nuremberg decided that burial, the local standard execution for women, was too cruel, so he initiated the practice of drowning instead.[22] Then, in the late sixteenth century, one of his successors took the initiative to end the practice of drowning and initiated beheading as the standard execution for women.[23] The shift observed in Nuremberg was part of a more general transformation in punishment, whereby most executions came to be relatively simple beheadings while a few cases were reserved as show executions, theaters of cruelty in which the mob was edified and entertained with the gruesome variety of traditional executions.[24] It may also have been connected to the growing voice in Nuremberg for restraint in criminal justice, evidenced by the history of torture in that city. Conversely, it may also be seen as a process of rationalizing criminal justice. If anyone survived an execution in the fifteenth century, they would be released, absolved by the miracle. The first known instance of re-execution comes from Nuremberg in 1525. The end of gallows miracles and of the practice of drowning women were signs of a changing understanding of the role of the divine in criminal justice.[25]

Whether restrained or zealous, urban authorities did not enact rituals of punishment in isolation; the public was an active presence at executions. In Nuremberg, for example, it was considered an act of piety for someone to step forward to support the head of the condemned man as he was dragged through the streets, to lessen his torment.[26] Thus Müllner, in his seventeenth-century history of Nuremberg, deemed it remarkable when, in 1453, a condemned murderer was denied this comfort by the crowd:

> On the Friday before All Saints', a journeyman baker was executed on the wheel. Desiring money, he had murdered his master in the night and seriously injured his wife with a blow to the head from a hatchet. [...] At this time it was the usual practice to place such a criminal on a plank [...] such that his head lay on the cobblestones, and to drag him thus out to the place of execution. Now and then there were people who, out of pity, would support his

head for him. For this murderer, no-one was willing to support his head.[27]

The public also interacted with the ritual at the execution itself. If the executioner botched his task, he suffered the danger of being stoned by the crowd. Such was the case at the execution of Ulrich Steinmeussel in 1506.

With this poor man the executioner missed and failed to execute him properly, for which the common people wanted to stone him, but the judge helped him escape.[28]

Indeed, without the compliance of the people, the authorities encountered substantial difficulties. As we have seen, when the city council in Basel confronted the problem of widespread Anabaptism in its territories shortly after the Reformation, its attempts to bring the religious deviants to justice were frustrated by the widespread refusal of local authorities and their deputies to arrest and deliver the suspects. Such rebellion threatened to undermine the city's authority.

Ceremonies of punishment could either reinforce or undermine the legitimacy and importance of criminal proceedings and, ultimately, of the authority behind them. Executions became complex public displays, intended for the masses.[29] The rituals of execution were already being expanded in the fifteenth century, as cruel displays of punishment and penance were developed for public edification. These ceremonies of criminal justice provide another way to examine judicial severity in the fifteenth century, as well as a means of judging the importance of punitive justice to the authorities.

The meaning of punitive justice, the logic of execution, has been described by Richard van Dülmen as transitioning from purification to deterrence. Van Dülmen identifies the urge for purification in such traditional punishments as drowning, burning, and burying alive, in which death was brought by the force of the elements, rather than directly by the executioner's hand.[30] That fire, in particular, was the preferred mode of execution for such crimes as sodomy, heresy, and witchcraft, argues for a purifying function of such a punishment. These are precisely the kinds of taboo-violating transgressions which, as Mary Douglas has argued, prompt societies to purge the transgressor, to purify the community.[31]

Yet it would be difficult to argue that there was no logic of deterrence in fifteenth-century rituals of punishment. The punishment of a woman convicted as a soothsayer in Nuremberg in 1432 reveals the deterrent function of such justice:

> Katharina, Hans Amberger's wife, was placed for a quarter hour in the stocks by the Pegnitz as a sorceress and a soothsayer, and a sign was placed upon her on which the Devil was painted, and thereafter a piece of her tongue was torn out.[32]

As was typical, Katharina's humiliation was public and her crime was displayed to the crowd. Her punishment was a permanent mutilation to serve as a constant reminder to herself and others of the retribution for such offenses. Not only did Katharina's mutilation serve a deterrent function, so did her humiliation. The dishonor which accrued from such public punishment was lifelong; the mere rumor of such was sufficient to cause the maligned party to sue for slander. In Lucerne, in 1480, a certain Staldeman brought slander charges against Hans im Holtz. Apparently, Hans had been spreading rumors that Staldeman had been arrested in Bern and imprisoned. Staldeman sued to protect his honor, and won. Hans had to pay a 10£ fine and take an oath that he had spoken falsely.[33]

The deterrent effect of criminal justice was part of the long course of the "civilizing process," in which the slow consolidation of power and the development of the modern state coincided with the formation of the civilized conscience in the individual. Following this argument, Richard Evans explains that during the early modern period, while the developing state was unstable and constantly threatened both internally and externally, criminal punishments were vicarious rituals of vengeance.[34] Through its deterrent effect, however, such cruel public retribution also served the purpose of social control in an age when internalized social discipline was largely absent.

Criminal justice can thus be linked to one of the central narratives of early modernity, the growth of the state. In the fifteenth century, the state in its modern sense did not exist. The process of territorial and jurisdictional consolidation was just beginning in such city states as Basel, Lucerne, and Nuremberg, and it suffered constant frustrations. The effect of overlapping jurisdictions and enclaves in undermining urban justice can be seen clearly in a 1478 case from Basel. The scion of the respected Strasbourg family Bisinger was condemned to die, because after having squandered his inheritance he had turned to theft to maintain his lifestyle. As Bisinger was taken to the place of execution, two university students, friends of his, cut the rope which bound him to the executioner and led him away to asylum in a nearby Franciscan cloister. In attempting to punish those who helped him escape, the council was frustrated on all sides. The two students, being under the jurisdiction of the University of Basel, were outside its reach. The officers and bailiffs who had stood by while the condemned man escaped were many; only the judge responsible for the execution proceedings was removed from his office. When the city council discovered that the plot to free Bisinger had included two powerful citizens of Basel, Niklaus Meyer and Hans Eberler, it attempted to apprehend them, but the two were warned in time and escaped into the house of the Teutonic Order of Knights. Thus most of the main perpetrators escaped the justice of the city council through the islands of separate jurisdiction and asylum which existed within the city walls. Eberler and Meyer later took citizenship in Zurich and Solothurn respectively, and their new cities began to put pressure on the Basel council to return their confiscated property to them.[35]

One of the primary functions of governments is the creation and exe-cution of law. In Basel, as elsewhere in the fifteenth century, a personal model of governance was beginning to be replaced by a territorial one. Bisinger's case reveals the tension which existed between the growing power of the city of Basel, which sought territorial dominance and juris-dictional monopoly, and the still powerful privileges of individuals and institutions. The pace at which the cities were able to eliminate or mar-ginalize such privileges varied. Already in the early fourteenth century, the Nuremberg council had established dominance over the guilds' claims of jurisdiction in matters of production, yet that city remained deeply enmeshed in the diplomatic limitations imposed by their posi-tion within the empire, and conflicts with the guilds continued in the fifteenth century.[36] Basel, Lucerne, and Nuremberg all enjoyed *de facto* autonomy in the fifteenth century, but remained in a condition of legal subordination to the emperor. They had also each recently expanded their control over lands outside the city walls. This meant a greater number of subjects who must be impressed by the authority of the city council and its effectiveness as an administrator of justice. This may have provided a political motor to increasing judicial severity, in the early phases of the process of territorialization.

Complex public displays of death were in part a fifteenth-century development. Aside from the sheer numbers of executions, it appears that the death penalty itself became more severe in the late fifteenth century.[37] This was done through the addition of physical torment and humiliation prior to the execution itself. The condemned might be torn with hot irons (once for each murder) or dragged feet first through the cobblestone streets to the place of execution. The road to the gallows was a reenactment of the Passion, drenched with religiously resonant ritual details.[38] Examining the details of these ritual displays as they developed in the three cities promises insight not only on the form, but also the meaning of the increasingly harsh criminal justice of the fifteenth century.

In the case of Lucerne, we have the least information. We only catch bare glimpses of the ceremonies which accompanied executions in that city, as for example, in a notation in the weekly expense record from 9 July 1519. That was the week when Hans Stächli, Andreas from Tschafel and Barbel Vermeggerin were burned at the stake. The best record of their trial is found in the city council records, which detail their confessions.[39] Along with the pay for the executioner and the *Stadtknechte* who escorted the prisoners and maintained order at the executions, however, the expense record also includes an extremely laconic reference to several shillings "to proclaim [their crimes] and for the monk who carried the cross before them."[40] Although the various expenses of an execution were often subsumed under the simple aside "and other costs," a survey of the expense records reveals that the various trappings of capital punishment were mentioned with greater frequency later in the period. From these hints we can compose a picture of execution in Lucerne. The condemned man spent the night before his execution in the tower, by candlelight, in the company of several employees of the city. His confession was heard by a priest, and then he was led out through the city to the place of execution. Before him walked the executioner and a monk carrying the cross, and he was surrounded by the civic henchmen. His crimes were proclaimed for the gathering public to hear, and he was executed in the manner judged fitting to his crimes. Usually, the corpse was left to the elements at the site of the execution. From time to time, gravediggers were sent out to bury any remains beneath the gallows.

These events, as far as we can discern them, conform entirely with general descriptions of executions in the period. What we cannot derive from the sources for Lucerne is any clear development in the rituals of execution, although the earlier entries lack any specific indication of the role of the monk in the procession and most other aspects of the ceremony. By contrast, the expense records of the city of Basel contain much more specific detail, allowing us to identify a trend toward more expensive and complex rituals of punishment as the fifteenth century waned and the sixteenth began.

In the earliest records examined, references to executions in Basel are quite brief. Around 1430 they usually consisted of only the executioner's pay of ten shillings. Occasionally other aspects of the execution come to light, such as expenses to guard the condemned man and to lead him to the gallows. An execution from 1428, in which the executed man was given the rare honor of being carried back into the city for burial, cost the city a total of one pound, eight shillings, and six pence.[41] A similar execution in 1453, again including the cost of burial, came to one pound, ten shillings, and four pence.[42] During this period, however, we see the first signs of the additional torments which were added to executions with greater frequency in late fifteenth-century Basel.[43] An example of this is found in the execution in July of 1460 of a man named Schynagel, whose crime is unknown to us. Schynagel was placed in the stocks before he was executed and was guarded there by several men who received as part of their pay a meal to eat while they waited. Then he was bound behind a horse and dragged through the city and out to the gallows, where his execution and dying were attended by a monk in addition to the executioner and his helpers. It is unlikely that Schynagel was hanged, as the executioner received one pound rather than ten shillings for his work, double pay being standard for more complex executions. Altogether, Schynagel's death cost the city two pounds, six shillings, and eight pence. By the turn of the century in Basel, the costs for even the most ordinary of executions, the hanging of a thief, had increased substantially. Although the executioner still received only ten shillings for his work, the total expenses to hang a thief in November of 1500 came to two pounds, five shillings. The additional expenses included soup for the condemned man's last meal, a priest to offer him the sacrament, a monk to walk before him as he was led out of the city, and a priest to accompany him.[44]

Not only were executions becoming more ceremonial and expensive in Basel during this period, so too were other punishments. In 1506, when a woman was placed in the stocks and swum as a thief, the city council spent one pound, nine shillings, and ten pence on the event.[45] To swim her, the executioner would have lowered her into the water under the bridge over the Rhine, and then slowly pulled her under the water to the other side of the bridge, where she would be lifted out again. Anyone subjected to this punishment suffered a fair chance of dying, so the council deemed it fitting to employ the same assortment of clergy as for an execution. She was given the sacrament and accompanied by monks to the place of punishment. Peter Schuster argues that these religious aspects of the execution appeared during the fifteenth century as a result of clerical unease with executions.[46] When Jacob Fissenstein had been swum for petty theft in 1430, there is no evidence in the city expense books of a clerical presence at his execution. The cost of his punishment was a mere seven shillings: five for the executioner and two for the guards who led him out to the bridge.[47] If clergy were involving themselves in the executions of the early fifteenth century without receiving compensation from the city, it is all the more interesting that the city council decided to begin paying them, to bring their religious rituals under the umbrella of the city council's authority.

During the same period in which the city councils were expanding and consolidating their power territorially, jurisdictionally, and ritually, they also oversaw the introduction of the practice of witch burning. As we have seen, this happened in the context of increasing judicial severity. Around the years in which the deadly practice appeared, both Basel and Lucerne experienced a jump in capital criminal cases, a surge in executions which initiated a new, higher norm in execution rates. Some of the additional cases were witch trials, but cases involving the combination of several capital crimes, increasing the probability of execution, also represented a substantial new element. This new element can be seen in the analysis of theft cases from Lucerne. While a wide range of possible judicial responses to theft existed, the late fifteenth and early sixteenth centuries were marked by a shift to more severe penalties, especially execution. When the details of the cases are examined, it is found that many of the later theft cases from Lucerne were mixed cases. A general trend toward compound accusations in capital cases coincided in Lucerne with a rise in cases involving murder. Turning away from the frequency of executions to examine the rituals which accompanied them, we observed a parallel trend. As executions were becoming more frequent, the ceremonies of death were becoming more intricate. Expensive displays put criminal justice on show.

What explanations can be found for this transformation? One possible explanation which presents itself is that of demographics. I have dealt here in raw numbers, not per capita execution rates. This is because precise population figures are unavailable for these cities during the fifteenth century. If, however, the populations of these cities were growing during the period, what appears as a modest increase in executions in Basel, for example, may in fact represent a per capita decline. It seems, however, that both Basel and Lucerne had relatively stable populations during these years. The population of Lucerne peaked in the fifteenth century and began a slow decline thereafter. As such, it is possible that the upsurge in executions there coincided with the pressure of relatively high population density. It is unlikely, however, that the increase in population during those years would have been large enough to account proportionately for the increase in capital crimes. In Basel, the population of the city would have been temporarily expanded during the Council of Basel and decreased again after the end of local military hostilities in 1449.[48] This means that during the earliest years surveyed, when the execution rates were lowest, the per capita execution rate would have been even lower. On the other hand, although the population of Basel was not growing in the late fifteenth century, the degree to which the criminal justice of the city included its rural subjects certainly was. The long process of judicial cooption described in Chapter 2 was not limited to witch trials. Yet here, as with the raw demographics of the city, close analysis confirms the trend rather than contradicting it. The city established high jurisdiction over its territories in stages but certainly did not see its authority diminishing in the late fifteenth century. The establishment of urban control over rural justice may help to explain the higher baseline at the end of the fifteenth century as compared to seventy years earlier, but it leaves the decades at mid-century to stand out as all the more remarkable.

It was during those decades that witch trials began in Basel territory, and then also that the city was establishing control over the countryside's criminal justice. As in Lucerne, the advent of witchcraft prosecution was bound up with a transformation of criminal justice. Clearly we cannot explain the changes as basically demographic. They were linked instead to the choices made by the city governments and to the new sensitization, as Alfred Soman would put it, to the crime of witchcraft.[49] What drove these changes in attitude?

We know that while the populations of these cities were not growing substantially, migration was a significant factor in the late fifteenth century. The medieval practice of adjudicating crimes by collective oaths, whereby if seven men were willing to swear to the innocence of the accused, that was sufficient to clear him, had largely fallen from use. The legal theory behind it, however, was not entirely absent either from legal practice or from the public mind. Oaths from several respected men, although rarely sufficient to clear the accused, were frequently used as the equivalent of posting bail. Using oaths backed by familial honor, respected families were often successful in intervening on behalf of their misbehaving scions. A substantial portion of strangers in the city presents a problem for such a system. The immigrants or passers-through generally had no-one (no citizen, that is) who would vouch for them. This made them far more vulnerable to punishment if they were accused of a crime. Moreover, the presence of strangers might well increase a general fear or suspicion of crime, as the presence of servants in a house increased the fear that a lost item might have been stolen. It appears, in fact, that foreign servants represented a disproportionate share of such disruptive crimes as violent quarreling.[50] Did migration increase actual crime? It is difficult to know for sure, but given the desperate circumstances of many of these individuals, it is certainly possible.

In the past, it has been argued that, historically, criminal justice mirrored the crime rate.[51] This position is difficult to maintain, however, given the conditions of fifteenth-century judicial practice. An accused thief might confess under torture to dozens of thefts and other crimes, although the authorities only had evidence of one instance of theft. Furthermore, what evidence the authorities had of crime – with the exception of the frequent violent conflicts in public – was drawn primarily from rumor or denunciation. With this in mind, it is difficult to maintain that criminal justice bore any direct relation to crime rates. Yet surely if more crimes were being committed, more cases would be brought, and greater attention would be given to criminal justice. Although we cannot estimate crime rates for the period, we do know that the urban authorities occasionally expressed concern with the frequency of particular crimes. It is possible that such concerns reflected an increase in crime.

Another potential explanation has already presented itself in the discussion of execution ceremonies. The increase in judicial severity could be a byproduct of the development of the nascent state, a mode of establishing or reinforcing the legitimacy of the authorities. The territorial growth of the cities during the fifteenth century brings with it the possibility of a demographic explanation for increasing execution rates. While many judicial proceedings would have taken place outside the central courts of the city council, some cases were brought to the center from the outlying areas. An expanded territory also helps explain the greater incidence of robbers before the courts: with more miles of highways within the responsibility of the city, more highwaymen might well have been caught and brought to justice. Increasing polarization of rich and poor was evident already in the fifteenth century and can be seen precipitating into urban justice in Augsburg.[52] Yet the timing for such an explanation is unsuitable. The great territorial expansions mostly happened before the period in question, well before the shift in execution rates.

It seems that the increasing judicial severity of the urban authorities in these cities was linked most immediately not to material causes but to political ones. As Schuster put it when reflecting on the case of Constance, city councils in the late Middle Ages went from being organs of self-administration to becoming governmental bodies.[53] These newly governmental city councils had to establish their autonomy and legitimacy with both subordinates and the emperor. They were competing for jurisdiction within the legally fractured spaces of the rural and urban landscapes with neighboring territorial powers and autonomous enclaves. The demographic factor of migration, in turn, provided a pool of particularly helpless objects for judicial demonstrations, as well as contributing to a public fear that crime was on the rise. It is not necessary to go so far as to propose that these city councils were engaging in cold and calculated demonstrations of authority at the expense of their most helpless subjects. Rather, the circumstances of the time provided them with what appeared to be a quite real need for a tough-on-crime stance, which in turn may have bolstered the apparent legitimacy and authority of the city state. In the end, the broad transformation of criminal justice in the fifteenth century can be ascribed to the mentalité of the men who governed these cities, to their new identity as a ruling coterie and to their personal sense of responsibility for the good of the community.

Part III

Reforming Zeal and Persecution in Lucerne

In both the particular history of witch trials and the general history of criminal justice, the city of Lucerne stands out as unusual in this tale. During the same years that the city was experiencing a late and accelerated adoption of inquisitorial process, with the torture and official investigation that accompanied it, Lucerne also picked up the relatively new stereotype of the diabolic witch and began regularly prosecuting witchcraft as a capital crime. These two developments are not unrelated. The very newness of the emerging mode of investigation made its use and practice all the more flexible, and the timing of its adoption seems to have encouraged a drastic increase in penal severity in the city. Yet the city fathers could just as well have been wary of the new techniques and evidentiary demands of inquisitorial process. Why were they so zealous in their pursuit of new modes of prosecution?

In order to shed light on the cultural climate from which the persecutory tendencies of urban justice grew, Chapter 7 will broaden the scope of the examination to look at social control generally. We will examine how the urban lords' efforts to reform their citizen subjects fit into late medieval social control, and the degree to which, once again, Lucerne stands out for its zeal in such matters. Then we will turn to a rather different question in Chapter 8, focusing in on the city of Lucerne, but broadening the chronological scope into the late sixteenth century. There we will examine the twin persecutions of witchcraft and sodomy, to see how Lucerne's zeal for prosecution and social control in the late fifteenth and early sixteenth centuries reached a climax that transformed the city's approach to witchcraft.

7
Urban Reform and Social Control

The fifteenth century was the golden age of the German cities. The power and independence they enjoyed was already eroding in the late fifteenth century, as they suffered important military and political losses in their power struggles with the territorial princes of the empire.[1] Within the bounds of the cities themselves, however, decline was nowhere evident. The vitality of late medieval cities was expressed in a variety of reforming efforts that aimed at perfecting the urban community and its governance. Bettina Günther argues that imperial cities make particularly good subjects for the study of early modern decency ordinances because their early state-like administration meant that, unlike larger territorial units, they could put late medieval reforming impulses into effect.[2] This longer view allows us also to move past the Reformation-focused work of older scholarship to understand the early modern innovations in a broader historical context. Among late medieval urban reforms must be counted the penal reformation described in Part II above, as well as the administrative efforts that produced increasingly extensive records in the urban archives as the century progressed. A wide range of efforts at social control were also part of these reforms, including some which were remarkably interventional, particularly in Lucerne.

In 1526, the Rager family of Lucerne fell to quarreling. Rager's son had taken a violent dislike to his stepmother, and the parents' marriage was soon in real trouble. Rager and his wife separated, which drew the matter to the attention of the city council. The council record reads:

> It is decided that Rager and his wife should come together again and keep house jointly as proper married people should, and as Rager's

> son has mistreated his stepmother and hit her, they must pay my lords 10£ as a fine.[3]

Interestingly, the city council did not merely fine the Ragers for their misbehavior. The entry continues:

> My lord the mayor should speak with both parties so that they will be peaceable with each other, as my lords will not suffer such behavior from them.[4]

Here we find an almost therapeutic impulse of the city fathers to teach their neighbors to behave as proper citizens should. When Rager failed in his duty as father and husband, allowing his son to become abusive, the city council stepped in and attempted to restore harmonious comportment. It looks like the council was acting as the "fathers" of the city, as Lyndal Roper has argued took place in post-Reformation Augsburg. Yet Lucerne remained Catholic in the Reformation and 1526 is far too early for any impact of post-Reformation Catholic confessionalization and discipline. Moreover, this was not the only time the city fathers intervened in family troubles; such intervention was fairly typical in late fifteenth- and early sixteenth-century Lucerne.

As we saw in Part II above, the rise of witch trials in Lucerne and Basel was due in part to an attitudinal shift on the part of the ruling class regarding their role in controlling crime. This shift was one of the products of the legal transformation of the late Middle Ages. Official prosecution meant an ongoing, personal responsibility on the part of city council members proactively to control crime. As we have seen, this resulted in a thorough and severe approach to hard crime. Yet in the details of social control, such as these from Lucerne, we also see an increasing tendency for the urban authorities to take on responsibility as arbiters of social mores and punishers of moral transgression. The late medieval cities pioneered methods of social control, prefiguring early modern social disciplining. In all three of the cities under examination, we find social control expanding over the fifteenth century, but in Lucerne the measures taken by the city council went further, with interventions aimed at reforming individuals.

In its broadest sense, social control could mean – as Bob Scribner put it – the entire process of socialization itself. To find a definition of social control which could be useful to the historian, Scribner narrowed the term to mean:

> Those forces maintaining the existing order which enable the continuance of established political authority and ensure the influence of political order over social formations.[5]

Scribner's emphasis on the political control over society is key to the use I make of the term here. For the purposes of this study, I use a narrower definition of social control, specifically *formal political control of social and moral comportment*. Although social control in a more general sense would include the punishment of crimes like theft and murder, here it is contrasted with criminal prosecution as the control of misbehavior not typically or necessarily considered criminal. Social control in this sense is the more general category of which social disciplining is a particular case.

The idea of social disciplining was first introduced by Gerhard Oestreich in the 1960s. Social disciplining, he argues, is the process by which people learned civilized self-control and became pious and obedient subjects. In Oestreich's view, social disciplining culminated in the seventeenth and eighteenth centuries, as both the prop and product of absolutist states.[6] Since Oestreich's time, the collaboration of church and state in the process of social disciplining has been elaborated. Social disciplining is now seen primarily as a feature of the age of confessionalization, from around the time of the Peace of Augsburg into the mid-eighteenth century. As Lutheran states became more Lutheran, Calvinist states more Calvinist, and Catholic states more Catholic, social discipline in its myriad forms was a means by which this confessionalization was achieved. In the process, subjects became more obedient as well as more pious, strengthening the state. The end product of social disciplining was the internalization of the moral strictures and behavioral codes of the confessional state.[7] It was, in this sense, a "civilizing process".

In this sense, social disciplining is a quintessentially post-Reformation phenomenon. In the restructuring which followed the Reformation, many states introduced special courts to oversee marriage and other aspects of social and religious life that had been policed by the Catholic church courts. Such was the case in Basel, where a marriage court, called the *Ehegericht*, was introduced as part of the reform of the city in 1529. The *Ehegericht* resolved conflicts within marriages and punished adultery, decided cases of disputed marriage promises, requests for separation from bed and board, and divorces.[8] Before 1529 in Basel, such cases (aside from divorce, which was then still impossible) had been heard by the ecclesiastical courts.

Courts designed to oversee social behavior more broadly were often introduced later, during the period of confessionalization. Such was the case with the *Chorgericht* of Bern, introduced in 1587. According to the mandate of the *Chorgericht*:

> The judges should be commanded not only to watch over matters of marriage, but also in general to maintain with the greatest industry and seriousness all the regulations of our Christian discipline, common order, and honor, and to send for the violators of the same, whether they be man or woman, and to judge and punish them according to the law.[9]

The work of the *Chorgericht* was the work of social disciplining, the effort by the state to impose moral order which went beyond public behavior into the private lives of their subjects.

The intense religious zeal that characterized the social disciplining of the confessional age was by no means unique to it. Religious reform was widespread at the end of the Middle Ages, from the high church politics of the Conciliarist movement to the intense lay piety of the beguines. As with all of these, late medieval social control laid the groundwork for the greater reforms to follow. Sin, public behavior, and the well-being of the community were all bound together, as in the words of the Basel preacher Johannes Heynlin in the late fifteenth century, "I say to you, people of Basel, if you do not cast off such public sin, God's wrath will not spare you, sooner or later!"[10] Indeed, fifteenth-century methods of social control may well have been a prerequisite for the Reformation, as tools to reinforce the fledgling reforms.[11] At times, attention to post-Reformation social disciplining has obscured this continuity. Lyndal Roper, for instance, discusses at length the role of the *Strafherren* (Discipline Lords) in Reformation Augsburg. The Discipline Lords served as an important tool of the city council's program of reform and discipline that began in 1537. Roper certainly presents a compelling case, but one could easily take away the false impression that the Discipline Lords were an innovation of the reforming council. In fact, the *Strafherren* had existed at least since 1507, although their role after the Reformation was vastly expanded and qualitatively transformed.[12]

Late medieval social control differed from the social disciplining of the confessional age in both quantity and quality, however. The sheer intensity and volume of the moral policing of the seventeenth century was unparalleled before the Reformation. Moreover, the difference was generally not only one of degree, but of kind. Gerhard Oestreich identifies the Renaissance-era precursor of social discipline as *Sozialregulierung*, social regulation. This social regulation, he argues, was typically urban and aimed at maintaining harmony and the *Stadtfriede*.[13] This harmony principle contrasts with the discipline and order sought by social control in the confessional age. Yet the need and desire for community harmony continued to play a role in later social disciplining. The work of reconciling quarreling neighbors was a key part of the role of the late sixteenth-century *Chorgericht* in Bern and, famously, of the Genevan Consistory.[14] Moreover, the driving quest for harmony itself could lead to more intrusive forms of social control, when private conflicts spilled out into the public arena.

An examination of social control in the normative literature of legal codes quickly reveals that the fifteenth century was a time of generally increasing concern over moral misbehavior. Joseph Baader's nineteenth-century collection of Nuremberg police ordinances covers the thirteenth through the fifteenth centuries. Unfortunately Baader does not provide dates for any of the ordinances he includes, dating them only broadly to the thirteenth and fourteenth centuries collectively or to the fifteenth century. Nonetheless, we can draw some conclusions by analyzing the broad categories which Baader provided. In the collection, nine ordinances are found from the thirteenth and fourteenth centuries which fall within the purview of the *Sittenpolizei*, the decency police. For the fifteenth century alone there are twenty-one.[15] Furthermore, the ordinances from the fifteenth century were far more extensive. The sumptuary ordinance from the earlier period fills about two pages in the edition, a dense list of forbidden luxuries and penalties:

> Every citizen, be he young or old, should wear no silver belt over a half mark's worth, nor any silver purse nor any silver Italian[16] knife, or any string of pearls.[17]

The clothing ordinance from the fifteenth century, by contrast, fills nearly fifteen pages, divided into subsections with headings for ease of use. Moreover, it includes a preface with the religious justification of the ordinance:

> Given, as has been manifoldly revealed, that almighty God has from the beginning, not only on earth but also in heaven and in paradise, hated and greatly punished the sin of pride and arrogance and has elevated humility, obedience, discipline and honorable good behavior with praise and has rewarded them [...] thus in order to glorify almighty God, to serve the common good, and to honor this honorable city of Nuremberg, and also that God might protect and shield us and the city through his mercy [...] therefore we, the mayor and council of the city of Nuremberg [...] have set forth the following ordinances.[18]

These sentiments would certainly not have been foreign to the council lords of the preceding centuries, but the lengthy exposition they receive here is significant. In the fifteenth century, the council not only designed an ordinance organized for easy reference, but also felt it necessary to explicitly justify it. This justification was probably intended for the patrician peers and even family members of the council, whose mercantile successes would have made such luxuries affordable. Bettina Günther's recent study of police ordinances in Frankfurt and Nuremberg across the threshold of the Reformation confirms the impression than normative expressions of concern over public decency were increasing during the fifteenth century, particularly after 1450. Among motivations for the regulation of sexual behavior, she cites – in addition to the Reformation desire to create a godly state – the particularly urban impulse of maintaining communal values and thus preserving the collective honor of the city, as well as a shift in the concept of decency during the late Middle Ages. Günther argues that in the fifteenth century not only the authorities but also large segments of the urban populace were uncomfortable with what they perceived to be sinful indecency and luxury.[19]

The legal sources from Lucerne reveal a similar concern with indecency in the fifteenth century, as evidenced by contrasts between ordinances of the thirteenth and fourteenth centuries and those of the fifteenth.[20] From the time prior to the Black Death only general law codes remain, the *Geschworene Briefe* that citizens swore to uphold. These codes included prohibitions and penalties for blasphemy, curfew violations, and forbidden gambling. From the 1350s onwards, specific ordinances appear, and after the turn of the fifteenth century many of these prohibit particular disruptive behaviors and indecencies. In 1409 a fine was set for talking during mass, in 1419 a penalty for obstinate public adultery. Such laws multiplied as the century progressed.

An examination of ordinances from Basel also shows an intensification of interest in social control during the fifteenth century.[21] Of fourteen decency ordinances passed between 1430 and 1490, nine were enacted in the 1440s and 1450s, during the same period when the practice of witch burning became established in the territory of Basel. This coincidence strengthens the argument that an ideological shift vis-à-vis crime and misbehavior in general lay behind the adoption of that deadly practice. Fifteenth-century social control legislation in Basel was crowned in 1498 with the *Alte Reformationsordnung* (Old Reform Ordinance). The *Alte Reformationsordnung* reiterated the long-standing focus of Basel decency laws on sexuality and blasphemy but also included a wide array of other moral transgressions, from the violation of holy days through dissipation via drinking and gambling.[22]

This normative intensification of concern over social mores was reflected in the punishment of misbehavior in all three cities during the fifteenth century. By far the most common response to minor transgressions of these normative strictures was to levy a fine. In Lucerne the standard punishment for gambling was a fine of five pounds, and one pound for breaking the peace (in this case fighting without drawing weapons). These hefty fines were specified in the ordinances, but judges could raise or lower the usual fine at their discretion. In Nuremberg, the yearly financial records list fines collected. For the early years of this survey, the entries include the reason for the fine: "for two skirts with a new cut," "for misbehavior in court," "for gambling."[23] Then, beginning around 1470, an increasing number of entries listed only the fine, eclipsing the various causes. After the turn of the century, fines were listed collectively, making a detailed analysis impossible. For the fifteenth century, however, some conclusions may be drawn.

Because most of the city financial ledgers from Nuremberg have been lost, fines levied for misbehavior can only be examined for the few years that remain. Of these, I have sampled the fines from about half, in an array stretching across the century (Figure 7.1). I have analyzed these fines for their sheer number, without regard to their individual heft. As is quickly apparent from a visual analysis of the data, the clearest conclusion which can be drawn is that the use of fines to punish minor misbehavior increased substantially over the latter part of the century. Incrementally, the number of fines levied in 1471–72

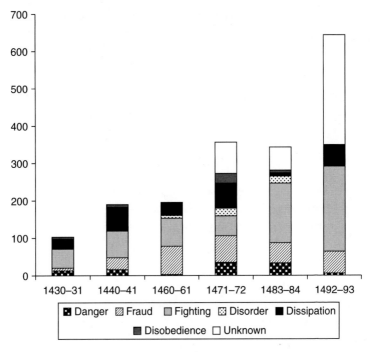

Figure 7.1   Nuremberg fines for misbehavior[24]

and 1483–84 represent an 85% increase over those from 1460–61, and the fines levied in 1492–93 an 82% increase over those from 1483–84. Essentially, the number of fines paid into the Nuremberg city coffers nearly doubled three times during the fifteenth century. While the rulers of Nuremberg were putting more time, energy and torment into the investigation of serious crimes, they were also paying more attention to ordinary misbehavior.

We can also make some broad observations about the categories of misbehavior for which these fines were imposed. A small number of the fines levied for misbehavior pertained to dangerous activities and illegal weapons (the category of *danger* in Figure 7.1), *disobedience* and general *disorder*. Discounting the fines of unknown cause, nearly half of all the fines levied related to *fighting*, principally fisticuffs, drawing weapons, and woundings. Over a fifth of the fines were assessed for *fraud*, generally for non-standard weights and measures. Roughly another fifth of fines pertained to *dissipation* and luxury, classic targets of social control.

Of these, one third (about one in twenty of all fines) were for gambling and another third were for violations of sumptuary laws. One purpose of sumptuary laws was to prevent excessive display of wealth and the social discord it could create. This is what the Nuremberg council meant when it cited the "common good" in the preamble to its fifteenth-century clothing ordinance.[25] Limits were set not only on luxurious clothing, but also on the costliness of gifts and the number of persons who might be invited to weddings and other private gatherings. The rest of these dissipation fines related to food and drink. Gluttony and drunkenness were only rarely punished specifically; most of these fines pertained to the serving of wine or rich foods at inappropriate times, such as after the evening bells or during a religious fast. Each year, for example, the council announced a prohibition against visiting wine houses during the first week of Lent.[26] Although an increasing number of fines fell under a veil of ambiguity as time went on, it is clear that the work of controlling misbehavior stepped up across the board.

A similar analysis for Basel and Lucerne is well-nigh impossible, as no comparable source exists to present detailed snapshots of fines. The sources which do exist, however, allow a more nuanced examination of the varied responses to particular forms of misbehavior. One constant concern was the disruptive and blasphemous potential of language. Hot tempers can lead to harsh words, which sow discord and could easily lead to more serious disorder such as armed conflict. For the mainte-nance of harmony and the *Stadtfriede*, verbal quarreling was controlled. Thus the first part of the Basel *Stadtfriede* ordinance of 1449 prohibited "breaking the peace with words."[27] This basic maintenance of harmony within the urban community was already an established part of urban justice. From 1430 we read:

> Greda Hechlerin should remain beyond the crosses [boundary stones] for half a year because she spoke evilly of Henbart Billung's wife, calling her a whore.[28]

Although entries were not always this specific, the essence of the crime was the violation of the peace with words. In 1431 a woman was ban-ished from the city for a year because "she violated the peace with words against Peter Herrenberg."[29] Similarly in 1450 a cloth cutter took the oath of banishment for a year because he broke the peace with words against another man.[30] Insults could also be taken as grounds for crimi-nal case against the insulted party. It pays to recall that ill repute was a valid cause for initiating criminal proceedings. The ordinary insults of "thief" and "whore" could have real repercussions if taken seriously by the court. In this context, relatively common heavy verbal abuses such as "witch" or "cow fucker" could be literally deadly insults.

Apart from the conflict it created, common verbal abuse could also be considered blasphemous, and efforts were made to curb the colorful and dirty language of the streets. A Lucerne ordinance from 1501 reads:

> When one says to the other, I would rather you had fucked a cow, a mare, or a donkey, and then another says to the same, well stick your penis in, this is ungodly and sinful and to hear it is shameful to all piety. [...] Whoever uses such terrible words henceforth will owe a fine of 5s.[31]

The ordinance went on to suggest the same fine for common oaths on Christ's humanity, "God's blood, God's body, God's gut, God's fear" and so forth. This suggested fine, however, represented a relatively mild punishment. In 1257, the Lucerne legal code stated that blasphemers were to be fined 12 shillings. In 1321, moreover, the Lucerne authorities established in writing that more serious cases of blasphemy deserved a more serious punishment: such persons should be swum.[32] This repertoire of punishments was expanded in the early fifteenth century, and three levels of the crime were described. Ordinary swearing was to be punished with fines, blasphemous oaths with the stocks and swimming, and heinous blasphemy was to be punished further on the body of the sinner as the city council saw fit. For example, an ordinance from 1497 reads:

> It should be announced in the churches that my lords will no longer suffer evil oaths, and whoever curses almighty God henceforth shall be placed in the stocks and thereafter [...] expect severe punishment.[33]

In fact, fines for blasphemous oaths appear to have been the exception rather than the rule. Most punishments were more severe.

This normative attention to blasphemy follows the general pattern for the urban communes in the late Middle Ages. Gerd Schwerhoff has recently argued that the cities played a pioneering role in establishing secular ordinances against blasphemy.[34] This battle with blasphemy was heightened in the fifteenth century, when many cities that previously had none established blasphemy ordinances. Schwerhoff identifies the mutilation of the tongue as the oldest trend in secular normative prescriptions of punishment, which was largely superseded by the widespread use of fines. As in Lucerne, however, the more detailed ordinances of the fifteenth century often delineated differing degrees of the crime and reserved the possibility of physical punishment or even execution for the worst offenders. Schwerhoff writes, "From a bird's eye view, one has the impression of directionless experimentation in the search for a better solution."[35] Although they followed general trends, secular ordinances against blasphemy were quite varied.

The actual practice of punishing blasphemy as we observe it in the fifteenth and early sixteenth centuries in Lucerne shows considerable variation from the norms laid out in the city's ordinances. Early on, cases of blasphemy were punished with the requirement that the transgressor confess and do penance, and physical punishment was added when the violation was considered especially serious. In 1424, Hensli of Winkle was banished from the city for half a year and required to confess and do penance after he indulged in blasphemous mockery of an oath taken in court.[36] In the same year, Jegkli Landwing of Zug suffered more extensive penalties for his blasphemy. Two witnesses had testified that while gambling with dice Jegkli had said that God and Saint Peter were sitting on a die and then had abused that die. Furthermore, they testified, he had blamed his losing streak on God and Saint Peter and another time had cursed God and His five wounds while gambling. Jegkli was placed in the stocks for the day and swum, after which he had to take an oath to confess and do penance and never to return to the city of Lucerne.

The idea that Saint Peter, in particular, might be affecting the roll of the dice was apparently not unique to Jegkli. Nearly sixty years later, Hans Weibel was punished for expressing a similar concern. A gambling companion of his testified that while they were gambling, Hans found one of the dice to be irregular. He drew his sword and said the die must be cut in two, and that Saint Peter sat upon it. His companion was shocked and exclaimed, "Hans, you do wrong, not to fear God in such matters." To which Hans replied, "Perhaps Saint Peter is there, perhaps not, but the die must be split."[37] While Hans's words and actions were questionable, they were not so clearly blasphemous as those of Jegkli Landwing. Hans was fined five pounds and had to swear not to gamble anymore.[38]

The practice of ordering blasphemers to confess and do penance continued in the late fifteenth century. In 1485 Jans Hut of Lucerne and Hans Weiss of Rothenburg appeared in the prison in Lucerne "on account of terribly unchristian oaths and sinful insults [...] as is fully proven on reliable testimony."[39] The two were beaten with rods out of the city gate in the direction of Constance to go see the bishop. They were told not to return unless they had confessed and done penance and brought a letter with them as evidence that they had done so. About ten years later, another case was resolved with punishment and penance:

> Hans Slatter of Rickenbach has come to our prison on account of some terrible words with which he insulted the holy virgin Saint Margaret. My lords have shown him mercy and allowed him to live and decided to place him in the stocks, as had been done. [...] And thereafter he should go to Constance and do penance for his evil deed, and bring back a letter and seal [proving] that he has done so.[40]

Similarly, in 1502, one year after the ordinance suggesting a five-shilling penalty for swearing by the body of Christ, Hans Reig of Reinach appeared before the court in Lucerne for using such oaths as "God's wounds, God's blood [...] God's weakness, God's strength, and God's corpse."[41] He was swum and had to swear that he would confess and do penance for his sin, bringing proof that he had done so if he returned to the city.

The religious element of penance in the punishment of blasphemy falls completely outside the sphere of those punishments suggested by written law. It represents an extra-legal tradition, employed by the city council throughout the fifteenth century. Schwerhoff notes that certain religious rituals were adopted into the early secular treatment of blasphemy, and such was the case in Lucerne.[42] In addition to being expected to confess and do penance for their sin, blasphemers were often banished from the city, subjected to corporal punishment, or both. It was important to the council of Lucerne that blasphemers should confess and repent their sin within the church, but also that they should suffer instructive public humiliation for their blasphemy.

The concern over dangerous language was certainly not unique to Lucerne. The punishment of blasphemy had long been a concern of the church, and in the thirteenth century the church requested that secular courts actively punish blasphemy as well. Laws passed against blasphemy in German cities during the following centuries introduced a wide variety of punishments. Among these were the fines, stocks, swimming, banishment, and pilgrimage imposed by Lucerne. More severe punishments are also evidenced, typically the mutilation or removal of the offending organ, the tongue. In extreme cases, even the death sentence was possible.[43] In light of these possibilities, the relatively mild and particularly reconciliatory nature of Lucerne blasphemy punishments becomes evident. Carl Hoffmann points out that the goal of reintegration persisted in the late medieval cities. This helps explain why many cities avoided the most extreme penalties on their books. In Hoffmann's view, the demands of ensuring peace won out over social discipline even in post-Reformation Augsburg.[44] Neither Basel nor Nuremberg shied away from the ultimate penalty in cases of blasphemy, and Lucerne's reconciliatory efforts in blasphemy cases cannot be explained merely as a traditional defense of urban harmony, given that the city's criminal justice was becoming increasingly deadly during these years. As we shall see, Lucerne's treatment of blasphemy fits into a larger pattern of innovation in social control in the city that seems to have focused on the moral reform of individuals.

In Basel, punishments for blasphemy varied from a five-pound penalty to time in the stocks, swimming, banishment, and even the cutting out of the tongue:

> Begelli the journeyman weaver shall be placed in the stocks, there-after swum and his tongue cut out and banished forever five miles from our city, on account of many evil and criminal oaths [...] which he made about God and Our Lady.[45]

Blasphemy was handled more frequently in Basel in the latter part of the fourteenth century than in the early fifteenth. Katharina Simon-Muscheid has counted 51 cases of blasphemy in the Basel banishment books between 1376 and 1406. From the following thirty years, she found only 18.[46] Nevertheless, a steady trickle of blasphemy cases appear in the Basel sources throughout the fifteenth century. Although most were punished variously with fines, stocks, swimming and banishment, worse was certainly possible. In 1527, Augustin Back was executed with the sword for some particularly vile, blasphemous comments he made to several women while working in the vineyard.[47]

Of the three cities, Nuremberg appears to have proceeded against blasphemy with the greatest severity. Although the earliest Nuremberg ordinance against blasphemy lists a minor penalty of six *Haller*, by the end of the fourteenth century harsher penalties appear, including mutilations.[48] In a fifteenth-century ordinance, the ultimate penalty is indicated:

> It may also be that such oaths and blasphemies are so criminal and crude that the council wishes to punish them, life or limb, as they [shall] decide for each case according to the nature of the matter.[49]

Nor did the authorities in Nuremberg shy away from such penalties. The punishments employed most frequently were banishment, execution, and the mutilation of the tongue.[50] Thus in 1436, the council condemned two iconoclastic blasphemers to death:

> Utz Ötterlein and Lorentz Wachleuel have been beheaded in Nuremberg through intercession, as they should have been burned alive because they shot at [the image of] a martyr and threw knives at the image of Christ, also on account of their great blasphemy.[51]

Blasphemy was a crime of many degrees, from the ordinary gutter language of the common people to conscious attacks against the central figures of Christianity. As such, it bridged the gap between religious crimes like heresy and witchcraft and the moral misbehavior of ordinary people. The authorities in Basel, Lucerne, and Nuremberg had to evaluate each case, to determine where it lay on this spectrum, and to assess the appropriate punishments. What is unusual about the approach of the Lucerne council is the emphasis their chosen punishments placed on the religious nature of ordinary cursing, and the goal of individual reform which the imposed pilgrimages seem to indicate. Although the religious aspect of the crime was mirrored in candle-carrying rituals in some late medieval cities, this appears to have been relatively infrequent.[52] The interest in the reform of individual subjects is what distinguishes the Lucerne efforts at social control from those in pre-Reformation Basel and Nuremberg.

Certain kinds of misbehavior reinforced each other. Blasphemy, as in the two cases from Lucerne involving Saint Peter and a game of dice, often arose in the context of gambling. Gambling often involved drinking and frequently took place among the journeymen of the cities, who were generally armed. This particular constellation was prone to violent and even deadly results. That the urban authorities sought to limit the dangerous potential of gambling is perfectly in keeping with Oestreich's harmony principle for late medieval social control. In order to maintain the peace of the city and to defuse the dangerous potential of the armed men among them, the city of Lucerne frequently used a dishonoring form of social control: the personal injunction. Injunctions against a given individual carrying a weapon, drinking, or gambling were essentially forms of punishment through dishonor.[53] As such, there was no necessary relationship between a specific injunction and the misbehavior it punished. The chief effect was to dishonor the misbehaving individual by marking him or her with a social disadvantage.

Most of the personal injunctions issued in Lucerne over the century under investigation fell between 1470 and 1510. Nearly all of the gambling injunctions occurred during this period; in the 1470s and 80s, gambling injunctions accounted for nearly half of all the personal injunctions issued. A case from 1471 seems to have initiated this trend in gambling injunctions. Several men of high standing appeared before the council:

> As my lords Hans am Achen, Hans Weibel, Hans an der Emen, Landös and other gamblers came to harsh words over cheating, my lords council and hundred have decided that all of the abovementioned [...] should henceforth never gamble again [...] nor should they host a game nor lay dice nor command anyone to do so on their behalf, and they should swear this on the saints.[54]

The incident seems to have elicited concern beyond the case itself, as the entry is immediately followed with a stern reiteration of the traditional gambling ordinance:

> On the same day my lords council and hundred have forbidden all games in their city and territory, except board games and chess, by a penalty of 5£ [...] and if anyone secretly or openly allows gambling against this prohibition in his house, from him also should the abovementioned fine be taken.[55]

Although neither this nor any other ordinance from the period mentions personal injunctions as a penalty for gambling, they featured prominently in the years which followed.

The first drinking injunctions appeared in 1477 in conjunction with a prohibition against gambling. Thereafter, the predominance in injunctions gradually shifted from injunctions against gambling to injunctions against drinking. A concentration of drinking injunctions dominated around the turn of the century, when drinking prohibitions accounted for more than half of the injunctions issued. The blasphemy ordinance from 1501 identified drunkenness as a cause of crude and dangerous insults, and prescribes sobriety as the penalty:

> Journeymen get drunk and in the blink of an eye call each other names [...] this my lords forbid and all those who drink so uncommonly and

contrary to our requirement, these same will be made to swear on the saints to drink no wine for a year and a day.[56]

Thus the authorities in Lucerne shifted their focus from gambling to drunkenness as a source of violent discord, a trend which was to continue through the 1520s. This may have been an attempt to get to the root of the problem; the Lucerne authorities drew a specific connection between the prohibited behavior and the misbehavior it was intended to rectify. Gambling often involved drinking, and it is evident that during the early sixteenth century, the Lucerne city council was inclined to see excessive drinking as the root of many other behavioral problems.

This examination of personal injunctions confirms the image of social control in Lucerne that emerges from the examination of the city's treatment of blasphemy. The lords of Lucerne appear to have used their authority in specific, somewhat experimental attempts to reform individuals whose behavior violated the religious integrity or social harmony of the city.

Lucerne was not the only one of the three cities which employed drinking injunctions in an attempt to curb misbehavior; Basel did as well. What is interesting is that drinking injunctions only appear in Basel after the city was reformed in 1529, in the flurry of social control which followed. In one case from 1530, Fridli Frütinger, who was employed by the city as a *Stadtknecht*, was arrested for drunkenness:

> He left the city without permission and went to Wyl, became overpowered with wine and handled himself entirely abnormally upon returning to Lesser Basel. [He was] however released on the Saturday after St. Sebastian, the twenty-second day of January. He has sworn that he will neither eat nor drink in any wine house, restaurant, or inn henceforth, unless he should first receive the permission of my lords.[57]

Fridli's behavior reflected particularly poorly on a reforming city which had recently issued a prohibition against drinking in excess. Such prohibitions were not new in the Reformation era, but they were certainly applied with a new earnestness. In sixteenth-century Augsburg we also find experimentation with injunctions against drinking that seem to have followed a logic similar to that evident in late fifteenth-century Lucerne. In Augsburg, also, the city fathers took a direct interest in the reform of individuals, coupling injunctions against drinking with reprimands.[58]

Another hallmark of early Reformation social control in Basel was an intense interest in marriage and sexual comportment. Following the Reformation, secular authorities moved quickly to establish control over marriage.[59] The secular marriage court that was founded in Basel with the Reformation would become a primary tool of social disciplining in the late sixteenth century, with over half of its business conducted *ex officio* – cases being initiated by the authorities rather than by complaints from the public. Even in its early years, in the first decade following the Reformation, the marriage court authorities initiated a quarter of cases themselves.[60] While in the early sixteenth century the court mostly handled marriage cases, particularly divorce suits, it also had competency in cases of sexual misbehavior. Essentially, the Basel marriage court replaced the ecclesiastical courts which had previously handled such matters.

Even before the Reformation, however, secular authorities frequently dealt with certain aspects of sexual comportment and marriage. There were some areas of city life, such as prostitution, in which the status quo diverged from strict church doctrine, and here the urban authorities stepped in to provide the primary regulatory influence.[61] Also, marriage had important ramifications for inheritance, and in cases where a marriage was annulled by the ecclesiastical court, or where partners received permission to separate from bed and board, property disputes were often brought before the secular authorities as a result. Moreover, loose sexual mores and discord within marriages could create conflict and disturb the civic peace. In such instances the city authorities might well intervene in their primary function of preserving the peace.

The most common urban solution to the problem of prostitution in the fifteenth century was the creation and maintenance of *Frauenhäuser*, communal brothels. Although these institutions were regulated and often even owned by the city government, fifteenth-century ordinances regarding them are relatively rare.[62] One exception to this tendency is found in Nuremberg. In the preamble to that ordinance, the authors explain their purpose:

> The honorable council of this city [...] is and should be more inclined to augment and increase respectability and good behavior than to allow sin and criminal existence.[63]

In order to increase respectability and good behavior as intended, the ordinance was mainly concerned with limiting the debts and restraints which compelled women to remain in the brothels:

> In order that the common women might more easily disentangle themselves and come away from the sinful existence in which they stand.[64]

The council was also concerned with preventing women from being improperly drawn into the brothel. The prohibitions against compelling a woman to become a prostitute through force and against the sale of women into the brothel provide a glimpse of the grim practices that existed.

The Nuremberg brothel ordinance ends with concern over the disruptive potential of prostitutes as lovers:

> Although the common women should be free and according to their name common, some of these common women have nonetheless had the audacity to take special lovers, whom they call their dear men, on account of which in past days much quarreling, indignation, discord and displeasure has come into being.[65]

The ordinance declared that such special relationships were not to be permitted, and sought to rein in the practice by having the women assigned to various men in turn. The possibility that brothel prostitution might become concubinage threatened the established social order.

Prostitution outside the brothels was much more difficult to control and could become an embarrassment to the city. In Basel, the prevalence of prostitution was especially problematic during the Council of Basel. In the banishment books of the city, sexual transgressions predominate in the years between 1426 and 1445. During the late fourteenth and fifteenth centuries, aside from the years of the Council, about one person was banished every two years for sexual transgressions. Between 1426 and 1445, however, 52 people were banished for such crimes, five every two years.[66] Many of these were women. The city authorities were clearly concerned with keeping prostitution hidden during Basel's time in the spotlight. In 1432 they also purchased two houses by the city wall to serve as brothels, pushing prostitution behind closed doors.[67]

Efforts were also made to bring prostitution within the walls of the city brothel in Lucerne. There, in 1469, the city council decreed that the *Hurenwirt*, owner of the brothel, should be allowed to force prostitutes who worked the streets to live in the brothel and work for him. If his brothel was already too full, he should report the "free prostitutes" to the city council, which would compel the prostitutes to limit themselves to the Kropfgasse or to leave the city.[68] In 1476 a similar ordinance places less responsibility on the *Hurenwirt*, ordering free prostitutes to register themselves with the city council and move into the brothel.[69] Later, in 1492, the authorities passed an ordinance that prohibited housing prostitutes, except in the city brothel.[70]

Prostitution in the city might give also occasion for concubinage. To prevent this, a Lucerne ordinance of 1499 threatened the female partners in such arrangements with banishment. It reads, "On account of the women of loose morals [...] if any man have such [living] with him, whether he is single or not, she will be forbidden the city by my lords."[71] Whether the women in such relationships were prostitutes or not, such cohabitation was a threat to marriage. Prohibitions against concubinage generally first appeared in the 1470s, including one unusual decree:

> Council and hundred have decided that as certain women live in sin, and were recently sick and were received by our lords and the priest and promised henceforth not to live in sin, and yet they still live with their lovers, these should swear on the saints from this hour forth to go four miles from our city forever and never again to return.[72]

It is interesting that the urban authorities would actively involve themselves in the desperate promises sick women made (probably during an epidemic) to improve their spiritual state should they recover. Yet not only did the city council impose punishment when these promises were broken; the council had apparently received the women along with the priest and probably encouraged them to make such promises in the first place. This active involvement of the city council in the personal spiritual state of their subjects was part and parcel of their unusual engagement with moral behavior.

While the authorities in all three cities were clearly concerned with controlling prostitution, a remarkably high degree of normative attention to sexuality is evident in Lucerne between 1469 and 1500. An ordinance in 1463 banning extramarital cohabitation is the only such ordinance found during the century but outside this period.[73] Tellingly, it came near the beginning of the period and might reasonably be considered a forerunner of the coming intensity of judicial attention to illicit sexuality. Two ordinances in 1470 and one in 1471 dealt with the same problem, but with a key difference. In 1463, the council was concerned with the behavior of council members. It decreed that any council member openly living in sin was to be temporarily removed

from the council until the situation was rectified. Furthermore, if anyone should persist in such sinful cohabitation, he was to be removed
permanently from the council, and his concubine banished from the
city.

In the 1470s, the focus was instead on the populace at large. The first
of two ordinances from 1470 specifies that any couple living in sin while
one of them had a proper spouse would suffer banishment. The second ordinance, two months later, is more specific. The pair are to be
banished for a week. An ordinance from 1471 matches closely actual
court decisions in such cases. That ordinance specified that the women
in such couples were to be banished, as common prostitutes were, four
miles from the city until such time as the council might have mercy
and allow them to return.[74] The 1472 case in which the council threatened lapsed concubines with banishment followed on the heels of these
ordinances. In an ordinance from 1474 the prohibition against cohabitation and concubinage was repeated once again.[75] Thus within less than
a decade, the normative utterances of the council shifted from laying
the blame for sinful cohabitation on the more powerful partners of such
unions, male council members, to the less powerful. In practice, women
nearly always suffered greater punishment in such cases than men.

Between the years of 1470 and 1500, the city council of Lucerne was
three times as likely to hear a case pertaining to sexuality as either
before or after. During this period, the council's concern shifted from
one problem to another in turn. After an early emphasis on controlling
prostitution, the focus of the 1470s was cohabitation. In the decade that
followed there was little normative attention paid to such matters but
cases continued to appear before the courts, such as the case of Richard
the furrier and a woman called Schoppenmanin. Richard's wife brought
charges of adultery against the pair, and the council decided:

> Richard must avoid Schoppenmanin, and have nothing more to do
> with her, and should take his wife back and do what is best and most
> proper for her. For if he mistreats her again, my lords will punish
> him as he deserves. And Schoppenmanin shall swear to leave the city
> by three miles for an entire year and not return without my lords'
> knowledge and permission.[76]

By the 1490s the focus of the council's energy turned to prostitution
once again. After the turn of the century, however, a new problem took
center stage. Cases pertaining to extramarital sexuality no longer predominated; instead, more cases over conflict within marriage appeared.

The intensity and frequency of marital conflicts had increased in Lucerne after 1470, but two altogether new kinds of cases appeared after about 1480: matrimonial disputes and separation cases. The matrimonial disputes consisted of contended marriages and suits over marriage promises. This was a realm in which the ecclesiastical court made a strong claim to authority. Although the church had claimed jurisdiction over marriage from the Carolingian era onwards, ecclesiastical courts never enjoyed exclusive marital jurisdiction in Germany. Nevertheless, general acceptance of the church's authority had been widespread since the thirteenth century.[77] The Lucerne council forwarded some matrimonial disputes to the ecclesiastical court in Constance, but others it decided on its own.

The second new kind of case appearing in Lucerne after 1480 pertained to separation. Whereas earlier the council had only intervened in the behavior of married couples if the situation were abusive, disruptive, or adulterous, beginning in the last decades of the fifteenth century the council began ordering peacefully separated couples to return to cohabitation. As they were sent back to live together, the separated couples were told to do what is best for each other and to treat each other as proper married people should. Thus in a case from 1512, Sager of Entlebuch and his wife were admonished:

> They should keep house together and do what is best for each other, and Sager should neither scold nor hit her, unless he should find her in circumstances which touch on his honor.[78]

In 1516 Jost Schlopper, listed with the appellation "woman hater," and his wife were chastised similarly. The two were told to return to keeping house together, as was proper for married people, and to treat each other well. Jost was warned further that he "should take back such words as he has used with his wife, for we do not have confidence in everything he says."[79] As they worked to reconcile couples and induce them to resume keeping house together, the Lucerne authorities instructed men on how to be proper husbands.

The council took on an almost pastoral role in the resolution of certain marital conflicts, occasionally sending the mayor to admonish couples to proper behavior and cohabitation. In 1526, a man named Schlesser had apparently thrown his wife out of the house. The council decided that the fault lay with Schlesser: "It is decided that my lord the mayor will speak with him [saying] that he should keep house with her and do the best for her."[80] It is surprising that the mayor should be given the task of delivering the message; clearly the high status of his person was intended to reinforce its effectiveness. Lucerne was a small city, and this may have affected how the urban lords viewed their relationship with their citizen subjects. In the effort to maintain harmony, the city-state took on a uniquely therapeutic aspect.

While matrimonial disputes and separation cases first appeared in Lucerne after 1480, they remained uncommon, occurring on the average once every four years until the 1520s. Then, between 1523 and 1530, the intensity of adjudication increased sharply, with more than two such cases being handled on average each year. Furthermore, a qualitative shift took place around the same time in the nature of disputed marriages. In earlier cases, from 1488–1516, all disputes were sent to Constance for resolution. A case from 1512 illustrates the deferral of the city council to Constance. In March of 1512, Conrat Truber and his wife were commanded to return to living together, "as my lords also decided sometime previously."[81] Clearly the matter had come up before, and the council was frustrated with the couple's insistence that they be allowed to separate. Only a few days later, however, the couple raised the matter again, this time bringing with them evidence that they had been formally separated in Constance. The council book reads:

> It is decided that she and he shall be separated as was done in Constance and that she should have and use her property, and he should have and use his property, so much as he has, each without worrying about the other.[82]

A third party was assigned as a steward over their child's inheritance, to ensure that neither father nor mother wasted it and left the child destitute. This concern over property was an expression of the primary legal responsibility of the secular government in marriage cases decided by the ecclesiastical court.

In the 1520s, however, the council of Lucerne appears to have taken more responsibility for resolving marriage cases itself; interesting timing given that the city remained staunchly Catholic. The last case which it explicitly referred to Constance in that decade came in 1524. In that case, the council seemed inclined to see a valid marriage, but referred the matter to Constance because the insistence of one party made it impossible for the council to resolve the case. The case involved a young couple and was contested by the girl's family. The council decided as follows:

> As the girl's family is of the opinion that not so much has taken place that a marriage should exist between them, and as the family

will not amicably allow the marriage to be, my lords cannot handle in the affair other than to allow them to take the matter before the ecclesiastical judge, but with this stipulation, that if the family wishes to use the church courts against Wendel,[83] than they should do this at their own cost, and neither at the girl's nor at Wendel's expense.[84]

Clearly, if the Lucerne council had been fully empowered to decide the case, it would most likely have insisted that the marriage stand, as seems to have been the wish of Wendel and the unnamed girl. This case highlights the limited nature of the city's authority in deciding marriage cases. As long as all parties would agree to abide by the city's decision, it could stand. As such, the council of Lucerne acted as a mediator in marriage cases, deciding them, in a sense, extra-judicially.

The case of young Wendel and his wife was, however, the last such case before 1530 that the city council hesitated to decide on its own. Thereafter, at least until the end of the decade, the council in Lucerne decided all the matrimonial disputes brought before it. This may have been a coincidence of tractable litigants, or due to a fear of contamination in the face of the spreading Reformation, resulting in a reluctance to send anyone north through Zurich on a religious errand. Whatever the reason, while the Lucerne council was on contested ground making decisions in matrimonial disputes, its interests do not seem to have been in conflict with ecclesiastical claims to authority, but rather to have supplemented them. If anyone insisted, the city readily deferred to the church in matters of marriage.

In balancing the autonomy of its own court with a calculated deference to the local bishop, Lucerne generally followed the trend for late medieval cities. Nuremberg established a firm de facto jurisdiction over clerics, another area where the church made a strong claim to jurisdiction. One case, in which Nuremberg did send an accused cleric to the bishop of Bamberg, appears to have been a carefully chosen demonstration of the city's willingness to cooperate with the bishop diplomatically, as it might with any foreign lord. In that case the accused was only nominally a cleric and, as the Nuremberg council may well have foreseen, he was returned by the bishop to the city for judgment.[85]

A comparative glance at the city of Constance helps to place the Lucerne city council's actions in perspective. In his study of adjudication in Constance, Peter Schuster found a stricter emphasis on sexual comportment in the late fifteenth century. In particular, the city council in Constance was concerned with threats to the institution of marriage. Like their counterparts in Lucerne, the secular authorities in Constance punished longstanding adultery and separated couples living in sin. Schuster also noted that the female partners in such relationships were consistently punished more severely. While the men were scolded, the women were often banished from the city. Women carried heavier blame in part because the accusation of prostitution, whether explicit or not, often overshadowed their participation in the informal and adulterous relationships.[86] In all of this, Lucerne and Constance exhibited similar practices. Schuster does not mention that the Constance city council ever separated married couples in the fifteenth century or ruled on whether a marriage was legitimate. In this, the actions of the Lucerne council appear to have been unusual. Also, although there is some indication that male partners in affairs were reprimanded for their misbehavior, no element of counseling appears such as that in Lucerne. This last element, which cannot be explained away by the distance between Lucerne and the episcopal city, thus emerges as the most significant element of innovation by the Lucerne council. It is evidence of the council's willingness to proactively intervene in the private lives of its subjects in order to ensure proper comportment.

While all three of the cities examined in this study, as well as the city of Constance, showed an increasing interest in social control during the late fifteenth century, the methods of the Lucerne city council stand out. The Lucerne authorities infused their attempts at social control with an active interest in the reform of individuals. The methods they used for punishment highlight this: penance and reconciliation; personal injunctions tailored to treat the root of the trouble; and scolding and counseling of feuding partners. These attempts at reform follow from the harmony principle which Oestreich identifies with late medieval social regulation, but also mimic the interests of later social disciplining, as the Lucerne authorities struggled to teach their citizen subjects proper comportment.

This kind of early social disciplining appeared in Basel immediately after the Reformation. Thus from 1530 we read:

> The abovementioned Hans Oswald, born in Freiburg in Breisgau, has been imprisoned on account of his gluttony and drunkenness, also because of some vulgar words which he shouted out a window.[87]

Hans was released with a warning to abstain from such things because they anger God. Hans was advised that a repeat offense would be punished harshly, and then released with a common oath of peace. As the council in Lucerne frequently did, the Basel court coupled threats of future punishment with mildness, trying to educate the wayward as it did so. In Lucerne, however, these methods appeared much earlier, and completely independently of the Reformation which that city ultimately rejected.

Social control in late medieval cities was the rule, not the exception. As cities were often filled to capacity, and with strangers frequently arriving for work, the level of crime was high and perceived by the authorities as a serious problem. Intensification of social control appears to have coincided with intensification of criminal justice; the concerns which drove the one also drove the other. Not infrequently, gambling or dancing ordinances expressly forbade one or another foreign form as degenerate. As conditions pressured the urban authorities to act, they also enjoyed substantial autonomy to do just that. In Lucerne, this autonomy was greater in matters of social control because of the distance to Constance. This distance in turn was effectively increased by the reformed lands which stood between them after the Reformation. Without directly challenging the authority of the church court, the council of Lucerne mediated marriage cases independently.

Is it a coincidence that the urban authorities most intensely interested in the moral comportment of their subjects were those who prosecuted witchcraft most intensely during the fifteenth century? The height of the early modern witch hunts coincided with the intense social disciplining of the confessional age and the birth of absolutism. This has led Robert Muchembled to argue that witch hunting was a means of acculturation, a tool in the war of elites against popular culture.[88] The idea that witch hunting was a clash of popular and elite culture has been largely debunked, and with it Muchembled's acculturation thesis. Yet the coincidence of social disciplining and witch hunting is not without meaning. They were, as Blauert also found in his examination of Speyer during the late sixteenth and early seventeenth centuries, both echoes of a general sense of crisis.[89] Social disciplining and judicial severity sought to eliminate ordinary evils; witchcraft prosecution was an attempt to eradicate the most evil crime imaginable.

8
Witchcraft, Sodomy, and the Demonization of Crime

In 1577, in the dark of November, Jacob Schmidli confessed to his Lucerne interrogators that he had denied God and raised storms at the Devil's bidding. In short, he confessed that he was a witch, opening his confession with the tale of his seduction. Thirteen years ago, Jacob related, he had encountered a priest to whom he complained of his poverty. The priest led him into a house to give him a meal, and there at the table sat three men dressed in green, with three women beside them. The men bade him sit with them and eat. When Jacob uttered a prayer, the three briefly disappeared, then returned. Their names were Spiegel, Fäderli, and Greßli. Reaching for a knife that had fallen under the table, Jacob saw that the three had goat's feet. He reflexively exclaimed a prayer, saying, "Jesus protect me!" and again they disappeared. This time the three women followed. Greasing their stools with a salve and chanting, "Howl, Devil, howl!" they flew off to the Heuberg, traditional meeting place of witches. The priest went with them, and when he returned he showed Jacob how to raise storms to spoil the hay and lay waste to Alpine meadows. Jacob said he later raised storms, used witchcraft to lame man and beast, and denied God and the saints.[1]

Jacob Schmidli's confession is typical in that it does not rigidly follow any script, yet contains certain recurring elements: his seduction in a time of need, his initial instruction in storm raising, and his apostasy. That Jacob was male immediately makes his trial stand out to us. As we have seen, until the early sixteenth century, witches in Lucerne were exclusively women. During the late sixteenth century witch hunt that saw the arrest of Jacob Schmidli, this was no longer the case. Most of the accused were still women, but the exclusive gendering of the indigenous witch stereotype no longer fully determined the range of possible suspects. The strict gendering of the witch stereotype in Lucerne had been broken during the course of a simultaneous persecution for witchcraft and sodomy. This persecution reached its climax with the trial that opened this book, but it began in the late fifteenth century. In order to put the trial of Andreas from Tschafel and his two companions into context, and in order to understand the full effects of the late fifteenth-century reforming zeal in Lucerne, we need to examine the city's history of sodomy prosecution.

The conceptual proximity of witchcraft and sodomy has been acknowledged, and Tamar Herzig has recently analyzed ways in which the diabolic witch stereotype forced intellectuals to reconsider the attitudes of demons toward sodomy. Yet the nature and extent of the relationship between actual persecutions of witchcraft and sodomy has never been fully examined. P. G. Maxwell-Stuart notes the coincidence of particular persecutions of witchcraft and sodomy, in this case during a military occupation by the armies of Cromwell's Protectorate, but his examination of the relationship between the two ends there. In a recent collection of bestiality and witchcraft cases from Basel, there is surprisingly little analysis of the relationship between the two persecutions.[2] The relationship between witchcraft and sodomy persecutions may be similar to the relationship found by Gary Waite between witchcraft and heresy trials. As Waite puts it, both persecutions were bent on "eliminating individuals who were believed to be in league with Satan and corrupting society."[3] Waite notes an imperfect alternation between periods of intensity in witch hunting and Anabaptist persecutions respectively. A similar alternation existed between persecutions of witchcraft and sodomy in Lucerne, but the relationship between the two persecutions was also dynamic.

When I use the term sodomy here, I am referring to all manner of "unnatural" or "unchristian" acts (as they were called) that were lumped together at the time, predominantly bestiality and homosexual relations. Using the term sodomy in this way avoids the anachronism of referring to early modern homosexuality. It also employs an early modern term for a rich and complex early modern category. One tendency among historians of sexuality, however, has been to use sodomy as a kind of shorthand for homosexual acts and to ignore the sheer breadth of the early modern term.[4] Others offer an important corrective to this by pointing out the use of the term for bestiality, "unnatural" intercourse between men and women, and even analogously for whole categories of non-sexual sin. Sodomy is a term with cognates in most, if not all, western European languages, with literally thousands of years of associations attached to it. The ambiguity that characterizes "sodomy" and its cognates is shared by vernacular synonyms. Helmut Puff discusses the conflation of bestiality and homosexual acts under the German term "Ketzer," and Erica Fudge and P. G. Maxwell-Stuart note that the English term "buggery" encompassed a similar range of actions.[5] The tendency to conflate sodomy and homosexual acts persists, however, in large part because one of the main inspirations for the field of the history of sexuality was queer scholarship with its search, explicit or not, for predecessors and heroes. It is a sign of the growing maturity of the field that this search is losing importance next to the broader effort to understand human sexuality in general.

One effect of expanding the category of sodomy beyond potential heroes is that it complicates the narrative of persecution. When historians of sexuality explicitly exclude cases of bestiality from studies of early modern persecutions of sodomy, this separation of subjects is a reflection of modern assumptions. Early modern individuals persecuted for homosexual acts make a sympathetic subject for the twenty-first-century historian of sexuality; those accused of bestiality significantly less so. The division reflects our modern conceptual separation of the two categories of action, the former as a frequently persecuted form of human sexuality, the latter as animal abuse. It should be noted, of course, that bestiality is also a frequently persecuted form of human sexuality – whether or not we wish to defend it. As Joyce Salisbury puts it, "It is likely that intercourse with animals has been one expression of human sexuality for as long as people have lived in close proximity with their animals."[6] In fact, bestiality was frequently the target of sodomy persecutions in German-speaking Switzerland, and no etymological distinction was made between homosexual acts and bestiality. It is also clear, as we shall see, that the region suffered deep fears of such acts, both for the divine wrath it might inspire and because it insulted Swiss honor.

Because judicial torture was generally employed in capital criminal cases, it is difficult to know for certain whether particular acts were actually committed. This is true not only for homosexual acts, of course, but also for bestiality, theft, arson, and murder. Early modern criminal justice in general was persecutory in nature. Lower status individuals, immigrants, and strangers were all particularly vulnerable to prosecution for crimes such as theft. Although jurists and lay judges were no doubt genuinely concerned with discovering the truth and punishing the guilty, the methods at their disposal were deeply flawed. As we have seen, they were guided by common sense in the process of torture and interrogation, and this arrangement powerfully confirmed any prejudices they might hold against the accused. From this perspective, tortured and executed criminals were persecuted, not just prosecuted. Thus even if we accept that bestiality was a real practice, and one we would scarcely approve of ourselves, we can still recognize its treatment within early modern criminal justice as persecution.

The persecutory nature of early modern justice generally is highlighted by its comparison here with witch hunting in particular. As discussed in Chapter 6, the patterns in witchcraft prosecution and criminal prosecution generally were strongly linked. They seem to have been driven by the same forces. It is difficult to argue that increasing witch trials are driven by rising rates of witchcraft; more sensible is the conclusion that the forces driving ordinary criminal prosecution are the same as those we generally see behind witch hunts: fear and the zeal for righteousness. Of all the various capital crimes I examined alongside witch trials in the course of this study, sodomy was the crime that had the closest conceptual proximity to witchcraft and the persecutions of the two have the most interesting relationship. A comparative analysis of witchcraft and sodomy trials in Basel and Lucerne (I found no sodomy persecution in Nuremberg) reveals that the conceptual proximity of the two had real effects on the course of the persecutions.

Shortly after the city of Basel was reformed in 1529, a former Franciscan named Hans Lüthard was preaching against the evils of adultery in Waldenburg and hit a sour note. In emphasizing the depravity of extramarital sex he compared it with bestiality, saying it would be easier for a man to be forgiven for having sex with a beast than for committing adultery. It is doubtful that he meant to defend bestiality, but he surely picked the wrong crowd for his hyperbolic comparison. In the city of Basel and its territories, every known instance of bestiality over the last century had been punished with death. Several of these cases had been discovered and punished in the rural district of Waldenburg. Apparently Hans Lüthard's audience complained of his words; the authorities in Basel took depositions from twenty witnesses in the matter.[7]

In the fifteenth and sixteenth centuries, bestiality was a touchy subject in Switzerland. The dominant discourse over sodomy was xenophobic and polemic.[8] During the period, Swiss Germans regularly expressed xenophobic suspicions of male–male sodomy against the French and Italians. In return, Swiss men were widely slandered as loving their cows more than their women. This highly polemical discourse over sodomy and nationality touched deeply on the individual and collective honor of the Swiss Confederates. It also had a profound impact on the fates of Swiss men accused of homosexual acts or bestiality, as well as those accused of slander in such matters.

In 1435 a certain Hans Zehend stood before the assembled representatives of the Swiss Confederates in Lucerne, accused of vile slander. Apparently Hans had said that cowherds were sodomizing their charges. He was accused of saying that he would not want to eat veal; "We must eat the children of many a Swiss man here." Imagine a wifeless man away on a lonely mountain all year, he reportedly said. He sees before him a cow with silky hair and has his way with her.[9] Whether his words were spoken in drunkenness or anger, or falsely reported by a companion, they constituted grave slander. What happened to Hans Zehend is unknown, but he certainly faced the possibility of execution. Thirty-five years later a brief entry in the Lucerne council records reads:

> A man named Hans Krucker has been drowned because he said that the Confederation was a good, free land, and if a man had sex with a cow, no-one would do a thing to him because of it.[10]

It is difficult to say which was worse – Zehend impugning that bestiality was rampant in Switzerland, or Krucker asserting that no-one would try to stop it. The master narrative of sodomy was and remains the story of Sodom and Gomorrah, destroyed by the wrath of God for the sins of their inhabitants. During the fifteenth century, this narrative was becoming increasingly important to how governors viewed their duties. Not only did they work to maintain the peace and harmony of the city, the medieval origins of urban law, they also averted the wrath of God by punishing transgressors and maintaining the moral order of the city. Thus Krucker's slander personally and professionally attacked the judge before him, a councilor of Lucerne. His sad end no doubt reflects this.

Talk of bestiality was part of the fabric of popular culture, not only on the level of national slander, but also on the individual level of insults bandied about in the streets. In 1501 the council of Lucerne passed an ordinance against certain oaths and insults current at the time, including among them the unforgettable line: "I would rather that you had fucked a cow." As we have seen, the councilors considered this crude oath and the usual response ("well, stick your penis in!") reprehensible, considering such language ungodly, blasphemous, and shameful to hear. However, the ordinance assigned a relatively small fine of five shillings: the same as was attached to other common blasphemous oaths. It would seem that such talk was simply so pervasive and petty that no harsher measures should be taken against it.[11]

There is a world of difference between a common, if crude, insult and a serious accusation. Charges of sodomy against individuals were usually handled as genuine. This was especially true if the content of the accusation were bestiality as opposed to homosexual acts. In 1516, Ulman Husser confronted Hans Schencker, saying that Hans had sodomized a cow. The initial confrontation was extra-judicial and most likely public. Hans could scarcely let the words lie, so he brought charges of his own before the court, accusing Ulman of slander. Ulman's words touched gravely on Hans Schencker's honor and reputation, the record reads formulaically, and as God is his witness, no truth can be proved in them. Ulman responded that he had discovered Hans "in circumstances in which no Christian man has any business being," demonstrating that his charges were not the repetition of slanderous rumors, but a specific accusation. Both of the men were then arrested and placed in the tower to be questioned, with torture if necessary. Five days later an entry in the council record begins, "Little Hans Schencker has confessed that he had sex with a cow in an Alpine meadow." Schencker confessed to multiple counts of bestiality and was burned at the stake.[12] His bid at countering slander legally had collapsed in the torture chamber.

The chance of surviving a charge of sodomy in Lucerne was quite small. Over three-quarters of men formally accused of sodomy in the city between 1480 and 1600 were executed.[13] When the handful of cases dealing with homosexual acts are removed from the figures, the total rises to 85%. Not only did the vast majority of sodomy cases pertain to bestiality in particular, bestiality was handled with much more consistent severity than sodomy between two human beings. This tendency bears out for Basel as well, and may well represent a regional trend for the German-speaking northern Alps. It may be that this reflects concern over the general slander against the Swiss as bestial sodomites, or it may reflect an actually higher instance of bestiality. Quite likely both played a role. In light of the concern over bestiality, it is interesting that prior to the 1480s very few cases appear in the records of either Basel or Lucerne. We know that the councilors of Lucerne were already concerned with slander pertaining to bestiality, from at least the 1420s. In addition to the slander against the Swiss Confederation mentioned above, in 1425 the Lucerne city council judged specific accusations of bestiality against a boy from their rural provinces to be slander.[14] As this is one of only a handful of bestiality cases to appear in the records before 1480, it is difficult to make generalizations. It does seem from the few cases we have, however, that early in the fifteenth century the council of Lucerne was more concerned about slander than about particular acts.

It is significant that the late fifteenth century witnessed the shift in Lucerne from occasional prosecution to active persecution of sodomy. Such active persecution seems to have been uncommon in the fifteenth century. Christine Reinle writes that the prosecution of homosexual sodomy in Regensburg during the time was haphazard. She identifies looming conflict with the Turks as the probable motivation for the one significant persecution that took place. The "silent sin" was attacked in a wave of spiritual housecleaning prior to war.[15] In Cologne at the end of the fifteenth century, the city council found itself unexpectedly confronted with intimations that hundreds of men in the city were involved in an active homosexual subculture. A case that had begun with the shocking deathbed confession of a single wealthy man threatened to involve a large number of people from all social ranks. Apparently more interested in maintaining harmony than in seeking to purify their city, the rulers of Cologne ceased their investigations and swept the case under the rug.[16] The persecution of sodomy is more often found in early modern confessional states, for which purity, inaccessible as it was in practical reality, was of fundamental importance.

Among those who have written on the subject, some, such as William Monter, have argued that early modern sodomy persecution was linked to post-Reformation religious zeal.[17] Monter analyzes a sixteenth-century persecution in Geneva that he claims was unrivaled before the Reformation. This may well be true for Geneva, but the persecution in late fifteenth- and early sixteenth-century Lucerne was proportionally more significant. In Lucerne there were 28 cases in 45 years – between 1485 and 1530 – most of which ended in execution. In Geneva (a larger city by a factor of nearly ten) there were 30 cases over the course of the sixteenth century, with nearly half of these ending in banishment or whipping. This level of prosecution apparently continued unabated or even increased in the seventeenth century; between 1555 and 1678, 30 people were executed for sodomy in Geneva.[18] Thus the post-Reformation persecution in Geneva was neither as extensive nor as severe as the earlier one in Lucerne. Nonetheless, an examination of the persecution in Lucerne confirms Monter's general thesis that sodomy persecution was greater during periods of religious zeal. Let us call it more generally "reforming zeal" and the similarities become unavoidable.

As illustrated in the previous chapter, a climate of urban reform and (at moments) moral panic gripped the city of Lucerne, beginning in the

late fifteenth century, and this gave rise to a wide variety of reforming measures in the city. During the witch hunting years of the 1480s
and 1490s, the city council engaged in a series of social disciplining
campaigns. The authorities in Lucerne infused their measures with
an active interest in the reform of individuals, using penance, reconciliation, personal injunctions, scolding, and counseling as they tried
to control misbehavior. This urban reform in Lucerne also inspired
harsher handling of crime and the outright persecution of sodomy that
culminated, as we shall see, in a general demonization of crime in the
early sixteenth century.

It seems also that a specific narrative of sodomitical mercenaries current during the Burgundian War (1474–1476) contributed to the focus
of this reforming zeal on sodomy and witchcraft. Swiss charges of sodomy against Charles the Bold of Burgundy, propagandistic as they were,
attached this narrative to the enemy as a whole.[19] In addition, there was
a conceptual connection between sodomy and witchcraft that caused
instances of the one to call to mind fears of the other. The case of Basel
demonstrates how powerful the combination of these factors could
be. In 1474, during the war with Burgundy, the Swiss Confederates
captured a number of prisoners of war, including mercenaries from
Lombardy. In messages to the emperor, the Swiss Confederates charged
that the Lombards had committed "murderous, sinful, unchristian and
unnatural acts." Meanwhile, the prisoners were taken to Basel, where
the authorities proceeded to question them regarding their supposed
war crimes. Under torture, the Lombard mercenaries were questioned
specifically about the crime of *florentzen*, sodomy between men, and
most of them confessed. On Christmas Eve, 1474, 18 Lombard mercenaries were burned as sodomites in Basel, a spectacle of execution
utterly unparalleled in the city.[20]

In the years immediately preceding those events, no-one had been
executed in Basel for witchcraft or for sodomy, although earlier prec-
edents did exist. After 1474, however, a number of deadly witchcraft and
sodomy trials took place in the territory of Basel.[21] The spectacle 1474
seems to have inspired not only concerns over sodomy, but witch trials
as well. One reason for this may have been quite simply that witchcraft
and sodomy were punished in the same way, with execution at the stake.
In a world in which executions were tailored to particular crimes and
the mode of execution was intended to telegraph the crime to spectators,
an execution might well call to mind other crimes punished similarly.

The resonance between witchcraft and sodomy went further, however. One short-hand for both of these crimes was heresy, *Ketzerei*,

another crime that might be punished at the stake. In fifteenth- and sixteenth-century Switzerland, the term *Ketzer* was ubiquitously used to refer to men who had engaged in homosexual acts or bestiality.[22] Heresy appears to have been used as a short-hand for witchcraft as well, as is made explicit in a written oath of banishment from Lucerne, in 1482, in which the accused proclaimed of herself: "I have a substantial reputation of being caught in heretical beliefs, that I should use witch-craft and sorcery."[23] The association of witchcraft and sodomy through the link to heresy actualized after witchcraft became defined as a form of diabolism in the first half of the fifteenth century, but it had roots in the ancient conceptual nexus of evil that linked secret worship, deviant sex, cannibalism, and magic. In the Roman world, the fears associated with this conceptual nexus had been attached to the mystery religions and to early Christians. During the Middle Ages these fears and the ster-eotypes associated with them were attached to heretics and the Jews. By the time of the persecutions of the Knights Templar and the Cathars, such imaginary diabolic sects had become an increasingly explicit and dangerous Other for medieval Christendom.[24] When these stereotypes were incorporated into the witch concept in the fifteenth century, the old baggage of deviant sex and sodomitical acts did not disappear. It remained a lesser leitmotif of witchcraft narratives through the end of the witch hunts. This association of witchcraft and sodomy was to play a crucial role in the particular history of witch trials in Lucerne.

There are a number of important similarities between Lucerne and Basel in this story. As we have seen, indigenous witch beliefs in the two cities were quite similar. In both cities, also, diabolism first began appearing in witch trials in the mid-fifteenth century. And in both Basel and Lucerne, parallels between witchcraft and sodomy prosecu-tion can be found, particularly in the late fifteenth century. A com-parison of the two cities is instructive, especially as they followed very different courses in witchcraft and sodomy prosecution later, during the sixteenth century. While waves of witch trials in Lucerne grew in intensity, culminating in a deadly period of witch hunting in the late sixteenth century, in Basel, after the deadly echoes of the 1474 show trial, interest in witchcraft died out. By the mid-sixteenth century, even the practice of banishing witches disappeared. The trajectory was simi-lar with sodomy; after a number of trials in the late fifteenth century, the crime again became very rare in Basel. In Lucerne, however, cases continue to appear with fluctuating regularity at least through the end of the sixteenth century. What accounts for these differences? I believe the answer lies in how the lords of the cities viewed their responsibilities as governors and judges. In Basel, their self-fashioning was marked by a distinct preference for mercy, while in Lucerne a strong interest in sin and reform, and the desire to search out the whole truth in criminal cases led to the demonization of all kinds of crime. This profound difference can be traced through the relationship between witch trials and sodomy prosecution in the two cities.

In Basel, as I mentioned previously, the generation after 1474 were marked by a deadly cluster of trials. Although the number of victims was not so high that we could speak of a witch hunt, it was by far the deadliest phase of witchcraft prosecution in Basel. Fourteen women were burned as witches, and nine men for sodomy. To put these numbers in perspective, the total number of women burned as witches in Basel between 1450 and 1550 was 20; the total number of men burned as sodomites during the same period (not counting the mercenaries) was eighteen.[25] The majority of all executions for witchcraft and sodomy that took place in Basel between the beginning of the fifteenth century and the end of the sixteenth were conducted during the generation following the sodomy trial of 1474. The apparent effects of the spectacle of mass execution were greater than those of the introduction of diabolism into witch trials in Basel during the 1450s.

After Basel became Swiss in 1501, there were few witch burnings in the city, and none at all after 1532. While sodomy, bestiality in particular, remained a capital crime in the territory, the flurry of executions at the end of the fifteenth century was unparalleled in the sixteenth. For both witchcraft and sodomy, this early sixteenth-century shift represented a return to prosecution trends of the early fifteenth century. The gentler handling of witchcraft and sodomy in the early sixteenth century was accompanied by a public presentation of mildness in criminal justice generally.

In 1530, Hans Eggle of Basel found himself in serious trouble. Having a history of gambling problems already, Hans had taken to fraud to support his losing streak. He took money from neighbors for wood which he then failed to deliver. Granted a contract to deliver 40,000 shingles to the city government, he delivered only half. When the shingles were counted, his fraud was discovered and Hans found himself before the court.

Said Hans Eggle has freely confessed to all of these articles on the Wednesday after the feast of the Holy Innocents, the 28th day of December, and has begged for mercy. Whereupon the worthy council, given the deeds listed above, had good grounds to punish him on life and limb. Nonetheless, on the abovementioned Wednesday, in consideration of his many young children [they] have mercifully released him, and he has sworn for all eternity not to gamble in or near the city of Basel, neither a little nor a lot, not with cards, dice, or bowling.[26]

Hans Eggle was certainly not an honorable man, and the only family mentioned is his miserable and impoverished wife and children. The mercy shown to Hans was not a mitigation granted in respect of an honorable person or his family; it was a display of pious compassion on the part of the city council as it actively refashioned its role in the first year after the Reformation.

Acts of mercy pepper the records from Basel, but when the language of mercy there is closely examined, a pattern emerges beyond the generational ebb and flow of attitudes toward justice. During the fifteenth century, most instances of mercy receive explanations despite the general brevity of the sources. Mitigated punishments were clearly rooted in the urban economy of honor, acknowledging the condemned person's connections with respectable citizens or institutions of the city. The dishonor that would accrue to the punished individual would also taint the honor of his associates. Most immediately, this meant his family had a vested interest in his treatment at the hands of the court and his behavior upon release. It also meant, however, that his friends, his neighbors, and his city had such an interest. Within the economy of honor, the honor of every individual was a shared investment. The greater his circle of associates, the more people held an interest in his honor. The higher the social position of the individual and his associates, the greater their investment in his honor. Even the city councils, being composed of individuals who were a part of this "economy," were invested in the honor of many of the people brought before their courts. Thus status and social networks were integrally linked and together bound up in the administration of justice.

Usually, such intercession took place within the local social network, in this case the city of Basel. In some unusual cases, defendants mustered support from the surrounding territories and even, in one extraordinary instance in 1439, from the king of Rome (the emperor elect) himself.[27] Often the language of mercy was used in such cases; although the council accommodated the political and social demands of the economy of honor. By framing this accommodation within the language of mercy they emphasized their sovereignty. Mercy was an ancient prerogative of rulers: the king's right to give pardon and the power of the urban authorities within their own orbit.

After the turn of the sixteenth century, the language of mercy became much more pervasive in Basel. Having long struggled to establish de facto autonomy, the Basel city council used its new independence after 1501 to refashion its approach to criminal justice. When it came to executing criminals, the lords of Basel began to show a distinct preference for the sword. The language used at such moments was the language of mercy, as in the case of a rebellion leader from 1513:

> This man was condemned to be executed with the axe, and all that goes with it [meaning quartering], but he has been shown mercy and ordered executed with the sword, as was done.[28]

This trend in Basel was a precursor, perhaps even a guide, to the general trend in early modern Germany.[29] In Basel, as the urban lords "turned Swiss" and joined the Confederation, they chose to highlight their increased practical sovereignty by exercising the power of pardon.

While it is wise not to take such language of mercy too literally, this change in modes of execution coincided with increasing mildness in the prosecution of witchcraft and then its cessation altogether. Why did the lords of Basel cease to punish witchcraft? In part, it may have been because they were intentionally presenting themselves as merciful rulers. As Schuster argues in the case of Constance, where mercy was also a frequently employed prerogative of the city council, milder justice fitted the medieval concept of just lordship better.[30] It may also have been that they were simply unconvinced of the validity of most witchcraft accusations. But it was probably also connected to the fact that the city had long shown restraint in the use of torture.

Torture was crucial to the witch hunts generally. Because witchcraft was a secret crime, like sodomy or theft, confession was considered the only fully reliable proof of guilt. In order to obtain a confession, whether true or false, torture was the most expedient method. It was not the use of torture to obtain confessions that was crucial to the witch hunts, however, but its use in further interrogations to acquire details of the witch's supposed crimes and, most importantly, the names of her accomplices. Through the brutal mechanism of forcing confessed witches to name further suspects, interrogation practices provided the motor for an ever-expanding circle of suspects.

Under the *Carolina*, the use of torture was to be carefully controlled. During the height of the witch hunts, these rules for the application of torture were blatantly violated. While the guidance of the *Carolina* suggested that torture should only be used once (or under particular circumstances, twice), repeated torture became the rule during witch hunts. The effects of the horrific pressure of torture are easily observed in witch trials. In 1557, Barbara Stenck was arrested, tortured, and executed for witchcraft in Lucerne. She confessed, but only after she had been in prison for about two weeks, during which time she had been tortured on at least four separate occasions.[31] It had no doubt become clear to her that she would be tortured until she confessed something. When she finally did confess, she provided a full narrative of her seduction into witchcraft and the requisite admission of harmful magic. Among acts of harmful magic performed with her devils, she confessed to acting alone on two occasions. On one, she caused a hailstorm by stomping in a brook. On the other, she lamed a cow belonging to Melchior Friedrich. This first confession, three pages long, was crossed out. The next day, Barbara produced another confession, superficially very similar to the first but subtly different. It does not seem that this was a case in which the interrogators were dissatisfied with her initial confession, but rather that Barbara was. In the second confession, she never admitted to having acted alone. Her Devil, Klein Heinrich told her to stomp in the stream, and no-one had been harmed by the storm that followed. Klein Heinrich suggested killing one of Melchior Friedrich's livestock. To this, Barbara reported, she replied, "I do not want to kill any creature belonging to anyone, but if you want to do so, you can."[32] Barbara must have been a very strong person. "I want to be an honorable woman," her testimony reads, and she defended her honor within the confines of her confession.

Others, when tormented and questioned not only offered up their own lives to end the pain, they offered up the lives of others; they named names. Such was the case of Catherina Schärerin, who was arrested in Lucerne while Barbara Stenck was resisting round after round of torture. Catherina was arrested on accusations of using magic to harm a certain Claus Meyer. A week after her arrest she began to confess, telling a strange tale of a demonic cat that came into her house, entered into conversation with her, and led her into witchcraft. She also began implicating others. On the strength of Catherina's denunciations, Barbara Rosenberg and Margreth Schächli were arrested a week later. Although neither confessed, Barbara mentioned a folk healer named Hans Riss, whom Catherina had also implicated. Arrested a few days later, Hans initially denied all charges of witchcraft, but freely admitted working as a healer. He was tortured until he confessed, becoming the star victim of the chain trial. Both Hans Riss and Catherina Schärerin were burned at the stake. Between the two of them they implicated or denounced at least five others, of whom three were arrested. Several of those tried in the case worked as healers. Catherina made healing salves from toads, Margreth worked as a midwife. Hans confessed to having learned his witchcraft from a woman he called the Selle Mutter (literally "soul mother"), who first appeared in his fractured narrative as a skilled healer and witch doctor herself. A sad footnote in the case was the brief arrest of Catherina's husband. He washed his hands of her, saying had he known she was a witch he would have turned her in, "even if she had been his own mother."[33] The extreme use of torture ruptured the bond between husband and wife and brought ordinary people to denounce colleagues, competitors, and acquaintances alike. Torture obtained denunciations, forging the essential dynamic of witch hunting.

When we speak of the abuses of torture during the witch hunts, do we mean to imply that the normal use of torture was not abusive? In fact, it certainly abused the individuals caught up in criminal justice, but it *was* controlled and limited – at least in theory – in ways that made false confessions less likely. Before the *Carolina*, and in most places even after its introduction, the use of torture was constrained only if local practices had developed which controlled it. In Basel, as we saw in Chapter 5, local practice had developed clear limits for the use of torture. The council compensated suspects who were tortured and found to be innocent, and the repeated application of torture was rare. This caution in using torture made it unlikely that the investigators would use torture in questioning confessed criminals for further details, as appears to have been the regular practice in Lucerne.

It seems that no steps were taken to limit torture in Lucerne during the period. Part of this may have been a matter of experience. While torture entered ordinary procedure in Basel around the turn of the fifteenth century, in Lucerne it first appeared later, as part of the mid-century revolution in criminal justice. The transformation began in the 1450s and 1460s, with the city's first wave of witch trials. During those decades the city ledgers record the costs of constructing torture devices.[34] Executions, which prior to 1450 had been extremely rare in the city, became a regular means of punishment. This revolution in criminal justice culminated when the city hired its own executioner in 1485. One of the duties of the executioner was to apply torture during interrogations, and once the council had an executioner on hand it appears to have employed torture with much greater frequency. More people were executed in Lucerne in the 1480s and 90s than during the first 80 years of the fifteenth century combined.

In Lucerne, the history of capital punishment in the fifteenth century is that of a bloody innovation that took on a life of its own. Across the second half of the fifteenth century and into the sixteenth, a generational ebb and flow of judicial severity was a secondary pattern within the overall growth of the death penalty. Witch burnings followed the same pattern, being most frequent during years of heightened judicial severity. Moreover, we have seen that when the witch trials and their victims are subtracted from the execution statistics, the general contours remain the same. Witch trials did not cause the periodic rise in executions; they complemented it. There was a fundamental relationship between severity in ordinary criminal justice and persecutions of witchcraft and sodomy. The reverse is also true. As the lords of Lucerne zealously hunted down witches and sodomites, this persecution impacted the practice of regular criminal justice, and all crime took on the tinge of diabolic evil.

The crucial moment for the history of witch trials in Lucerne was a fusion of the crimes of sodomy and witchcraft, which was driven by the heavy-handed use of torture. This fusion took place during the early sixteenth century. The early witch trials in Lucerne had come in waves; a deadly group of trials in the 1450s, another in the 1480s and 90s, and a third beginning in 1519. Thereafter, however, witch trials took place in Lucerne almost every year through the end of the sixteenth century, increasing in frequency as the century waned. In the last twenty-five years of the century, the frequency of witch trials in the city reached the density of a major witch hunt: 224 individuals were accused, of whom 99 were executed.[35] In 1519, sodomy and witchcraft had been fused in Lucerne, in a triple trial and execution that seemed designed to draw and hold the crowd's attention.

It was in 1519 that the trio of thieves we met at the beginning of this book were arrested in Lucerne. Hans Stächli, Barbel Vermeggerin, and Andreas from Tschafel were tortured – presumably – until they confessed all manner of depravity. Hans's confession began by listing his thefts, then abruptly shifted to a confession of bestiality:

> Also he has confessed how he had sex with a horse and some cows. [The cows] belonged to Rudi Ferren [...] and Jakob Christas [...] and the horse was his father's. He has committed such depravity so often and with so many cows that he does not know how many.[36]

Upon encountering this confession, we might think any number of things. We might assume that it is most likely a manifestation of an obsession on the interrogator's part, or perhaps a reflection of acts which Hans himself actually committed. Either of these might be true, but what is interesting about the confession of bestiality is not that it is bizarre but that it was in fact rather commonplace. As it turns out, men accused of theft in Lucerne would occasionally confess under torture that they were also guilty of bestiality. There is no logical reason why thieves should have a greater penchant for abusing animals than any-one else, so it stands to reason that this association likely originated in the questions chosen by the interrogators.

People somehow suspected that individuals who were willing to vio-late the sanctity of a house by sneaking through a window to steal a purse of coins might well be willing to violate the sanctity of a barn by sneaking into a stall and assaulting its occupant. The sanctity of the barn was quite a serious matter. The penalties attached to a crime increased if it were committed at night or secretly, but also if it were committed in the house or barn of the victim. Like the house, the barn was a magical, protected space. The undesired and unexpected appear-ance there of a neighbor or a stranger might well motivate suspicions of witchcraft against the interloper.[37] In an agrarian society, especially one as heavily dependent on cattle as Switzerland had become by this period, the protection of livestock was secondary only to the immediate protection of family members.

The sexual violation of a cow or a horse was not merely a matter which inspired disgust or moral condemnation as it might today. It was a pollution of the highest order, it meant that the meat and milk of the beast were tainted and the highly valued creature would have to be destroyed.[38] It is for this reason that Hans's confession names the owners of the beasts. Although the Lucerne council records do not generally record the destruction of violated animals, in Basel the authorities usually obtained the creature and burned it together with the man who had confessed bestiality. The violated animal was a total loss.

As the thief Hans became a sodomite under torture, so the woman of the trio, Barbel Vermeggerin, became a witch. The summary of her con-fession began with a list of thefts, listing thirteen specific acts of thiev-ery before an abrupt change of subject. Without any narrative segue, her confession then describes how she met a goat-footed Devil who taught her to make hail in return for her veneration of him and renun-ciation of Christianity.[39] Barbel's confession thus became a witchcraft confession. There are two key elements to her confession of witchcraft: the first is the role of the Devil, the second is the power to make hail. Together these two elements embodied the melding of popular and elite ideas of witchcraft, a combination crucial to the incendiary power of the witch concept.

Although they were executed together, it is unclear if Hans and Barbel were suspected of being accomplices. The fusion of witchcraft and sodomy was completed in the confession of the other thief, Andreas from Tschafel. Like the other two, Andreas's confession began with thefts he had supposedly committed. After only a few specific confessions of theft, however, the summary reads, "he has confessed that he has stolen so much money that he cannot remember the amount,"[40] a formula which most often appeared at the end of very long lists of specific thefts. But Andreas's confession was not at an end. "Also he has admitted to having sex with a cow," it read, "and he has confessed to having florentinized six boys."[41] This mention of pederasty is our first indication that Andreas's confession was something unusual, that it went beyond the established stereotype of the sodomitical thief. Although no more accepted than bestiality, homosexual acts appeared far less frequently in the criminal records of Swiss cities during the period. As mentioned above, sex acts between men or between men and boys were often associated with foreign and specifically Italian influences. This clearly was the case here, as it had been in Basel, in 1474. In Florence, sexual relations between young men and teenage boys enjoyed a certain degree of acceptance, and the city had entered the Swiss-German vocabulary to represent homosexual relations.[42]

Although the confession of sodomy was already sufficient to condemn Andreas to death at the stake, his confession goes on to describe how he sacrificed his little finger to the Devil in hopes of winning at gambling. Also in the vein of anti-religious crimes was his admission to a fifteen-year avoidance of the sacrament of confession, required yearly of all Christians after Lateran IV in 1215. Then, like Barbel, Andreas confessed to having renounced Christianity altogether and having given himself to the Devil in order to learn storm raising.[43] Andreas's confession thus also became a confession of witchcraft. It is interesting here that Andreas confessed two different stories about his diabolism; in the first he presented an unusual story about gambling and a missing finger,[44] in the second he repeated the standard formula of confessing witches. This may indicate that his unusual confession of diabolism prompted his interrogators to press him for a confession of witchcraft. He went on to confess several murders and more theft.

At the end of Andreas's confession, the summary describes his execution. It reads, "My lords [the councilors of Lucerne] have had him torn in all four directions, and bound to the wheel, and thereafter burned to ashes."[45] This display made his death the showcase of the triple execution. In part, his punishments represented his crimes, as punishments generally did during the fifteenth and sixteenth centuries. He was broken on the wheel as a murderer and a robber and burned as a sodomite and a witch. His quartering, however, was a symbol loosed of its original meaning and employed in a new way. Quartering was the traditional punishment for treason. One might argue that Andreas had committed treason against God through his renunciation, and thus the punishment was a direct reflection of his crime. This makes sense at first glance, but I have found no other case of diabolism in which this was done. It seems rather that Andreas was being used to represent crime incarnate. As the worst criminal imaginable, his punishment included the execution for treason as a symbolic representation of his abject criminality.

The combination of sodomy and witchcraft embodied in Andreas's confession and condemned through his unusual execution took place at the heart of a series of deadly sodomy cases. In the mid-1480s, during an intense phase of witch trials, accusations of sodomy, most often bestiality, began appearing before the Lucerne court. In the previous century, sodomy had been mentioned only twice, and in both cases the accusation had been treated as slander. Between 1480 and 1530, however, 39 cases of sodomy appeared in Lucerne, and after 1490 *all* of them ended in execution.[46] The trial of Andreas, Hans, and Barbel in 1519 came at the end of the most intense phase of this persecution, and appears to have helped the persecution shift gears. After 1519, the number of sodomy trials decreased, while a cycle of deadly witch trials took center stage. Throughout the mid-sixteenth century, witch trials remained common. Between 1550 and 1580, another sodomy persecution took place, reaching its peak in 1575 – the same year that the witch hunt in Lucerne began. As appears to have been the case in Basel after 1474, sodomy persecutions in Lucerne seemed to trigger witchcraft persecutions. The conceptual association of the two crimes had measurable effects on the realities of criminal justice.

The fusion of witchcraft and sodomy in 1519 had another important effect. Although it did not create a permanent fusion of the two crimes – witch trials and sodomy trials remained distinct thereafter – it did break down the traditional gendering of witchcraft. The Alpine witch I have described was exclusively female in fifteenth-century Lucerne. It was only after Andreas's confession – which would have been read aloud at his theatrical execution – that men began to be accused of witchcraft in Lucerne. Not only did this broaden the base of potential victims, it is significant for the fact that it signals a partial collapse of the traditional witch stereotype of the region, and not only with regards to gender. Andreas's narrative entry into witchcraft, the context in which his confession became a witchcraft confession, was unequivocally diabolism. In Andreas's confession we can see that the narrative of diabolism, which had first entered witch trials in Lucerne about 70 years earlier, had finally gained the upper hand. This opened the door to new questions in the witch trials later in the sixteenth century, questions which had been absent in earlier trials. In particular the concept of the witches' sabbath crept into the trials, providing a narrative framework in which denunciations could take place. So it was that Adelheit Fritschin, accused of witchcraft in 1580, testified:

> Approximately ten weeks ago, her [demon] lover had given her a black salve, which [she] smeared it on a chair and rode to Brattlen Matt. She knew no-one [there] except a certain Margaret, who has long resided in Agers.[47]

After 1519, the stage was set for a mass witch hunt.

Over the long decades between 1480 and 1650, the death penalty held sway in Lucerne. That those same years witnessed several waves of witch hunting and a steady trickle of individual witch trials is no coincidence. What was true during the first witch hunt in Lucerne in the late fifteenth century remained true during the later witch hunts: the number of executions in the city rose independently of the number of witch hunt victims.[48] The motivation that provided the well-spring for witchcraft and sodomy persecutions was the same that fed increasingly severe criminal justice. In the course of a sincere effort at urban reform, moral crusading had turned into a moral panic, and it seemed that evil was everywhere.

If Andreas, Hans, and Barbel had been arrested a century earlier they might have been executed as thieves. But it is very unlikely that they would have been questioned further, pressed for details of bestiality or diabolism, avoidance of confession or witchcraft. While the councilors in Basel were fashioning themselves as merciful lords, the lords of Lucerne sought to purify their city. Investigators suspected that ordinary criminals were harboring darker secrets, and not only witchcraft but *all* crime took on a tinge of diabolism. Armed with torture, the more details the investigators sought, the more details they found, confirming the sense that crime threatened the city and its way of life not only physically, but spiritually. The Devil, it seems, lurked in the details.

Conclusion

Why did the city of Lucerne become obsessed with crime when it did? Perhaps the most striking thing about this story is the profundity of the revolution in criminal prosecution in Lucerne, which transformed the city from one that rarely used capital punishment to one that employed a spectacular triple execution as a symbolic attack on crime. Certainly there were practical changes that facilitated this transformation, including the adoption of aspects of inquisitorial process, the acquisition or production of torture devices, and the employment of a full-time executioner. But each of these changes required a decision, the reasoning for which is hidden from us. Although the decisions are lost to us, the objects of Lucerne's crime fighting campaign reveal much about the concerns that fueled it.

Insofar as the records reflect the origins of the men and women prosecuted over the century, most of them appear to have been foreigners. This was certainly true of Andreas, Hans, and Barbel, whose confessions reveal lives of marginal wanderers. This was less true of witchcraft suspects. For these the work of Stefan Jäggi has revealed a social profile of the resident stranger – long-term immigrants from near or far whose failure to fully integrate socially spelled their doom when witchcraft accusations arose.[1] A third group of strangers also appears from time to time in the concerns voiced in the council minutes: beggars and vagrants. The details of the city's concern over these marginal individuals reveals a worldview in which outsiders in particular were vectors of chaos and suffering. The city council not only profiled beggars and vagrants as likely criminals, they also voiced clear suspicions about the ostensible virtue of pilgrims and readily believed that a conspiracy of men clad as beggars was on the roads, determined to set the Confederation ablaze. Strangers, outsiders, and immigrants appeared threatening and dangerous to the citizens of Lucerne and their ruling elite.

In all of the cities examined here and in the legal history of Germany as a whole we can observe profound ramifications of the simple demographic fact of an increasing ratio of outsiders to insiders during the late Middle Ages: the transformation of the role of reputation in criminal prosecution from the central consideration in medieval proceedings to an important but secondary consideration in early modern investigation-driven criminal process. As we have seen, this change happened at different paces in different places, and in Lucerne it came relatively late for a German city.

There remains one last, crucial consideration regarding the timing of Lucerne's prosecutorial transformation, and this is the observation that key moments in the process coincided with witchcraft panics in the city and its rural possessions. One or even two such coincidences might be judged chance, but the pattern of coincidence in Lucerne is too strong to be discounted in this way. The idea of the witch (the ultimate stranger-within) and her ally the Devil (the original outlaw) proved a perfect catalyst for fears and concerns that had probably been mounting for decades. When rumors of witches reached Lucerne in the 1440s, they lit the tinder of a far greater fire than the tragedy of the witch hunts that followed. The early witch trials in Lucerne were crucial to promoting that city's shift to a far bloodier, more modern mode of criminal prosecution.

History exists in the tension between contingency and pattern. Perhaps the most important contingencies for historians of the fifteenth century are those that determined which records were lost and what sources remain to us. For example, execution statistics from the crucial 1440s in Basel are lost to us entirely. We are left guessing whether judicial severity came on the heels of witchcraft prosecution, or witchcraft prosecution emerged at the crest of a wave of judicial severity. The loss of expense records from the 1470s in Lucerne creates a similarly problematic puzzle. Very few capital cases appear in the city council records, but this period of apparent mildness cannot be confirmed through an examination of the generally more reliable expense records. It *seems* that the decade after 1470 was a benign period: the sun shone warmly, the grain grew high, the executioner's axe lay idle, and the whispering fear of witches subsided. In Basel, where records from that decade do exist, we find a substantial drop in executions and no witch trials at all. Contingency has been most cruel to the archives of the city of Nuremberg; I must often pass over my third case in silence.

For Basel and Lucerne, however, conclusions may be drawn. We can see a regular pattern of ebb and flow in judicial severity, possibly the product of generational infusions of fresh blood and new ideas into the city councils. We can also see larger patterns superimposed over the lesser tide of generations. In Basel, the uncommon severity of the mid-century stands out, marking as unusual the generations during which the practice of witchcraft prosecution was adopted in that city. In Lucerne, the history of capital punishment in the fifteenth century is that of a horrifying crescendo of judicial violence. Beginning in the same generation that adopted witchcraft prosecution, capital punishment was established as a normal part of criminal justice in that city. In the years that followed, the ebb and flow of judicial severity was a secondary pattern within the overall growth of the ultimate punishment. As with executions generally, so it was with witch burnings. The worst years were those of the 1480s and 1490s, but the decades which followed offered no real reversal of the trend. The executioner dominated the criminal court in Lucerne well into the sixteenth century.

When we turn from the analysis of imperfect execution statistics to an examination of judicial procedure, we find clues for the interpretation of this dominance of the death penalty in Lucerne and garner insight from the case of Nuremberg. The history of judicial procedure in these fifteenth-century cases is one of innovation and experimentation. The practice of using judicial torture to obtain confessions, details of crimes, and the names of accomplices takes center stage in this story. It seems, however, that the use of judicial torture carried with it the seeds of doubt in its efficacy and that the first fruit of this doubt was not the abolition of torture but the limitation of abuses.

In Nuremberg, the limitation of torture came gradually and only in the wake of extreme abuses. The city council experimented with giving the investigating prosecutors full discretion over when, how, and how often to apply torture. Ultimately, though, the opinion came to dominate practice in that city that, with torture, less was more effective. While in Basel this realization appears to have come even earlier, we do not have evidence of a corresponding development of legal skepticism in Lucerne during the period. It is likely that this and the unusual judicial severity of late fifteenth-century Lucerne were both products of the relatively late adoption of inquisitorial procedure, torture, and execution into regular judicial practice there. Moderation, where it appeared at all, was apparently the product of experience, and in Lucerne during the period of this study that experience was still accumulating.

The different course taken in Lucerne, however, was not the simple result of a passive lack of experience with new techniques. It was instead bound up with an active interest on the part of the Lucerne city council in new techniques and experimentation which went beyond criminal justice into other areas of social control. In this, as in the other aspects examined in this study, the course taken by Lucerne, though not wholly divergent from that of other cities during the period, was marked by an unusual amount of energy dedicated to urban reform and to the peace and moral order of the city. On the question of social control we cannot say much about Basel during the fifteenth century, but the case of Nuremberg demonstrates the general concern over moral control which was present in fifteenth-century cities. In Nuremberg we observe a shift in both the normative sources and the prosecution of moral transgressions. The number and verbosity of ordinances increased considerably as compared to previous centuries, and throughout the fifteenth century we can see a continuing increase in the number of fines levied for misbehavior. What we do not see is the kind of innovation that we find in Lucerne. There the city fathers experimented with various modes of intervention, in an apparent effort to teach their citizen-subjects self-control. This remarkable social disciplining coincided with the greatest fifteenth-century concentration of witch trials in Lucerne.

When we examine the history of the witch trials in these three case studies, the relationship between witchcraft prosecution and the prosecution of criminal and moral transgression becomes clearer. Witchcraft was neither prosecuted nor persecuted in isolation. In Lucerne, we find witchcraft prosecution integrated into a growing campaign against crime both real and imagined. In their zeal to root out evil, interrogators in Lucerne extracted confessions as various as sodomy, murder, blasphemy, and witchcraft from accused or suspected thieves. The persecution of women for witchcraft was matched in both Lucerne and Basel with a growing persecution of men for sodomy. In Lucerne these two came together in the early sixteenth century, destroying the rigid gendering of the local witch stereotype and opening the way for the persecution of diabolic witchcraft in mass witch hunts.

We can also observe the importance of witch trials in neighboring territories to the adoption of the practice of witchcraft prosecution. In Basel, we can examine this development most closely and see how the practice was first adopted in the rural hinterlands of the city. The rural residents of the territory of Basel were not passive subjects; their relationship with the urban authorities was contentious and dynamic. In the case of witchcraft, the city's efforts to control the countryside eventually resulted in the adoption of witchcraft prosecution in the city itself. The crucial role played in Basel and Lucerne by witch trials in neighboring territories makes the divergent course of Nuremberg all the more interesting. In that city, although the idea of diabolic witch-craft was demonstrably available and accusations of harmful magic were being brought to the authorities, the example of a witch burning in nearby Schwabach had, if anything, a negative impact. Ultimately, the Nuremberg city council actively and explicitly rejected the idea of witchcraft. Clearly, other factors were at play.

Although accusations of witchcraft arose from the populace and the fear of witchcraft may be viewed as the proper motor of the witch trials in these case studies, the will of the authorities to prosecute witchcraft was the deciding factor in whether and how the practice of witchcraft prosecution came to be adopted. In the case of Basel, we can see the attitude of the urban authorities vis-à-vis witch trials being actively influenced by the demands of their rural subjects. In Nuremberg, legal skepticism had a crucial impact on the city council's perspective on witchcraft. In Lucerne, however, the will of the urban authorities to reform their city, ensure harmony, and root out crime, evil, and misbe-havior actively contributed to the adoption of witchcraft prosecution in that city.

In the past, explanations of the early witch trials have hinged on the adoption of the diabolic interpretation of witchcraft. The idea of diabolic witchcraft still plays an important role in the story as I have told it, but I have relegated its influence to a secondary status. This has allowed us to see the importance of other factors in the development of fifteenth century witchcraft prosecution. Most importantly, it has facil-itated a newly integrated perspective on witch trials and other legal pro-ceedings. As long as we insist on the central importance of diabolism in the history of the European witch trials, we will continue to be blinded by the exceptional nature of the crime of witchcraft. In this study, I have worked to shed a different light on the matter, to illuminate the terrifying ordinariness of witchcraft prosecution. When ordinary witch trials are returned to the context of daily criminal justice, the persecu-tory nature of early modern justice becomes clearer. Although the mass witch hunts of the late sixteenth and early seventeenth century were a departure from normal criminal procedure in practice, in spirit they were well-suited to the landscape of early modern justice.

Appendix
Selected Trial Documents

Hans Stächli, Andreas from Tschafel, and Barbel Vermeggerin

Staatsarchiv Luzern Ratsprotokolle 11, fol. 103v–105r

July 13, 1519

Hans Stächli from Meerschwand has confessed how he climbed into Heini Brülman's house, where he found a purse lying on a chest and took eleven shillings from it.

He has also confessed that he stole twenty Rössler from Big Peter from Buscheswil, out of his purse.

Also he has confessed how he had sex with a horse and some cows, which belonged to Rudi Ferren am Far and one to Jakob Christas from Willisau, and the horse was his father's. He has committed such depravity so often and with so many cows that he does not know how many.

Therefore based on his confession my lords have had him burned.

Andreas from Tschafel in the Eschland has confessed how he stole eight good Vierer from a purse.

He has also confessed how he stole a gown, a cloak, and a pair of pants during the Bavarian war.

Also he has confessed how he was once given a collar for safekeeping, which he accepted and then sold for six good Kreuzen.

He has confessed that he has stolen so much money that he cannot remember the amount.

Also he has admitted to having had sex with a cow.

And he has confessed to having florentinized six boys.

Also he has confessed how he was gambling once and could not win, and so he gave the little finger on his left hand to the Devil, that he might make him win. But it never helped him.

Also he has admitted that he has not been to confession in fifteen years.

Moreover, he has confessed that he has renounced God, His worthy Mother, and the whole heavenly host, and has given himself to the Devil and believed in him. And the Devil instructed him, taught him how to make hail and overcome good.

Also he has confessed that he made a storm in Güns, not far from Chur, but it was not a big storm. This he attempted often; at times he succeeded, others not.

He has also confessed how in the lands of the Bishop of Salzburg he stabbed a shoemaker who shared a room with himself and another man. This he did, just because that same shoemaker had a dog that tried to bite him and since the shoemaker had not protected him, he had stabbed him with a knife. And he did not know whether the man died of the wound or not, because he left right away.

Also he has confessed how he found a man sleeping in a hut not far from Chur, and had stabbed that man in the back from behind with a sharpened stick and thus murdered him, and took the two pounds which he found on him.

According to his confession, my lords have had him torn in all four directions, and bound to the wheel, and thereafter burned to ashes.

Barbel Vermeggerin from König in the territory of Bern has confessed that she stole a pair of sleeves and a sheet.

Also she has confessed that she found a purse in Hitzkirch, in which she found three pounds.

She has also confessed that she stole four shillings from her brother-in-law.

Also she has confessed that she stole five pounds from her friend Peter Wältin.

She has also confessed that she stole eight shillings from Peter Sager of Burgdorf.

Also she has confessed that she stole six shillings from Peter Gerwer of Burgdorf.

Also she stole a cloth from her aunt.

Also she stole two pounds of wool from her brother-in-law.

And she stole two cloths from her sister Anne in Solothurn.

She has also confessed that she stole a pot from her cousin Peter Wältin and sold it for five Batzen.

Also she stole a wedge from the abovementioned Peter Wältin.

She has also confessed that she stole a pillow from her friend Hansen Müllenberg.

Also she stole a jacket in Hitzkirch.

Also she has confessed how the Devil came to her in the shape of a man with goat's feet, and won her over with good words, [saying] that he would teach her to make hail. So she believed in him, and renounced God, His worthy Virgin Mary, and all of the saints, and gave herself to the Devil.

And afterwards he taught her how to make hail, which she attempted to do many times but only succeeded twice. One time the hailstones were the size of peas, the other time like beans.

She has also confessed how the abovementioned Andreas from Tschafel, with whom she has been for six years, and whom she herself brought to do such things, had anal intercourse with her twice.

Therefore based on her confession, my lords have had her burned to ashes.

These abovementioned three persons were executed with the fire together on the same day.

Else of Meersburg

From Hoffmann-Krayer *Luzerner Akten zum Hexen- und Zauberwesen* p. 4–7

circa 1450, possibly summer 1448.

Else of Meersburg has confessed the following.

First that she knows the [black] art and has taught it to more than one woman, so that their husbands would have to be good to them and would not wish to beat them.

Also she has often cursed people evilly when she became enraged. These curses also came true, and she believed that she had [efficaciously] wished evil on them.

Also on the Monday of the most recent hailstorm, she has confessed, she was between Malters and the city. There a beggar approached her and tried to rape her, so that she would marry him and have relations with him. She became angry and went from him to a brook and threw water into the air with both hands behind her back, in the names of all the devils and especially of Beelzebub and Krütli, who was her chief master among the devils, and to whom she had devoted herself. And she cursed the beggar with the falling sickness, and if he had been struck by hail and lightening, it would have pleased her. Then the hailstorm came that she had made.

Also she has devoted herself to the evil spirit, he met her three times and wanted to lead her away.

Also she had resided openly with the priest of Kilchberg for 26 or 27 years. The matter had this form: He had been her husband, and after she gave him up and he became a priest, she moved back in with him and kept house for him for that many years. And for all the years that he was in Kilchberg until his death, hailstorms never struck there [because] he could command them. But after his death hail struck rather frequently there.

Also her master the Devil is called Krütli, and she was possessed by him for a time, and he came to her as a spirit.

Also she has also confessed that over 40 years ago, while she was still a child [living] with her father, there was a great hail maker in Meersburg named Else Schiesserin who, as far as she knows, now lives in Erfurt. This woman came to her with many friendly words and taught her with what words and gestures she should devote herself to the Devil during the Ember Days. This she did, and devoted herself to the Devil at that time, so that he would help her gain riches and whatever she asked of him. The same woman, her teacher, also taught her then how to raise a hailstorm, and [the storm they called] struck the people of Constance and Meersburg with great devastation.

Also the people of Constance once did something against her and hers, for which she is still their enemy today. So she called another great hailstorm with the aid of her master the Devil, and it struck the people of Constance causing great damage. This was 30 years ago.

One time, about 40 years ago, she also raised a hailstorm in Frauenfeld, but it was not large and did not do much damage.

Note regarding the witch. Investigate whether she supposedly lives over the Rümlig, and whether she knows anyone else.

Also note regarding the great hailstorm.

Also note the three met below Strasbourg and spoke together and said they would go from theirs to the ones in Mulhouse and let themselves be reverse baptized and thereafter have to avoid such things.

These same women and she also raised a great hailstorm seven years ago, because their 13 companions complained saying that the [Swiss] Confederation had ruined them, so they should also bring ruin. It happened in Menznau. One [of the women] was called Wissenbacherin of Strasbourg. Thus they were behind the watch in Menznau during the Ember Days. Also they rode dogs and wolves. ~~These were burned~~. Also she had to go there or they would hurt her.

Note supposedly there were two beggars living or residing in Escholzmatt or in the Entlebuch, one of whom had a small child. The one with the child was named Anna Stellin and the other was Gret Jägerin, who also had a little girl in Langnau. She was a weaver and is also a witch. She was with them but she ran off.

Also she also confessed that she and the others could not do these things unless it suited the Devil.

Note regarding Thann [in Alsace]. The twelve were together in a grove in the monastery and whenever they were together hay became more costly. It was a Thursday in the Ember Days, and they were jousting and holding tourney with hemp stalks. Some of them rode on dogs. She [does not] know if they were dogs or wolves.

Also the head witch was Agnes of Liperheim, from Ettenheim below [i.e. north of] Kenzingen. It [presumably a hailstorm] took place before the battle at Basel. [Battle of St. Jakob an der Birs, 1444]

Note she advises that we should drive the beggars from the land.

Also a tall, beautiful woman lives in Schaffhausen. She is one of the chief witches. Also and the innkeeper is named Else of Mundelsheim. The beautiful woman is named Beata and lives on the Rindermarkt. This was 14 years ago.

Also when the others salved their stalks and rode, she wanted to also ride her stalk, but it would not work.

Also there are two witches in Sipplingen. One is named Anna Bäschin, the other Else Schudin, whose father was hanged.

Note if [anyone] wants to arrest them, he should search them thoroughly, and take from them any little boxes or other things.

Also as soon as soon as they returned to God and His Mother, they could no longer do anything with their witchcraft.

Also she threw her [magical] gear into a stream.

Rüschellerin of Reiden

From Hoffmann-Krayer *Luzerner Akten zum Hexen- und Zauberwesen* p. 19–23
Banished April 1486 according to StALU RP 6, fol. 117v.

Testimony

Also Reider of Langnau testified first that when he lived in Reiden, he was in conflict with the Rüschellerin and his cow gave nothing but blood. He complained of this to a number of honorable men, and it went on for so long that he moved from Reiden to Langnau because of it.

Also Heini Fuchs testified that one morning just as the day had begun to break, he encountered her coming out of a forest, some distance from Reiden. She ran toward the village with her skirts hitched up high. She came in such a dreadful manner, her mouth nearly blue, that he became so terrified of her that his hair stood on end and from that day onward his mouth was covered in sores. But what she had done or what her business had been he knew not.

Also Fuchs said further that he was once in his garden. Then she came before the garden and spoke: I have always had the most beautiful garden in Reiden, until you came here and [now] your garden is prettier than mine; I must come in with you. Then she came into the garden and went to and fro and touched the onions. From that hour the onions began to wither and the next morning they were entirely rotten, and no good came of them.

Also Reider also testified further, that in summer he saw her twice in one day going suspiciously about a meadow. Then Reider said to his neighbor: you can count on it; we'll have a huge storm today. And as he had guessed, a great furious storm came that day.

Also Gassenrumer has testified that about ten years ago he was working for the governor. One morning, he saw the Rüschellerin going toward a wood in which there was a pond. She had bound her skirts up high and was running so fast that he would not have been able to recognize her except that he rode after her on his horse so he could recognize her. Then he let her run and rode home and told his lord about it. The whole day there was a cloud over the pond; many people saw that cloud. And the whole day they had to ring the bells against storms, but toward evening a powerful storm came, with rain but no hail. If they had not been so quick to ring the bells, it would have been worse. The whole day the storm hung over the pond, until evening. The Gassenrumer saw it the next morning from Reiden and said there would be a storm that day.

Also Rudi Metziner has testified that he once quarreled with the Rüschellerin; shortly thereafter one of his good cows died. He testified further that the Rüschellerin once approached his wife and grasped her breast, saying: how could you be so ill-advised with your breasts! As soon as she grabbed her breast, [his wife] was stabbed with such a pain that she had to take to her bed and they all commended her to the saints. Further he testified that his child once sat with the Rüschellerin's child. There were a number of other children, also Metziner's. And the children said: we have baby birds! And some children said: we have baby geese! Then the Rüschellerin's child said: but we have baby foxes and baby wolves, and when my father is away, my mother feeds them on the barn floor.

Also Metziner, Fuchs, and Gassenrumer have testified further that they were [once] fishing in a brook, when a man from Reitnau, a trustworthy man, approached them and said: I saw a woman from Reiden riding a wolf on a mountain. It was on the equinox, and she did not notice [him]. Then they said: who was she? And he answered, saying: she has green sleeves with buckles. Around that time the Rüschellerin also wore green sleeves with buckles. So Gassenrumer went to Reiden into the village and said to the women: you shed God's blood, you women of Reiden! Why do you not ride horses instead of wolves?

Also Metziner and Fuchs also testified that they had both heard the miller of Unterwasser, who is now dead, say that he recognized all witches when he first laid eyes on them. So they said: what do you think of the Rüschellerin? And he said: she is a witch and a truly evil woman. I once encountered her near Reiden in a field and she bound up her skirts and ran at [me] and fell on [my] neck and put her arms around [me] saying: my godfather, [surely] you are not afraid of me? And [I] said: get away, I know full well who you are.

Also Hans Uli zum Sarbaum has testified that the miller of Unterwasser had bought a house in the village and wanted to move out of the mill. Then the Rüschellerin moved into the same alley. Then the miller no longer wanted to move into the house. Hans Uli zum Sarbaum asked him: when do you want to move into your house? And the miller said: the Devil take the house! I would have to see a witch every morning, and she knows full well that I recognize her and know that she is a witch.

Also Schlucher the tailor has testified that his brother has been before the law against the Rüscheller and his wife. When Schlucher's case was winning over Rüscheller's, right then a good horse of his died. And the Rüscheller came to Schlucher the tailor and said: do you not see that your brother has also encountered bad luck?

Also Uli Kalt of Wigen testified that his father and another mower were mowing in Reiden. The Rüschellerin came to them and asked them to come and mow at her place the next day. They said that they could not do that [because they could not just leave his meadow][1] when they had just begun to mow it. Then she swore, saying: if you do not come mow for me tomorrow you can be certain that it will come to no good for you. The next day the other mower suffered in bed, and lay there a good while. When he got up then he caught a chill and lay for six weeks in bed.

Also Uli Meiger testified that the Rüschellerin once came to him and said: why is it that you have been made deputy sheriff and because of you my husband cannot testify? And she scolded him. After this one of his horses died, which had cost him ten gulden. Later he had two young geese that lay as if mad before his house and they fell down and died. So he had the [dead] geese thrown before the Rüschellerin's house. And she said: did he mean to imply that I killed them? He might have bad luck and suffer further losses. And the next day one of his cows lay down and was crippled so she could not stand up. She would eat and drink what they brought to her but would not rise. [The cow] lay a full fifteen days and then died. It happened to three of his cows the same as the first – they became lame and all four died.

Also Kleiwi Meiger testified that he once quarreled with her husband. She heard of this and right away one of his horses became ill so that it sweat blood through its whole hide such that [the blood] dripped down. Then he saw the Rüschellerin by the well. He went over to her and said: great God's blood! One of my horses has been bewitched and if it dies, I am going to turn [the witch] in so she has to burn. As soon as he came home, his horse stood there eating, and it was cured. Shortly thereafter the other [horse] also became ill. But he went to [the Rüschellerin] and used the same words, and the horse recovered. Then Kleiwi Meiger went to his comrades and bragged about how he had cured his horses with angry words. But when she heard of this, one of his horses died. He could not help it with angry words any longer. Also he testified how he and his brother were driving into the wood called Twerenfelt early one morning as day first began to break. She came running out of the woods, and he and his brother were terribly startled and greatly frightened.

They have all sworn aloud to God and the saints that they speak the truth in this.

On top of all this there is a general rumor throughout Reiden that [the Rüschellerin] is a witch. Some say it to her face, but she does not sue anyone for this. Her mother died under the rumor of being a witch.

Also dear lords, if it pleases you as it pleases me, please sent Klaus, the big bailiff up here with my son, and he can take her away to Willisau.

Hans Schürpf

This is my handwriting.

Notes

Introduction

1. StALU RP 11 fol. 103v–104r.
2. Brian Levack reviews this impulse and its early fruit in "Crime and the Law" in Jonathan Barry and Owen Davies, eds, *Palgrave Advances in Witchcraft Historiography* (Basingstoke, 2007).
3. Andreas Blauert "Kriminaljustiz und Sittenreform als Krisenmanagement?" in Andreas Blauert and Gerd Schwerhoff, eds, *Mit den Waffen der Justiz: Zur Kriminalitätsgeschichte des Spätmittelalters und Frühen Neuzeit* (Frankfurt, 1993).
4. It may be noted that this definition excludes healers who were persecuted as witches, but I submit that most if not all of these were accused because they were suspected of using their power for evil, either through fraud or outright magical harm.
5. For Nuremberg see Hartmut Kunstmann, *Zauberwahn und Hexenprozess in der Reichsstadt Nürnberg* (Nuremberg, 1970). Basel and Lucerne, having richer sources for the study of fifteenth-century witchcraft prosecution, have drawn the attention of many scholars. The best recent work on Basel has been produced by Dorothee Rippmann. Dorothee Rippmann, "Hexenverfolgungen und soziale Unrast. Der Forschungsstand zum Basler Raum (Nordwestschweiz) im Spätmittelalter," *Schweizerische Zeitschrift für Geschichte* 52 (2002); Dorothee Rippmann, "Hexen im 15. und 16. Jahrhundert" in Dorothee Rippmann, Katharina Simon-Muscheid, and Christian Simon, eds, *Arbeit – Liebe – Streit: Texte zur Geschichte des Geschlechterverhältnisses und des Alltags, 15. bis 18. Jahrhundert* (Liestal, 1996). For Lucerne, the work of Andreas Blauert and Lucerne Archivist Stefan Jäggi has dominated recent scholarship. Andreas Blauert, "Hexenverfolgung in einer spätmittelalterlichen Gemeinde: Das Beispiel Kriens/Luzern um 1500," *Geschichte und Gesellschaft* 16 (1990); Andreas Blauert, *Frühe Hexenverfolgungen: Ketzer-, Zauberei- und Hexenprozesse des 15. Jahrhunderts* (Hamburg, 1989); Stefan Jäggi, "Luzerner Verfahren wegen Zauberei und Hexerei bis zur Mitte des 16. Jahrhunderts," *Schweizerische Zeitschrift für Geschichte* 52 (2002); Stefan Jäggi, "Hexen im Rontal und im Habsburgeramt," *Rontaler Brattig* (2004).
6. This intriguing possibility remains beyond the bounds of this study but has been recently examined by Edward Bever, *The Realities of Witchcraft and Popular Magic in Early Modern Europe: Culture, Cognition, and Everyday Life* (Basingstoke, 2008).
7. Joy Wiltenburg, "True Crime: The Origins of Modern Sensationalism," *American Historical Review* 109 (2004).
8. See for example Eberhard Schmidt, *Inquisitionsprozess und Rezeption* (Leipzig, 1940).
9. Dagmar Unverhau, "Akkusationsprozeß – Inquisitionsprozeß. Indikatoren für die Intensität der Hexenverfolgung in Schleswig-Holstein? Überlegungen

und Untersuchungen zu einer Typologie der Hexenprozesse," in Christian Degn, Hartmut Lehmann and Dagmar Unverhau, eds, *Hexenprozesse. Deutsche und Skandinavische Beiträge* (Neumünster, 1983).

10. Gerd Schwerhoff, "Kriminalitätsgeschichte im deutschen Sprachraum. Zum Profil eines 'Verspäteten' Forschungszweiges," in Gerd Schwerhoff and Andreas Blauert, eds, *Kriminalitätsgeschichte. Beiträge zur Sozial- und Kulturgeschichte der Vormoderne* (Constance, 2000).
11. For more on this demonological development see Chapter 1 below.
12. Wolfgang Behringer, *Witches and Witch-Hunts: A Global History* (Cambridge, 2004), p. 61.
13. Michael Bailey and Edward Peters, "Sabbat of Demonologists: Basel 1431–1440," *The Historian* 65:6 (2003): 1375–95.
14. Richard Kieckhefer, *European Witch Trials: Their Foundations in Popular and Learned Culture, 1300–1500* (London, 1976), pp. 125–47.
15. Andreas Blauert, "Die Erforschung der Anfänge der europäischen Hexenverfolgungen," in Andreas Blauert, ed., *Ketzer, Zauberer, Hexen* (Frankfurt, 1990), p. 20.
16. Isabelle Terrier and Charlotte Touati, "Procès de sorcellerie à Neuchâtel au XVᵉ siècle. Quelques aspects," *Schweizerische Zeitschrift für Geschichte* 52 (2002); Bernard Andenmatten and Kathrin Utz Tremp, "De l'hérésie à la sorcellerie: l'inquisiteur Ulric de Torrenté OP (vers 1420–1445) et l'affermissement de l'inquisition en Suisse romande." *Zeitschrift für Schweizerische Kirchengeschichte* 86 (1992): 69–119. The inquisitor in question was Ulric de Torrenté; on his career see Chapter 1.
17. Niklaus Schatzmann, *Verdorrende Bäume und Brote wie Kuhfladen. Hexenprozesse in der Leventina 1431–1459 und die Anfänge der Hexenverfolgung auf der Alpensüdseite* (Zurich, 2003); Niklaus Schatzmann, "Hexenprozesse in der Leventina und die Anfänge der Hexenverfolgung auf der Alpensüdseite (1431–1459)," *Schweizerische Zeitschrift für Geschichte* 52 (2002).
18. E. Hoffmann-Krayer, *Luzerner Akten zum Hexen- und Zauberwesen* (Zurich, 1900), p. 4.
19. Rippmann, "Hexen im 15. und 16. Jahrhundert," p. 210.
20. Joseph Hansen, ed., *Quellen und Untersuchungen zur Geschichte des Hexenwahns und der Hexenverfolgung im Mittelalter* (1901; reprint, Hildesheim, 2003), p. 535.
21. Blauert, *Frühe Hexenverfolgungen*, pp. 67–71.
22. Behringer, *Witches and Witch-Hunts*, pp. 3–4. For a fuller discussion of definitional concerns see Chapter 1.

1 Evil by Any Other Name: Defining Witchcraft

1. Hansen, *Quellen*; Joseph Hansen, *Zauberwahn, Inquisition und Hexenprozess im Mittelalter und die Entstehung der grossen Hexenverfolgung* (1900; reprint, Frankfurt a.M., 1998). Another version of the review of literature that follows has been published as Laura Stokes, "Prelude: Early Witch-Hunting in Germany and Switzerland," *Magic, Ritual, and Witchcraft* 4:1 (2009): 54–61.
2. Hansen, *Zauberwahn*.

3. Kathrin Utz Tremp, *Waldenser, Wiedergänger, Hexen und Rebellen: Biographien zu den Waldenserprozessen von Freiburg im Üchtland (1399 und 1430)* (Freiburg, 1999).

4. Kathrin Utz Tremp, "Von der Häresie zur Hexerei. Waldenser- und Hexenverfolgungen im heutigen Kanton Freiburg (1399–1442)," *Schweizerische Zeitschrift für Geschichte* 52 (2002): pp. 117–8.

5. Most recently, Wolfgang Behringer has interpreted this transformation of Waldensianism into witchcraft from the perspective of conspiracy theory. Wolfgang Behringer, "Detecting the Ultimate Conspiracy, or How Waldensians became Witches," in Barry Coward and Julian Swann, eds, *Conspiracies and Conspiracy Theory in Early Modern Europe: From the Waldensians to the French Revolution* (Aldershot, 2004).

6. Blauert, *Frühe Hexenverfolgungen*, pp. 62–3. Pierrette Paravy, "Zur Genesis der Hexenverfolgungen in Mittelalter: Der Traktat des Claude Tholosan, Richter in der Dauphiné (um 1436)," in *Ketzer, Zauberer, Hexen*.

7. Martine Ostorero et al., eds, *L'imaginaire du sabbat: Édition critique des textes les plus anciens (1430 c.–1440 c.)* (Lausanne, 1999), p. 273.

8. Andenmatten and Utz Tremp, "De l'hérésie à la sorcellerie." Martine Ostorero, "Itinéraire d'un inquisiteur gâté: Ponce Feugeyron, les juifs et le sabbat des sorciers," *Médiévales* 43 (2002): 103–117.

9. Martine Ostorero, "Les chasses aux sorciers dans le Pays de Vaud (1430–1530). Bilan des recherches," *Schweizerische Zeitschrift für Geschichte* 52 (2002): p. 109–14.

10. Martine Ostorero, "Le procès d'Aymonet Maugetaz d'Épresses, en 1438," in *L'imaginaire du sabbat*, p. 342.

11. Georg Modestin, *Le diable chez l'évêque: Chasse aux sorciers dans le diocèse de Lausanne (vers 1460)* (Lausanne, 1999), Martine Ostorero, *"Folâtrer avec les démons" Sabbat et chasse aux sorciers à Vevey (1448)* (Lausanne, 1995).

12. Pierrette Paravy, "Claude Tholosan: Ut magorum et maleficiorum errores..." in *L'imaginaire du sabbat*. See also Paravy, "Zur Genesis der Hexenverfolgungen."

13. On Nider's *Formicarius* see Michael Bailey, *Battling Demons: Witchcraft, Heresy, and Reform in the Late Middle Ages* (University Park, Pennsylvania, 2003). See also Werner Tschacher, *Der Formicarius des Johannes Nider von 1437/38: Studien zu den Anfängen der europäischen Hexenverfolgungen im Spätmittelalter* (Aachen, 2000). A translation into French of the key passages pertaining to witchcraft is found in Catherine Chène, "Johannes Nider, *Formicarius* (livre II, chapitre 4 et livre V, chapitres 3, 4, et 7)," in *L'imaginaire du sabbat*.

14. Bailey, *Battling Demons*, p. 120.

15. Arno Borst, *Medieval Worlds: Barbarians, Heretics, and Artists in the Middle Ages*, Eric Hansen trans. (Chicago, 1992), p. 105. Borst argues that Peter of Greyerz was most likely Nider's informant, but Catherine Chène has identified three different Peters who served as judge in the Simmental between 1492 and 1437/38, throwing this identification into doubt. Chène "Johannes Nider," pp. 224–27.

16. Ibid., pp. 105–7.

17. Ibid. See also Blauert, *Frühe Hexenverfolgungen*, pp. 56–9.

18. Blauert, *Frühe Hexenverfolgungen*, pp. 58–9.

19. Norman Cohn, *Europe's Inner Demons: The Demonization of Christians in Medieval Christendom* (Chicago, 2000). For a recent analysis of the late medieval prosecution of Waldensians beyond Fribourg, see Georg Modestin *Ketzer in der Stadt. Der Prozess gegen die Straßburger Waldenser von 1400* (Hanover, 2007).

20. In Lucerne, for instance, diabolism appears in 13 of 21 cases for which at least some details are known. See Chapter 4.

21. Notable exceptions being those trials conducted under the centralized Inquisitions of Italy and Spain. See Gustav Henningsen, *The Witches' Advocate: Basque Witchcraft and the Spanish Inquisition, 1609–1614* (Reno, 1980); Ruth Martin *Witchcraft and the Inquisition in Venice, 1550–1650* (Oxford, 1989).

22. Siegfried Leutenbauer, *Hexerei- und Zaubereidelikt in der Literatur von 1450 bis 1550. Mit Hinweisen auf die Praxis im Herzogtum Bayern* (Berlin, 1972), p. 110.

23. Schroeder, Friedrich-Christian, ed., *Die Peinliche Gerichtsordnung Kaiser Karls V. von 1532 (Carolina)* (Stuttgart, 2000), p. 73.

24. Aside from the following three reasons, there is another that extends beyond the framework of this study into the realm of comparative witchcraft research. Wolfgang Behringer has argued that a definition of witchcraft based on Christian theology is no longer acceptable, because such a theological definition clearly separates European witch beliefs and historical witch hunting from witch beliefs and persecutions that exist throughout the world today. Behringer, *Witches and Witch-Hunts*, p. 3. Witchcraft persecution is a pressing human rights issue in the twenty-first century. In order to make research on historical witch hunts in Europe accessible and pertinent to those struggling with witch hunting today, we need to step back from the rigid definition of witchcraft as diabolism and recognize this as a special case in the early modern European experience.

25. Oliver Landolt, "'Mit dem Für zuo ir richten und si zuo Bulfer verbrennen' Zauberwahn und Hexenverfolgungen im spätmittelalterlichen Schaffhausen," *Schaffhauser Beiträge zur Geschichte* 78 (2004): p. 170.

26. StALU RP 3, fol. 61; StALU URK 392/7235.

27. Landolt, "Mit dem Für zuo ir richten," p. 171. The term used here was *Hegsen*.

28. StABS Leistungsbuch II, fol. 111r. Further analysis of the indigenous witch concept of the Rhine-Alpine region follows below.

29. Johannes Franck ,"Geschichte des Wortes Hexe" in Hansen, *Quellen*, pp. 614–70, here pp. 635–36.

30. Hoffmann-Krayer, *Luzerner Akten*, pp. 4–8, 12–18.

31. See for example Johannes Dillinger, *"Böse Leute" Hexenverfolgungen in Schwäbisch-Österreich und Kurtrier im Vergleich* (Trier, 1999), pp. 44–6, 55–7.

32. For a recent, thorough, and comprehensively footnoted summary of these events, see Tschacher, *Der Formicarius*, pp. 293–340. Unless otherwise noted, the details in the following summary are drawn from Tschacher.

33. Translation taken from Alan Charles Kors and Edward Peters, eds, *Witchcraft in Europe 400–1700: A Documentary History*, 2nd ed. (Philadelphia, 2001), p. 164. An edition of the Latin text of the treatise with commentary and a translation into modern French is available in Paravy, "Claude Tholosan."

34. Kors and Peters, *Witchcraft in Europe 400–1700*, p. 161.
35. Ibid., p. 157.
36. Blauert, *Frühe Hexenverfolgungen*, p. 68.
37. Hansen, *Quellen*, p. 536.
38. Jeffrey Russell and Mark Wyndham, "Witchcraft and the Demonization of Heresy," in Brian P. Levack, ed., *Articles on Witchcraft, Magic and Demonology*, vol. 2 (New York, 1992), p. 313. For the history of this nexus down through the Middle Ages see also Cohn, *Europe's Inner Demons*.
39. Walter Wakefield and A. P. Evans, eds, *Heresies of the High Middle Ages* (New York, 1965), pp. 78–9.
40. Kors and Peters, *Witchcraft in Europe*, pp. 160–1.
41. Ibid., p. 160.
42. Hansen, *Quellen*, p. 537.
43. Kors and Peters, *Witchcraft in Europe*, pp. 167–8.
44. StABS Leistungsbuch II fol. 111r.
45. Heinrich Wittenweiler, *"Der Ring"* trans. by Bernhard Sowinski (Stuttgart, 1988) pp. 374–77.
46. Hoffmann-Krayer, *Luzerner Akten*, p. 32.
47. Ibid., p. 28.
48. E. William Monter, *Witchcraft in France and Switzerland. The Borderlands During the Reformation* (Ithaca, 1976), pp. 145–50.
49. Monter refers to some German Swiss witches as werewolves, although the sources contain only wolf riding. Although Monter acknowledges the primacy of wolf riding in the German sources, he bundles the cases imprecisely under werewolvism. See Monter, *Witchcraft in France and Switzerland*, p. 151, note 28.
50. Willem de Blécourt, "A Journey to Hell: Reconsidering the Livonian "Werewolf"," *Magic, Ritual, and Witchcraft* 2:1 (2007): 49–67, here p. 54, note 13.
51. StABS Criminalia 4,3.
52. StABS Criminalia 4,3 fol. 1r.
53. StABS Criminalia 4,3 fol. 11r–12r.
54. StABS Criminalia 4,3 fol. 12r.
55. Lyndal Roper, *Witch Craze: Terror and Fantasy in Baroque Germany* (New Haven, 2004), pp. 93–94.
56. StALU COD 4450 fol. 110v, 111r, 112r, 113r–v, 115v, 116v–118r.
57. StALU COD 4450 fol. 116v.
58. StALU RP 9 fol. 316v.
59. Jacob and Wilhelm Grimm, *Deutsches Wörterbuch* (Leipzig, 1854–1960). Online edition: http://germazope.uni-trier.de/Projects/DWB.
60. Dillinger, *"Böse Leute,"* 49.
61. Wolfgang Behringer, "Climatic Change and Witch-Hunting: The Impact of the Little Ice Age on Mentalities" *Climatic Change* 43 (1999): 335–51.
62. Hoffmann-Krayer, *Luzerner Akten*, p. 4
63. Ibid., p. 6.
64. Ibid., p. 10.
65. Nicholas Remy, *Demonolatry*, trans. by E. A. Ashwin (Secaucus, New Jersey, 1974), p. 74.
66. Ibid.

67. Monter, *Witchcraft in France and Switzerland*, pp. 151–56.
68. Rippmann, "Hexen im 15. und 16. Jahrhundert." Gret escaped the Basel trial and moved into the countryside, only to be caught up in witchcraft accusations in 1458 with another woman, Verena Symlin. The two were successfully prosecuted during that second trial, providing among other things the first confession of diabolic witchcraft from the territory of Basel. Neither woman ever confessed to raising a hailstorm.
69. Ibid., p. 200.
70. StALU URK 392/7235.
71. StALU RP 17 fol. 166v–167r. Entire case transcribed in Hoffmann-Krayer, *Luzerner Akten*, pp. 96–105.
72. StALU RP 7 p. 113.
73. Barbara's case began in 1576 and continued through two periods of imprisonment and multiple interrogations. StALU COD 4450 fol. 61v–62r, 114r, 115r/v, 116r, 118r–119v, 120r–121r.
74. StABS Leistungsbuch II fol. 111r; Hoffmann-Krayer, *Luzerner Akten*, p. 47.
75. Grimm, *Deutsches Wörterbuch*. As Franck notes, *Unholde* was also a powerful inversion of the "good women" who were believed to ride with the Germanic goddess Holda through the night. Franck, "Geschichte des Wortes Hexe."
76. This is the logical companion to Bailey's argument that the concept of the witches' sabbath "provided an explanation by which authorities familiar with the learned tradition of demonic magic, or necromancy, could understand what they believed to be demonic magic practiced by uneducated people." Michael Bailey, "Medieval Concept of the Witches' Sabbath," *Exemplaria* 8:2 (1998): 419–39.

Part I   Witch Trials in the Cities

1. Alison Rowlands, *Witchcraft Narratives in Germany: Rothenburg, 1561–1652* (Manchester, 2003).
2. Johannes Dillinger, "Hexenverfolgungen in Städten," In *Methoden und Konzepte der historischen Hexenforschung* (Trier, 1998), p. 129.
3. Dillinger, "Hexenverfolgungen in Städten."

2   Basel: Territorialization and Rural Autonomy

1. René Teuteberg, *Basler Geschichte* (Basel, 1986), pp. 150ff.
2. Gustav Schönberg, "Basels Bevölkerungszahl im 15. Jahrhundert," *Jahrbücher für Nationalökonomie und Statistik* 40 (volume 6 of new series) (1883): 378.
3. Andreas Heusler, *Verfassungsgeschichte der Stadt Basel im Mittelalter* (Basel, 1860), pp. 206–7.
4. Teuteberg, *Basler Geschichte*, pp. 162, 180ff.
5. Hans Rudolf Guggisberg, *Basel in the Sixteenth Century. Aspects of the City Republic before, during and after the Reformation* (St. Louis, 1982), p. 4.
6. Hans-Rudolf Hagemann, "Basler Strafjustiz im Mittelalter," *Basler Juristische Mitteilungen* 5 (1979): p. 225.
7. Ibid., pp. 225–6.

8. StABS Leistungsbuch II fol. 52y. The trial dossier has been transcribed in Carl Buxtorf-Falkeisen, *Basler Zauber-Prozesse aus dem 14. und 15. Jahrhundert* (Basel, 1868). The following is taken from this work unless otherwise noted.

9. StABS Leistungsbuch II fol. 51v.

10. It is possible that some were later pardoned and allowed to return. Although I have not found evidence of that in this particular case, the practice was common enough.

11. Hagemann, "Basler Strafjustiz im Mittelalter," p. 225. In many cases, however, friends and relatives could and did successfully intervene in the judicial process in Basel.

12. Rippmann, "Hexen im 15. und 16. Jahrhundert."

13. On Peter zum Blech, see ibid., p. 168.

14. The term *Hexenmeister* appears to have had two entirely different meanings in the fifteenth and sixteenth century. The meaning it held in this case was that of an expert on witches and bewitchments. At other times and places, *Hexenmeister* meant the master of the witches' sect, or sometimes simply a male witch.

15. Rippmann suggests that Verena and Gret may have been midwives, and that this may help explain the focus on small children. Rippmann, "Hexen im 15. und 16. Jahrhundert," p. 172. As Lyndal Roper has recently shown, however, the witch as a destroyer of small children and as an antithesis of fertility is a topos which goes far beyond cases involving midwives; Roper, *Witch Craze*. Midwives were no more likely to be accused as witches than other women. See Richard Horsley, "Who Were the Witches? The Social Roles of the Accused in the European Witch Trials," in Brian Levack, ed., *Articles on Witchcraft, Magic and Demonology*, vol. 10 (New York, 1992).

16. Rippmann, "Hexen im 15. und 16. Jahrhundert," p. 210.

17. Ibid., p. 216.

18. Brian P. Levack, ed., *The Witchcraft Sourcebook* (New York, 2004), p. 48.

19. Buxtorf-Falkeisen, *Basler Zauber-Prozesse*, pp. 20–21. As peculiar as the connection between the gallows and love magic may seem at first encounter, the remains of the executed dead were believed to hold powerful magic throughout the Middle Ages and the early modern period. It is possible also that the central Christian mystery of the executed God imbued all executions with greater magical valency. Ruggiero discusses the use of the suffering God in Italian love magic. Guido Ruggiero *Binding Passions: Tales of Magic, Marriage, and Power at the End of the Renaissance* (Oxford, 1993), p. 106.

20. StABS Leistungsbuch II fol. 47r, 50r, 51v, 52y, 76v, 78v, 80v, 81v, 82v, 103v, 107v, 111r, and 114r; StABS Urfehdenbuch I pp. 152, 210–11, and 250. Of the thirteen separate incidents involved, six are included in the following: Hansen, *Quellen*; Buxtorf-Falkeisen, *Basler Zauber-Prozesse*; Rippmann, "Hexen im 15. und 16. Jahrhundert."

21. StABS Leistungsbuch II fol. 50r.

22. StABS Leistungsbuch II fol. 80v.

23. Threats of execution coupled with banishment were effectively a reiteration of the implied threat of execution due to oathbreaking. In actuality, most people who violated banishments were simply banished again as a result.

24. Rippmann, "Hexen im 15. und 16. Jahrhundert."
25. Bernard Harms, *Der Stadthaushalt Basels im ausgehenden Mittelalter*, 3 vols. (Tübingen, 1909), vol. 1, p. 173. Although the entry does not specify who the men in question were, they were most likely a retinue that went to Waldenburg to facilitate the execution.
26. Of these fourteen cases, three are found in Harms, *Stadthaushalt Basels*, vol. 1, p. 173 and StABS Leistungsbuch II fol. 129v, 134r. For the remainder see Rippmann, "Hexen im 15. und 16. Jahrhundert."
27. Rippmann, "Hexen im 15. und 16. Jahrhundert," p. 200.
28. Rippmann, "Hexen im 15. und 16. Jahrhundert," p. 189; Rippmann, "Hexenverfolgungen und soziale Unrast," p. 168.
29. StABS WAG 11 pp. 483–4, 538–545, 763, 766–7ff, 768, and 771: StABS WAG 12 pp. 286, 291, 328, and 939–942: StABS WAG 13 pp. 102, 103, 105, and 523–24: StABS WAG 15 pp. 88, 92: StABS Urfehdenbuch II p. 72, Urfehdenbuch IV p. 160: StABS Criminalia 4, 1 and 4, 2. Two of these cases are also listed in Hansen, *Quellen*. One case is drawn from Rippmann, "Hexen im 15. und 16. Jahrhundert."
30. StABS WAG 13 p. 102.
31. StABS WAG 13 p. 101.
32. StABS WAG 13 p. 105.
33. StABS WAG 11 p. 767.
34. Rippmann, "Hexenverfolgungen und soziale Unrast," pp.153–4.
35. Juliane Kümmell, *Bäuerliche Gesellschaft und städtische Herrschaft im Spätmittelalter. Zum Verhältnis von Stadt und Land im Fall Basel/Waldenburg 1300–1535* (Constance, 1983), p. 146.
36. Dorothee Rippmann, *Bauern und Städter. Stadt-Land-Beziehung im 15. Jahrhundert* (Basel, 1990), pp. 311–12.
37. A complete survey of StABS WAG 15 and StABS Urfehdenbuch IV for 1530 reveals 75 cases related to Anabaptism, many with multiple references. One can scarcely scan two pages without finding another "Täufer".
38. StABS Urfehdenbuch IV pp. 77–9.
39. Siegfried Frhr. von Scheurl, "Näher am Original? Zur Verfassung der Reichsstadt Nürnberg 1516." *Mitteilungen des Vereins für Geschichte der Stadt Nürnberg* 86 (1999): 21–46, here p. 45.
40. Gary Waite, *Heresy, Magic, and Witchcraft in Early Modern Europe* (Basingstoke, 2003).
41. For example in the case of Hans Oswald from 1530. StABS Urfehdenbuch IV, p. 154.
42. On the effect of such providential theology on the witch trials more broadly, see Erik Midelfort, *Witch Hunting in Southwestern Germany 1562–1684: The Social and Intellectual Foundations* (Stanford, 1972).

3 Nuremberg: The *Malleus* that Never Struck

1. Emil Reicke, *Geschichte der Reichsstadt Nürnberg von dem ersten urkundlichen Nachweis ihres Bestehens bis zu ihrem Uebergang an das Königreich Bayern (1806)* (Nuremberg, 1896), p. 558.
2. Gerald Strauss, *Nuremberg in the Sixteenth Century* (New York, 1966), p. 6–7.

3. Strauss, *Nuremberg*, p. 4. As Strauss points out, these comments should be taken in their context. Silvius was using the successes of Nuremberg as proof that cities had flourished under the Catholic church.

4. Hermann Kellenbenz, "Gewerbe und Handel am Ausgang des Mittelalters," in Gerhard Pfeiffer, ed., *Nürnberg – Geschichte einer europäischen Stadt* (Munich, 1971), p. 176.

5. Reicke, *Geschichte der Reichsstadt Nürnberg*, p. 578.

6. Ibid., p. 556.

7. Gerhard Hirschmann, "Zeitalter des Markgrafen Albrecht Achilles," in *Nürnberg – Geschichte*. See also Fritz Schnelbögl, "Zwischen Zollern und Wittelsbachern," in *Nürnberg - Geschichte*.

8. Wolfgang Leiser, "Nürnbergs Rechtsleben," in *Nürnberg - Geschichte*, pp. 171–2. See also Scheurl, "Näher am Original?" p. 42–5.

9. From Christoph Scheurl's 1516 letter on the constitution of the city of Nuremberg, as transcribed in Scheurl, "Näher am Original?," p. 42.

10. All but one of these trials is detailed in Kunstmann, *Zauberwahn*. The remaining case is that of Heintz Ritter's widow Agnes, who was released on an oath of peace in 1468 after accusations of enchanting livestock were not proved against her. StAN Rep 52B AStB no. 206, fol. 202r.

11. *Chroniken der fränkischen Städte. Nürnberg* (Leipzig, 1874), vol. 5, p. 550.

12. Gerhard Hirschmann, ed., *Johannes Müllner: Die Annalen der Reichsstadt Nürnberg von 1623* (Nuremberg, 1984), p. 576.

13. Kunstmann, *Zauberwahn*, pp. 33–4.

14. StAN AStB 226a fol. 26r.

15. Kunstmann, *Zauberwahn*, pp. 42–4.

16. Rudolf Endres, "Heinrich Institoris, sein Hexenhammer und der Nürnberger Rat," in Peter Segl, ed., *Der Hexenhammer. Entstehung und Umfeld des Malleus maleficarum von 1487* (Cologne, 1988), pp. 195–216; and Heinrich Kramer, *Nürnberger Hexenhammer 1491. Faksimile der Handschrift von 1491 aus dem Staatsarchiv Nürnberg, Nr. D 251*, ed. Günter Jerouschek (Hildesheim, 1992).

17. StAN RV 350 fol. 19v.

18. StAN Diff-Akt fol. 130a, 146a, 157a. These three cases are discussed by Kunstmann, *Zauberwahn*, pp. 34–5.

19. Details of Barbara's case are drawn from Traudl Kleefeld, et al., *Hexenverfolgung im Markgraftum Brandenburg-Ansbach und in der Herrschaft Sugenheim mit Quellen aus der Amtsstadt Crailsheim* (Ansbach, 2001), pp. 28–30.

20. For more on the history of torture in Nuremberg, see Chapter 6.

21. Presumably she had, as was customary, later confirmed or repeated the confession originally made under torture. This confirmation would have been made without torture, but under at least the implicit threat of further torment if she recanted.

22. *Chroniken der fränkischen Städte. Nürnberg*, vol. 5, p. 694.

23. Ibid.

24. Ibid.

25. *Chroniken der deutschen Städte. Nürnberg*, vol. 5, p. 536.

26. Kunstmann, *Zauberwahn*, pp. 186–7.

27. Ibid., p. 187.

28. All of the details of this case have been drawn from Kunstmann, *Zauberwahn*, p. 54–65.
29. Ibid., p. 62. Kunstmann quotes StAN Ratschlagbuch 9 fol. 107r, where the phrase is "fantasma und gesicht."
30. Kunstmann, *Zauberwahn*, p. 197. The phrase used for pure madness is "lauter wahn."
31. Wolfgang Behringer, *Hexenverfolgung in Bayern. Volksmagie, Glaubenseifer und Staatsräson in der Frühen Neuzeit* (Munich, 1988), pp. 432–66. In addition to the execution of Els Gernoltin, six people were executed as witches in Nuremberg during the late sixteeth through mid-seventeenth centuries. Kunstmann, *Zauberwahn*.
32. Arnd Müller, *Geschichte der Juden in Nürnberg 1146–1945* (Nuremberg, 1968), pp. 33–4; H. C. Ernst Mummenhoff, "Die Juden in Nürnberg bis zu ihrer Austreibung im Jahre 1499," in *Aufsätze und Vorträge zur Nürnberger Ortsgeschichte* (Nuremberg, 1931), pp. 314–19.
33. Reicke, *Geschichte der Reichsstadt Nürnberg*, p. 578.
34. StAN Stadtrechnungen 9 fol. 8v–10r.
35. A pound in local currency was worth 92.3% of one gulden (in this case *Landwährungsgulden*). See Paul Sander, *Die reichsstädtische Haushaltung Nürnbergs dargestellt auf Grund ihres Zustands von 1431 bis 1440* (Leipzig, 1902), p. 26.
36. StAN Stadtrechnungen 9 fol. 9r.
37. Hermann Knapp, *Das Lochgefängnis, Tortur und Richtung in Alt-Nürnberg. Auf Grund urkundlicher Forschung* (Nuremberg, 1907), p. 33; Irene Stahl, ed., *Die Nürnberger Ratsverlässe. Heft 1 1449–1450* (Neustadt a.d.A., 1983), pp. 173–74, 176, and 303–4.
38. Mummenhoff, "Juden in Nürnberg," p. 326. H. E. B. Briegleb, *Die Ausweisung der Juden von Nürnberg im Jahre 1499* (Leipzig, 1868), p. 20. Briegleb quoted an unnamed contemporary of his, who wrote, "Around this time [1480] the Israelite citizens of Nuremberg refused to acknowledge the new, reformed legal code of the city, because they were substantially damaged by it."
39. StAN Stadtrechnung 19a fol. 99r.
40. Franco Mormando, *The Preacher's Demons: Bernardino of Siena and the Social Underworld of Early Renaissance Italy* (Chicago, 1999), p. 179. The Trent case was quite famous in its time and after. Schoeps argues that this was due in part to the high number of victims, but nearly as many Jews were executed in Nuremberg twenty years later. Hsia is more convincing; he argues that the process of venerating "little Simon" as a saint propelled word of the case surrounding his murder around Europe. R. Po-chia Hsia, *Trent 1475: Stories of a Ritual Murder Trial* (New Haven, 1992); Julius Schoeps, "Justizfolter und Geständis. Der Trienter Ritualmordprozeß von 1475" *Zeitschrift für Religions- und Geistesgeschichte* 49:4 (1997): 377–81.
41. R. Po-chia Hsia, *The Myth of Ritual Murder: Jews and Magic in Reformation Germany* (New Haven, 1988).
42. StAN AStB 226a fol. 23v.
43. Edict from July 21, 1498 as transcribed by Briegleb, *Ausweisung der Juden*, p. 14.
44. Details of the case from Kunstmann, *Zauberwahn*, pp. 65–72.
45. "Irs warsagens und zauberns halben," "teufelsegen." Ibid., p. 66.

4 Lucerne: Urban Witch Hunters

1. Fritz Glauser, "Zur Verfassungstopographie des mittelalterlichen Luzern," in *Luzern 1178–1978. Beiträge zur Geschichte der Stadt* (Lucerne, 1978).
2. Fritz Glauser "Der Gotthardtransit von 1500 bis 1660. Seine Stellung im Alpentransit." *Schweizerische Zeitschrift für Geschichte* 29:1 (1979): 16–52.
3. Martin Körner, "Luzern als Finanzplatz im 16. Jahrhundert," in *Luzern 1178–1978*.
4. Werner Schnyder, "Reich und Arm im spätmittelalterlichen Luzern," *Geschichtsfreund* 120 (1967): p. 60.
5. Wilhelm Schnyder, Karl Meyer, and Peter Xavier Weber, *Geschichte des Kantons Luzern von der Urzeit bis zum Jahre 1500* (Lucerne, 1932), pp. 421, 692ff., 757ff., 783–4.
6. Ibid., pp. 651ff.
7. For the early period through 1550 see Jäggi "Luzerner Verfahren." Jäggi has also surveyed the late sixteenth-century witch hunt in Lucerne, and he provides brief figures on those trials in "Waldbruder, Prophet, Astrologe. Ein Luzerner Eremit am Ende des 16. Jahrhunderts," in *Der Geschichtsfreund* 158 (2005), p. 163–94. More general statistics for the whole period from 1551 through 1798 are found in Michael Harrer, "Statistik der Hinrichtungen in Luzern von 1551 bis 1798," in Jürg Manser, ed., *Richtstätte und Wasenplatz in Emmenbrücke (16.–19. Jahrhundert) Archäologische und historische Untersuchungen zur Geschichte von Strafrechtspflege und Tierhaltung in Luzern* (Basel, 1992). Analysis on the late trials in Lucerne with particular attention to the regional context is available in Philippe Bart, "Hexenverfolgungen in der Innenschweiz 1670–1754," in *Der Geschichtsfreund* 158 (2005) p. 5–161.
8. StALU URK 198/2893 fol. 7v.
9. StALU RP 3 fol. 61r; StALU URK 392/7235.
10. StALU RP 5A fol. 7r. No other mention of the case remains.
11. Hansen, *Quellen*, pp. 548–51.
12. Rippmann, "Hexenverfolgungen und soziale Unrast," p. 152.
13. Hoffmann-Krayer, *Luzerner Akten*, p. 4; Hansen, *Quellen*, p. 553.
14. 1£ 6s 8p to Cuntzlin Tamanen for the keep of "schwartz Ellsin," dated the Saturday after John the Baptist, 1448. StALU COD 8200 fol. 6r.
15. Hoffmann-Krayer, *Luzerner Akten*, p. 4–8. The rings and notes of "nichil" described by Hoffmann-Krayer were most likely added as a later confession was being compared to Else's. This may well have been the confession of Margaret Jägerin, whom Else had denounced. A translation of Else's confession is contained in the appendix.
16. Epilepsy.
17. Hoffmann-Krayer, *Luzerner Akten*, p. 4.
18. Carlo Ginzburg, *The Night Battles: Witchcraft and Agrarian Cults in the Sixteenth and Seventeenth Centuries* (Baltimore, 1983), p. 44. Ginzburg reaches the Swiss cases through werewolves in northern Europe (the Thies case in particular). As de Blécourt points out, the tendency to regard German Swiss wolf riding as a variant of werewolfism is highly problematic. De Blécourt, "Journey to Hell," p. 54.

19. Joseph Schacher, *Das Hexenwesen im Kanton Luzern, nach den Prozessesn von Luzern und Sursee 1400–1675* (Lucerne, 1947), p. 16.
20. Hoffmann-Krayer, *Luzerner Akten*, p. 6–7.
21. StALU COD 8280 fol. 14r.
22. StALU URK 397/7332.
23. For an extensive discussion of the correlation of execution rates generally and witch trials see Chapter 7 below.
24. Rüdiger Glaser, *Klimageschichte Mitteleuropas. 1000 Jahre Wetter, Klima, Katastrophen* (Darmstadt, 2001), pp. 61–92.
25. Wolfgang Behringer, Hartmut Lehmann, and Christian Pfister, "Kulturelle Konsequenzen der "Kleinen Eiszeit"? Eine Annäherung an die Thematik," in Behringer, et al., eds, *Kulturelle Konsequenzen der "Kleinen Eiszeit." Cultural Consequences of the "Little Ice Age,"* (Göttingen, 2005), p. 10.
26. This lull in witchcraft trials was reflected also in Basel and Nuremberg, but the small number of cases in those cities makes such trend analysis more problematic.
27. The purpose of the *Urfehde* was to prevent the oathtaker from seeking vengence for his treatment while in prison. See Chapter 5 for a more complete discussion of *Urfehde*.
28. StALU COD 8435 fol. 19r–21r; StALU COD 8440 fol. 10r–v, 11v–12r. The city council minutes do exist for this period, but no trace of these trials remains in them.
29. Hansen, *Quellen*, p. 582.
30. Glaser, *Klimageschichte Mitteleuropas*, pp. 61–92.
31. Hoffmann-Krayer, *Luzerner Akten*, pp. 19–23; see translation in Appendix.
32. StALU RP 6, fol. 117v.
33. For a full analysis of the evidentiary principles at play during the period, see Part II below.
34. Hoffmann-Krayer, *Luzerner Akten*, p. 23.
35. Ibid.
36. Hoffmann-Krayer, *Luzerner Akten*, p. 21.
37. Ibid., pp. 21–22. The narrative in the original shifts from first to third person mid-sentence.
38. Ibid., p. 19.
39. Literally "his hair stood toward the mountain"
40. Hoffmann-Krayer, *Luzerner Akten*, pp. 19–20.
41. Ibid., p. 20.
42. Ibid., p. 21.
43. Ibid.
44. Dillinger, *"Böse Leute."*
45. Jäggi, "Luzerner Verfahren," p. 150.
46. Blauert, "Hexenverfolgung," pp. 20–1 and passim.
47. StABS Criminalia 1A,G1; StABS WAG 15 pp. 76, 82.
48. Susanna Burghartz, "The Equation of Women and Witches: A Case Study of Witchcraft Trials in Lucerne and Lausanne in the Fifteenth and Sixteenth Centuries," in Richard Evans, ed., *The German Underworld: Deviants and Outcasts in German History* (London, 1988).
49. StALU RP 10 fol. 80r and StALU COD 8730 fol. 18r.
50. StALU RP 11, fol. 103v–105r; see translation in Appendix.

51. StALU RP 11 fol. 105r.
52. StALU RP 11 fol. 107v.
53. See Chapter 8 below for a full analysis of the case from 1519 and its larger significance.

5   Between Two Worlds: Fifteenth-century Justice at the Threshold of the Early Modern

Parts of this chapter have appeared previously as Laura Stokes, "Experiments in Pain: Reason and the Development of Judicial Torture," in Marjorie E. Plummer and Robin Barnes, eds, *Ideas and Cultural Margins in Early Modern Europe: Essays in Honor of H.C. Erik Midelfort* (Aldershot, 2009). I am grateful to Ashgate Publishing for permission to reprint selections here.

1. Andreas Blauert, *Das Urfehdewesen im deutschen Südwesten im Spätmittelalter und in der Frühen Neuzeit* (Tübingen, 2000).
2. Rudolf His, *Das Strafrecht des deutschen Mittelalters*, vol. 1 (Aalen, 1964), pp. 476–7.
3. His, *Strafrecht*, vol. 1, p. 533.
4. Katharina Simon-Muscheid, "Gewalt und Ehre im spätmittelalterlichen Handwerk am Beispiel Basels," *Zeitschrift für Historische Forschung* 18 (1991): 1–31. Martin Schüßler, "Statistische Untersuchung des Verbrechens in Nürnberg im Zeitraum von 1285 bis 1400," *Zeitschrift der Savigny-Stiftung für Rechtsgeschichte, Germ. Abt.* 108 (1991): 117–93. Schüßler has been critized by Schwerhoff for engaging in naive statistical analysis of these sources. Gerd Schwerhoff, "Falsches Spiel. Zur kriminalhistorischen Auswertung der spätmittelalterichen Nürnberger Achtbücher." *Mitteilung des Vereins für Geschichte der Stadt Nürnberg* 82 (1995): 23–35.
5. Günter Jerouschek, "Die Herausbildung des peinlichen Inquisitionsprozesses im Spätmittelalter und in der frühen Neuzeit," *Zeitschrift für die gesamte Strafrechtswissenschaft* 104 (1992). As Jerouschek points out elsewhere in reaction to pejorative over-simplification of inquisitorial process, during the last twenty years, the literature on early modern German criminal justice has developed into a field in its own right. Günter Jerouschek, "'Mit aller Schärpffe angegriffen undt gemartert.' Überlegungen zur Folter als Institut des gemeinrechtlichen Strafverfahrens," in Jost Hausmann and Thomas Krause, eds, *"Zur Erhaltung guter Ordnung." Beiträge zur Geschichte von Recht und Justiz. Festschrift für Wolfgang Sellert zum 65. Geburtstag* (Cologne, 2000), pp. 351–2.
6. Schmidt, *Inquisitionsprozess und Rezeption*. Schmidt argues that the emergence of inquisitorial process in Germany was an indigenous development. Langbein accepts Schmidt's argument but refines the question of influence, pointing out that models from Roman-Canon law no doubt affected the process. John Langbein, *Prosecuting Crime in the Renaissance: England, Germany, France* (Cambridge, Massachusetts, 1974).
7. Alfred Soman has argued that in France this process of transformation was not complete until the end of the eighteenth century. Alfred Soman, *Sorcellerie et justice criminelle: Le Parlement de Paris (16e–18e siècles)* (Aldershot,

1992). On the mixture of styles in early modern witch trials see Unverhau, "Akkusationsprozeß – Inquisitionsprozeß."

8. Schwerhoff "Kriminalitätsgeschichte."

9. Rudolf His, *Geschichte des deutschen Strafrechts bis zur Karolina* (Munich, 1967), p. 58.

10. Hermann Knapp, "Das alte Nürnberger Kriminalverfahren bis zur Einführung der Karolina," *Zeitschrift für die gesamte Strafrechtswissenschaft* 12 (1892): p. 229.

11. As quoted in ibid., pp. 231–2.

12. Philipp Anton von Segesser, *Rechtsgeschichte der Stadt und Republik Luzern*, 5 vols. (Lucerne, 1850–1858), pp. 693–4.

13. Langbein, *Prosecuting Crime in the Renaissance*, p. 151.

14. StALU RP 12 fol. 89r.

15. Hans-Rudolf Hagemann, *Basler Rechtsleben in Mittelalter* (Basel, 1987), p. 212.

16. StABS Urteilsbuch 48 fol. 157 as quoted in Hagemann, *Basler Rechtsleben*, p. 212.

17. Hermann Knapp, *Das alte Nürnberger Kriminalrecht. Nach Rats-Urkunden erlautert* (Berlin, 1896), p. 21. Knapp's sources here are sixteenth-century Polizeiordnungen.

18. Helmut Martin, *Verbrechen und Straf in Spiegel der spätmittelalterlichen Chronistik Nürnbergs* (Cologne, 1996), p. 108; Peter Schuster, *Eine Stadt vor Gericht: Recht und Alltag im spätmittelalterlichen Konstanz* (Paderborn, 2000), pp. 315–16; See also Rolf Sprandel, "Die Strafrechtswirklichkeit im Spiegel der spätmittelalterlichen Chronistik. Ein Überblick über den Forschungsstand des Würzburger Teilprojekts," in Hans Schlosser and Dietmar Willoweit, eds, *Neue Wege strafrechtsgeschichtlicher Forschung* (Cologne, 1999), pp. 147–54, here pp. 147–50.

19. StAN AStB 226a fol. 23r.

20. StALU RP 9 fol. 325v–326r.

21. See Chapter 7 below.

22. StABS Criminalia 21 S,1; StABS WAG 14 p. 557.

23. Jerouschek, "Mit aller Schärpffe angegriffen," pp. 355–7.

24. Hansen, *Zauberwahn*, p. 118.

25. Langbein, *Prosecuting Crime in the Renaissance*, p. 149: Dieter Baldauf, *Die Folter. Eine deutsche Rechtsgeschichte* (Cologne, 2004), pp. 71–75. The best recent survey of the history of torture in Germany is Robert Zagolla, *In Namen der Wahrheit. Folter in Deutschland vom Mittelalter bis heute* (Berlin, 2006).

26. Jerouschek, "Mit aller Schärpffe angegriffen," p. 268.

27. Müller, *Geschichte der Juden*, p. 33; Mummenhoff, "Die Juden in Nürnberg," p. 317.

28. Adrian Staehelin, "Von der Folter im Basler Strafrecht," *Basler Stadtbuch: Jahrbuch für Kultur und Geschichte* (1965): p. 100.

29. Henry Charles Lea, *Torture* (Philadelphia, 1973), p. 79.

30. Langbein, *Prosecuting Crime in the Renaissance*, p. 149.

31. StABS WAG 1 p. 115 as quoted in Hagemann, *Basler Rechtsleben*, p. 200.

32. StABS WAG 6 pp. 500, 523, 541; StABS Leistungsbuch II fol. 103v, 105r.

33. StABS WAG 6 p. 481.

34. StABS Leistungsbuch II fol. 103v; StABS WAG 6 p. 525.
35. StABS WAG 6 pp. 506–8.
36. StABS WAG 9 p. 58.
37. In general, "gichtigen" meant to interrogate with or without judicial torture. Grimm, *Deutsches Wörterbuch*. The use of the term in Basel, however, seems to have been limited to cases where torture was used. Hagemann, *Basler Rechtsleben*, p. 204.
38. StABS WAG 11 p. 483.
39. StABS WAG 11 p. 253.
40. See Chapter 8 below.
41. See for example Baldauf, *Die Folter*, p. 71.
42. Scheurl "Näher am Original?" p. 45.
43. As cited in Knapp, *Das Lochgefängnis*, p. 23.
44. StAN Rep. 60a Ratsverlässe. Published editions exist for the Ratsverlässe from 1449 through 1471: Irene Stahl, ed., *Die Nürnberger Ratsverlässe. Heft 1 1449–1450* (Neustadt a.d.A., 1983); Martin Scheiber, ed. *Die Nürnberger Ratsverlässe. Heft 2 1452–1471.* (Neustadt a.d.A., 1995).
45. Stahl, *Nürnberger Ratsverlässe. Heft 1*, pp. 68, 70.
46. Ibid., p. 92. The language used in these entries is of particular interest. Rather than using a specific term for torture, such as *Folter*, the council minutes frequently referred to the process vaguely as causing pain (*Weh tun*). Here as elsewhere, we get a hint of the distance between these lay judges and formal theories of criminal justice. They seem to have shared the assumption that pain could draw out the truth, but they did not use language that identified this particular kind of pain as a distinct category, part of the repertoire of criminal justice.
47. Ibid., pp. 83, 85, 91.
48. Knapp, *Das alte Nürnberger Kriminalrecht.*
49. Knapp, *Das Lochgefängnis*, p. 45.
50. The case of Niclaus Muffel is widely reflected in archival sources, chronicles, and other contemporary sources. See Gerhard Fouquet, "Die Affäre Niklas Muffel. Die Hinrichtung eines Nürnberger Patriziers im Jahre 1469," *Vierteljahrschrift für Sozial- und Wirtschaftsgeschichte* 83, no. 4 (1996): 459–500.
51. Ibid., p. 41.
52. Fouquet, "Die Affäre Niklas Muffel," p. 462.
53. A similar case is that of the Landvogt Peter von Hagenbach, who was tortured and executed in Breisach in 1474. Sven Lembke "Folter und gerichtliches Geständnis. Über den Zusammenhang von Gewalt, Schmerz und Wahrheit im 14. und 15. Jahrhundert," in Peter Burschel, et al., eds, *Das Quälen des Körpers. Eine historische Anthropologie der Folter* (Cologne, 2000), pp. 171–74.
54. StAN AStB 226a fol. 17v.
55. Schieber, *Nürnberger Ratsverlässe. Heft 2*, p. 169.
56. StAN RV 23 fol. 9v through RV 25 fol. 11r, passim. Knapp *Das Lochgefängnis*, p. 35. I have not found the record that was mentioned here.
57. Somewhat confusingly called the Nuremberg Reformation, this legal reform was completed in 1479 and printed in 1484. Daniel Waldmann, "Die Entstehung der Nürnberger Reformation von 1479 (1484) und die Quellen

ihrer prozessrechtlichen Vorschriften," *Mitteilung des Vereins für Geschichte der Stadt Nürnberg* 18 (1908): 1–98.
58. StAN RV 156 fol. 17v through RV 157 fol. 10r, passim; StAN Stadtsrechnungen 19a fol. 157v.
59. Lisa Silverman, *Tortured Subjects: Pain, Truth, and the Body in Early Modern France* (Chicago, 2001).
60. Hans Fehr "Zur Erklärung von Folter und Hexenprozeß" *Zeitschrift für Schweizerische Geschichte* 24 (1944): 581–585. On the role of demons in early modern thought, see Stuart Clark *Thinking with Demons: The Idea of Witchcraft in Early Modern Europe* (Oxford, 1997).
61. Lembke "Folter und gerichtliches Geständnis," p. 192.
62. StAN RV 470 fol. 9v.
63. StAN RV 470 fol. 7v–14r, passim.
64. StAN RV 470 fol. 11v.
65. Andrea Bendlage and Ulrich Henselmeyer, "Zur Monopolisierung des Strafrechts. Gesellschaftliche Relevanz und Reichweite obrigkeitlicher Normen in der Reichsstadt Nürnberg im 15. und 16. Jahrhundert," in Hans Schlosser, et al., eds, *Herrschaftliches Strafen seit dem Hochmittelalter: Formen und Entwicklungsstufen* (Cologne, 2002), 311–29, here p. 320.
66. Knapp *Das Lochgefängnis*, pp. 25–27.
67. Scheurl, "Näher am Original?" p. 42.
68. StAN RV 659 fol. 20r through RV 661 fol. 9r, passim.
69. Kroeschell describes the German investigating juries as drawing mainly on unwritten procedural law. Karl Kroeschell, *Deutsche Rechtsgeschichte* (Opladen, 1989), vol. 2, p. 125.
70. Kunstmann, *Zauberwahn*, 60–1. Kunstmann notes that Scheurl was a legal consultant for the Nuremberg city council from 1512 through 1542.
71. Knapp, *Nürnberger Kriminalrecht*, pp. viii–ix.
72. Stokes, "Experiments in Pain."
73. Segesser, *Rechtsgeschichte*, vol. 2, p. 712.
74. Ibid.
75. Susanne Burghartz's monograph on late fourteenth-century Zurich, for example, demonstrates the high incidence of officially-initiated criminal trials there. Susanne Burghartz, *Leib, Ehre und Gut. Delinquenz in Zürich Ende des 14. Jahrhunderts* (Zurich: Chronos, 1990). For discussion see also Esther Cohen "Inquiring once more after the Inquisitorial Process" in Dietmar Willoweit, ed., *Die Entstehung des öffentlichen Strafrechts. Bestandsaufnahme eines europäischen Forschungsproblems* (Cologne: Böhlau Verlag, 1999); and Schwerhoff, "Kriminalitätsgeschichte."
76. I have not completely surveyed the *Ratsprotokolle* of the city prior to 1430; it is quite possible that earlier traces exist.
77. StALU RP 1 fol. 310r; StALU URK 391/7228 and URK 391/7229.
78. StALU RP 3 fol. 61r.
79. StALU RP 4 fol. 89v and 142r.
80. See Chapter 6, Figure 6.4. Further data and analysis regarding the execution rate in Lucerne is also available in Chapter 6.
81. StALU RP 4 fol. 142r.
82. StALU COD 8260 fol. 17r: StALU COD 8280 fol. 9r.
83. StALU COD 8440 fol. 14v.

84. StALU COD 8440 fol. 23r.
85. StALU RP 6 fol. 55v.
86. StALU RP 6 fol. 141r.
87. StALU RP 8 fol. 128v.

6   The Advancing Death Penalty and the Re-imagining of Magical Crimes

1. Schuster, *Eine Stadt vor Gericht*, p. 316.
2. StABS WAG 12 through WAG 15.
3. StALU COD 8470 fol. 20r.
4. The following statistics are drawn from a survey of the Basel weekly expense records from 1428 through 1532. StABS WAG 6 through WAG 15.
5. Execution statistics for Lucerne are drawn from a complete survey of the Lucerne weekly expense records from 1430 through 1530. StALU COD 8035 through COD 8920.
6. See also Chapter 4 above.
7. For general discussion of the parallels between judicial severity generally and witchcraft trials in particular, see Burghartz "The Equation of Women and Witches" p. 70.
8. Gerd Schwerhoff, *Köln im Kreuzverhör: Kriminalität, Herrschaft und Gesellschaft in einer frühneuzeitlichen Stadt* (Bonn, 1991), p. 148. Carl Hoffmann, "Der Stadtverweis als Sanktionsmittel in der Reichsstadt Augsburg zu Beginn der Neuzeit.," in Hans Schlosser and Dietmar Willoweit, eds, *Neue Wege strafrechtsgeschichtlicher Forschung* (Cologne, 1999).
9. See Chapter 8 below.
10. Hirschmann, *Müllner: Annalen*, vol. 2, p. 349.
11. StALU RP 6 fol. 140v.
12. The distinction in late medieval German law between *Mord* and *Todschlag* was not one of intent, as it is in contemporary Anglo-American law, but secrecy and openness. It was during the same long transition in criminal justice from medieval to early modern that the element of intent began to play a more significant role in the distinction between murder and manslaughter.
13. StALU RP 9 fol. 57r.
14. On sodomy and theft in Lucerne, see Chapter 8 below.
15. Bob Scribner argued for the possibility that such arson conspiracy theories had a kernel of truth in them, but noted that the panic that surrounded them far outstripped any such reality. Robert W. Scribner, "The Mordbrenner Fear in Sixteenth-Century Germany: Political Paranoia or the Revenge of the Outcast?" in Richard Evans, ed., *The German Underworld: Deviants and Outcasts in German History* (London, 1988).
16. StALU RP 7 p. 212.
17. Bever, *Realities of Witchcraft*.
18. For more recent interpretive frameworks, see Mitchell Merback, *The Thief, the Cross, and the Wheel: Pain and the Spectacle of Punishment in Medieval and Renaissance Europe* (London, 1999); Peter Schuster, "Hinrichtungsrituale in der Frühen Neuzeit. Anfragen aus dem Mittelalter," in Harriet Rudolph and

Helga Schnabel-Schüle, eds, *Justiz = Justice = Justicia? Rahmenbedingungen von Strafjustiz im frühneuzeitlichen Europa* (Trier, 2003), 213–33.

19. Schuster, "Hinrichtungsrituale," pp. 218–19.
20. See Chapter 8.
21. StAN RV 23 through RV 32: StAN RV 156 through RV 169.
22. StAN AStB 226a fol 23v.
23. In 1580, three women were condemned for infanticide. The executioner's diary reads: "As murderesses, all three were executed with the sword and their heads were nailed to the gallows. Never before had a woman been executed with the sword in Nuremberg. I and two priests brought this about, as the established practice was that all three should have been drowned." Jürgen Carl Jacobs and Heinz Rölleke, eds, *Das Tagebuch des Meister Franz Scharfrichter zu Nürnberg. Nachdruck der Buchausgabe von 1801* (Harenberg, 1980), p. 11–12.
24. Richard van Dülmen, *Theatre of Horror: Crime and Punishment in Early Modern Germany*, Elisabeth Neu, trans. (Cambridge, 1990), p. 88.
25. Schuster, "Hinrichtungsrituale," pp. 217, 219.
26. Knapp, *Nürnberger Kriminalrecht*, pp. 59–60.
27. Hirschmann, *Müllner: Annalen*, vol. 2., p. 501. See also StAN AStB 226a fol. 18r.
28. StAN AStB 226a fol. 24v.
29. Karl Metzger, *Die Verbrechen und ihre Straffolgen im Basler Recht des späteren Mittelalters I. Teil: Die Verbrechen und ihre Straffolgen im allgemeinen* (Basel, 1931), pp. 54–5.
30. Van Dülmen, *Theatre of Horror*, p. 88.
31. Mary Douglas, *Purity and Danger: An Analysis of Concept of Pollution and Taboo* (New York, 1966).
32. Hirschmann, *Müllner: Annalen*, vol. 2, p. 315.
33. StALU RP 5A fol. 509r.
34. Richard Evans, *Rituals of Retribution: Capital Punishment in Germany, 1600–1987* (New York, 1996), pp. 14–15.
35. Hagemann, *Basler Rechtsleben*, pp. 318–19.
36. Bendlage and Henselmeyer, "Zur Monopolisierung des Strafrechts," pp. 313, 315.
37. Hagemann, *Basler Rechtsleben*, p. 221.
38. Schuster, "Hinrichtungsrituale," p. 221.
39. StALU RP 11 fol. 103v–105r. See also Chapter 4 and Chapter 8 for further discussion of this case.
40. StALU COD 8805 fol. 12r.
41. StABS WAG 6 p. 388.
42. StABS WAG 9 p. 84.
43. Hagemann, *Basler Rechtsleben in Mittelalter*, p. 221.
44. StABS WAG 12 p. 627.
45. StABS WAG 12 p. 950.
46. Schuster, "Hinrichtungsrituale," pp. 221–23
47. StABS WAG 6 p. 541.
48. Jürg Bielmann, *Die Bevoelkerung Basels vom Mittelalter bis zur Gegenwart. Begleitheft zur Ausstellung im Staatsarchiv Basel-Stadt vom 1. Februar bis 31. März 1974* (Basel, 1974), p. 2.

49. Soman, *Sorcellerie et justice criminelle*.
50. Hagemann, *Basler Rechtsleben*, p. 161.
51. Ibid., p. 156. Blauert has noted more recently that modern criminal historians are entirely skeptical regarding the possibility of making statements about actual crime rates. Blauert, "Kriminaljustiz," p. 124.
52. Hoffmann, "Der Stadtverweis als Sanktionsmittel," p. 212.
53. Schuster, *Eine Stadt vor Gericht*, p. 312.

7   Urban Reform and Social Control

1. In particular, the cities' war and the weak position of the imperial cities in the reformed imperial constitution of 1495. See Strauss, *Nuremberg*.
2. Bettina Günther, "Sittlichkeitsdelikte in den Policeyordnungen der Reichsstädte Frankfurt am Main und Nürnberg (15.–17. Jahrhundert)," in Karl Härter, ed., *Policey und frühneuzeitliche Gesellschaft* (Frankfurt a.M., 2000), pp. 121–48.
3. StALU RP 12 fol. 160r.
4. Ibid.
5. Robert Scribner, *Popular Culture and Popular Movements in Reformation Germany* (London, 1987), p. 176.
6. Winfried Schulze, "Gerhard Oestreichs Begriff 'Sozialdisziplinierung' in der Frühen Neuzeit," *Zeitschrift für Historische Forschung* 14 (1992).
7. R. Po-chia Hsia, *Social Discipline in the Reformation: Central Europe 1550–1750* (London, 1989).
8. Susanna Burghartz, "Ehen vor Gericht. Die Basler Ehegerichtsprotokolle im 16. Jahrhundert," in Heide Wunder, ed., *Eine Stadt der Frauen. Studien und Quellen zur Geschichte der Baslerinnen im späten Mittelalter und zu Beginn der Neuzeit (13.–17. Jahrhundert)* (Basel, 1995).
9. As cited in Heinrich R. Schmidt, "Die Christianisierung des Sozialverhaltens als permanente Reformation. Aus der Praxis reformierter Sittengerichte in der Schweiz während der frühen Neuzeit," in Peter Blickle and Johannes Kunisch, eds, *Kommunalisierung und Christianisierung* (Berlin, 1989), p. 113.
10. As cited in Teuteberg, *Basler Geschichte*, p. 181.
11. Scribner, *Popular Culture*, pp. 175–84.
12. Lyndal Roper, *The Holy Household: Women and Morals in Reformation Augsburg* (Oxford, 1989); Reinhold Schorer, "Die Strafherren – Ein selbständiges Organ der Rechtspflege in der Reichsstadt Augsburg in der Frühen Neuzeit," in Hans Schlosser and Dietmar Willoweit, eds, *Neue Wege strafrechtsgeschichtlicher Forschung*, p. 175–77. Schorer critizes Roper for adopting older assessments of the *Strafherren* that focused exclusively on the office in its Reformation context.
13. Schulze, "Gerhard Oestreichs Begriff 'Sozialdisziplinierung'," p. 267.
14. Schmidt, "Christianisierung des Sozialverhaltens," p. 152.
15. Joseph Baader, *Nürnberger Polizeiordnungen aus dem XIII. bis XV. Jahrhundert* (1861; reprint Amsterdam, 1966).
16. The term used, "Welsch", usually denoted Italian or French in early modern German. Christa Baufeld, *Kleines frühneuhochdeutsches Wörterbuch*.

Lexik aus Dichtung und Fachliteratur des Frühneuhochdeutschen (Tübingen, 1996).

17. Baader, *Nürnberger Polizeiordnungen*, pp. 65–6.
18. Ibid., p. 95.
19. Günther, "Sittlichkeitsdelikte," pp. 127, 141–44.
20. Konrad Wanner, ed., *Die Rechtsquellen des Kantons Luzern*, 3 vols. (Aarau, 1998).
21. Johannes Schnell, ed., *Rechtsquellen von Basel Stadt und Land* (Basel, 1856).
22. Hagemann, *Basler Rechtsleben*, p. 72–3.
23. StAN Stadtsrechnungen 11 fol 8v.
24. Based on StAN Stadtsrechnung 9 fol. 9r–11r: StAN Stadtsrechnungen 11 fol. 7r–11r: StAN Stadtsrechnungen 14 fol. 10r–13r: StAN Stadtsrechnungen 17 fol. 15r–24r: StAN Stadtsrechnungen 19a fol. 9r–19v: StAN Stadtsrechnungen 22 fol. 10r–17v.
25. Baader, *Nürnberger Polizeiordnungen*, p. 95.
26. Joseph Baader, "Polizeiliche Massregelungen des Rates der Stadt Nürnberg gegen Luxus und Unsittlichkeit gerichtet," *Anzeiger für Kunde der deutschen Vorzeit. Organ des Germanischen Museum* (1862): p. 326.
27. Schnell, *Rechtsquellen*.
28. StABS Leistungsbuch II fol. 104v.
29. StABS Leistungsbuch II fol. 106v.
30. StABS Leistungsbuch II fol. 133r.
31. StALU RP 9 p. 3.
32. Wanner, *Rechtsquellen des Kantons Luzern*, p. 42.
33. StALU RP 8 p. 87.
34. Gerd Schwerhoff, *Zungen wie Schwerter. Blasphemie in alteuropäischen Gesellschaften 1200–1650* (Constance, 2005), pp.131–47.
35. Ibid., p. 138.
36. StALU RP 4 fol. 54r.
37. StALU RP 5A fol. 526r.
38. StALU RP 5A fol. 526r–v.
39. StALU RP 6 fol. 78v.
40. StALU RP 7 p. 366.
41. StALU RP 9 fol. 60v.
42. Schwerhoff, *Zungen wie Schwerter*, p. 145.
43. His, *Geschichte des deutschen Strafrechts*, pp. 107–8. Pope Gregory IX requested the intervention of the secular arm in a decretal released between 1227 and 1234. Gerd Schwerhoff, "Blasphemie vor den Schranken der städtischen Justiz: Basel, Köln und Nürnberg im Vergleich (14.–17. Jahrhundert)," *Ius commune. Zeitschrift für europäische Rechtsgeschichte* 25 (1998): p. 40.
44. Hoffmann, "Stadtverweis," pp. 228, 235.
45. From 1396, StABS Leistungsbuch II fol. 18v as cited in Hagemann, *Basler Rechtsleben*, p. 250.
46. Simon-Muscheid, "Gewalt und Ehre," pp. 30–1.
47. StABS Criminalia 1A,B1.
48. Schwerhoff, "Blasphemie vor den Schranken," pp. 49–50. A *Haller* was worth about half a penny.
49. Baader, *Nürnberger Polizeiordnungen*, p. 114.
50. Knapp, *Das alte Nürnberger Kriminalrecht*, p. 277.

51. Hirschmann, *Müllner: Annalen*, p. 321.
52. Schwerhoff, *Zungen wie Schwerter*, p. 146.
53. Ann Tlusty, *Bacchus and Civic Order: The Culture of Drink in Early Modern Germany* (Charlottesville, VA, 2001), pp. 118–19.
54. StALU RP 5A fol. 285r.
55. StALU RP 5A fol. 285r.
56. StALU RP 9 p. 4.
57. StABS Urfehdenbuch IV p. 67.
58. Hoffmann, "Stadverweis," pp. 193–95. See also Tlusty, *Bacchus and Civic Order*.
59. Joel Harrington, *Reordering Marriage and Society in Reformation Germany* (Cambridge, 1995).
60. Susanna Burghartz, *Zeiten der Reinheit, Orte der Unzucht. Ehe und Sexualität in Basel während der Frühen Neuzeit* (Paderborn, 1999), pp. 114, 118–19.
61. Although some clerics did consider prostitution a necessary evil, its regulation was generally left to the secular authorities.
62. Beate Schuster, *Die freien Frauen. Dirnen und Frauenhäuser im 15. und 16. Jahrhundert* (Frankfurt a.M., 1991), p. 88.
63. Baader, *Nürnberger Polizeiordnungen*, p. 117.
64. Ibid., p. 118.
65. Ibid., p. 121.
66. Simon-Muscheid, "Gewalt und Ehre," p. 30–1.
67. Rudolf Wackernagel, *Geschichte der Stadt Basel*, 3 vols. (Basel, 1907–1924), vol. 1, p. 490.
68. Wanner, *Rechtsquellen des Kantons Luzern*, vol. 3, p. 57.
69. Ibid., p. 166.
70. StALU RP 7 p. 259.
71. StALU RP 8 fol. 148v.
72. Wanner, *Rechtsquellen des Kantons Luzern*, vol. 3, p. 351.
73. StALU RP 5B, fol. 208v, 213v.
74. StALU RP 5A, fol. 272r, 276v, 309v.
75. Wanner, *Rechtsquellen des Kantons Luzern*, vol. 3, p. 148.
76. StALU RP 5B 382r.
77. Harrington, *Reordering Marriage*, p. 107.
78. StALU RP 10 fol. 103r.
79. StALU RP 10 fol. 207v.
80. StALU RP 12 fol. 151r.
81. StALU RP 10 fol. 108r.
82. StALU RP 10 fol. 110r.
83. The would-be groom.
84. StALU RP 12 fol. 96v.
85. Sprandel, " Strafrechtswirklichkeit," pp. 148–49. Sprandel is reviewing some of the findings of Martin, *Verbrechen und Strafe*.
86. Schuster, *Eine Stadt vor Gericht*, pp. 111–19.
87. StABS Urfehdenbuch IV p. 154.
88. Robert Muchembled, *Popular Culture and Elite Culture in France 1400–1750* (Baton Rouge, 1985).
89. Blauert, "Kriminaljustiz und Sittenreform," p. 130.

8 Witchcraft, Sodomy, and the Demonization of Crime

1. StALU COD 4450 fol. 182v.
2. Tamar Herzig "The Demons' Reaction to Sodomy: Witchcraft and Homosexuality in Gianfrancesco Pico della Mirandola's *Strix*" *Sixteenth Century Journal* 34 (2003): 53–72. For an example of the rather vague use made of the relationship between witchcraft and sodomy, see Vern Bullough "Postscript: Heresy, Witchcraft, and Sexuality" in Vern Bullough and James Brundage, eds, *Sexual Practices and the Medieval Church* (Buffalo, 1982), pp. 206–217. P. G. Maxwell-Stuart, " 'Wild, Filthie, Exacrabill, Detestabill, and Unnatural Sin': Bestiality in Early Modern Scotland," in Tom Betteridge, ed., *Sodomy in Early Modern Europe* (Manchester, 2002), p. 89. There is surprisingly little analysis of the relationship between sodomy and witchcraft trials in Dietegen Guggenbühl, *Mit Tieren und Teufeln: Sodomiten und Hexen unter Basler Jurisdiction in Stadt und Land 1399 bis 1799* (Basel, 2002). Despite Guggenbühl's contribution, a serious gap has persisted in the scholarship.
3. Waite, *Heresy, Magic, and Witchcraft*, p. 8.
4. This was especially the case in the 1980s, but the tendency persists. Recently Maria Boes, in an interesting essay on apparent toleration of homosexual acts in early modern Frankfurt, notes but disregards two cases of bestiality during the same period. Maria Boes, "On Trial for Sodomy in Early Modern Germany," in Tom Betteridge, ed., *Sodomy in Early Modern Europe*.
5. Helmut Puff, *Sodomy in Reformation Germany and Switzerland, 1400–1600* (Chicago, 2003), p. 18; Erica Fudge, "Monstrous Acts. Bestiality in Early Modern England" *History Today* 50, August (2000): 20–25; Maxwell-Stuart, " 'Wild, Filthie, Exacrabill," pp. 82–93.
6. Joyce E. Salisbury, *The Beast Within: Animals in the Middle Ages* (New York, 1994), 84.
7. StABS Criminalia 1A, B12. Several of these depositions are transcribed in Guggenbühl, *Mit Tieren und Teufeln*, 212–213.
8. See Puff, *Sodomy in Reformation Germany and Switzerland*, pp. 115–117; Helmut Puff, "A State of Sin: Switzerland and the Early Modern Imaginary," in Katherine O'Donnell and Michael O'Rourke, eds, *Queer Masculinities, 1550–1800: Siting Same-Sex Desire in the Early Modern World* (Basingstoke, 2006), pp. 94–105.
9. StALU RP 5A fol. 43r.
10. StALU Ratsprotokoll 5A fol. 232v.
11. StALU Ratsprotokoll 9 fol. 3r.
12. StALU RP 10 fol. 218r, 219r.
13. These data were gathered from a survey of the Ratsprotokolle and Umgeldrödel of the Staatsarchiv Luzern from 1400 through 1599.
14. StALU RP 4 fol. 78v.
15. Christine Reinle, "Zur Rechtspraxis gegenüber Homosexuellen. Eine Fallstudie aus dem Regensburg des 15. Jahrhunderts," *Zeitschrift für Geschichtswissenschaft* 4 (1996): 307–26.
16. Bernd-Ulrich Hergemöller, "Die unsprechliche stumme Sünde in Kölner Akten des ausgehenden Mittelalters," *Geschichte in Köln* 22 (1987): 5–51;

Hergemöller, "Homosexuelle als spätmittelalterliche Randgruppe," *Forum Homosexualität und Literatur* 2 (1987): 59–91; Iwan Bloch, "Homosexualität in Köln am Ende des 15. Jahrhunderts," in Wayne Dynes and Stephen Donaldson, eds, *History of Homosexuality in Europe and America* (New York, 1992), pp. 1–9.

17. William Monter, "Sodomy and Heresy in Early Modern Switzerland," in Salvatore Licata and Robert Petersen, eds, *The Gay Past: A Collection of Historical Essays* (New York, 1985).

18. William Naphy, *Sex Crimes from Renaissance to Enlightenment* (Stroud, 2002), p. 90. See also William Naphy, "Sodomy in Early Modern Geneva: Various Definitions, Diverse Verdicts," in *Sodomy in Early Modern Europe*.

19. Claudius Sieber-Lehmann, *Spätmittelalterlicher Nationalismus. Die Burgunderkriege am Oberrhein und in der Eidgenossenschaft* (Göttingen, 1995), pp. 251–300; Puff *Sodomy in Reformation Germany and Switzerland*, pp. 43–44. For an interesting example of how this manifested in actual charges see Helmut Puff, "Localizing Sodomy. The Priest and Sodomite in Pre-Reformation Germany and Switzerland," *Journal of the History of Sexuality* 2 (1997): 184.

20. Sieber-Lehmann, *Spätmittelalterlicher Nationalismus*, pp. 143–149.

21. These cases are found in the StABS WAG 11 and 12.

22. This is apparent from an examination of the court records from places like Lucerne. For a general discussion of this etymological link between sodomy and heresy, see Puff, *Sodomy in Reformation Germany and Switzerland*, p. 18.

23. StALU URK 398/7351.

24. See Chapter 1.

25. These figures are garnered from a survey of the Basel expense records (StABS WAG 9 through 15), banishment books (StABS Leistungsbuch II and Urfehdenbücher I through IV), and trial dossiers (StABS Criminalia series 4) from 1450 through 1530, supplemented for the seventy years following with the cases collected in Guggenbühl *Mit Tieren und Teufeln*.

26. StABS Urfehdenbuch IV p. 180.

27. StABS StrPolAkt S13.

28. StABS Criminalia 6 M1 fol. 4v.

29. Evans, *Rituals of Retribution*.

30. Schuster, *Eine Stadt vor Gericht*, p. 312.

31. StALU COD 4450 fol. 118v–121r.

32. StALU COD 4450 fol. 114r, 115r–116r, 118v–121r

33. StALU COD 4440 fol. 127r. For the entire chain trial see StALU COD 4450 fol. 116r–135v *passim*. The official version of Hans Riss's confession is found in StALU COD 4450 fol. 158v–161r.

34. StALU COD 8260 fol. 17r; StALU COD 8280 fol. 9r. See Chapter 5 for a fuller treatment of the history of torture in Lucerne.

35. Jäggi, "Waldbruder, Prophet, Astrologe," p. 181. Guido Bader, *Die Hexenprozesse in der Schweiz*, (Affoltern a.A., 1945), listed a total of 626 persons accused of witchcraft in Lucerne between 1450 and 1600. Bader's figures are greater than those of Stefan Jäggi, and my own research confirms Jäggi's figures. It may be that Bader was including all persons named in confessions, many of whom were never prosecuted.

36. StALU RP 11 fol. 103v.

37. See for example Dillinger *"Böse Leute."*
38. The execution or destruction of the violated animals was a widespread practice in early modern Europe. See Katherine Crawford, *European Sexualities, 1400–1800* (Cambridge, 2007), pp. 162–63.
39. StALU RP 11 fol. 105r.
40. StALU RP 11 fol. 103v.
41. StALU RP 11 fol. 103v.
42. Michael Rocke, *Forbidden Friendships: Homosexuality and Male Culture in Renaissance Florence* (Oxford: Oxford University Press, 1996); Puff, *Sodomy in Reformation Germany and Switzerland.*
43. StALU RP 11 fol. 104r.
44. A similar story was told by Rudolf Erenbolder, who was burned for diabolism in Lucerne in 1511. StALU RP 10 fol. 80r and cod 8730 fol. 18r. Perhaps the missing-finger narrative was an underworld glorification of thieves' penal mutilation. At any rate, it was uncommon but not unique.
45. StALU RP 11 fol. 104r.
46. These figures on sodomy cases and those which follow are drawn from a survey of the Lucerne Ratsprotokolle 1480–1599 (StALU RP 5A through 46), Umgeldrödel 1480–1530 (StALU COD 8435 through 8905), and Turmbücher 1554–1599 (StALU COD 4435 through 4480).
47. StALU COD 4450 fol. 462v.
48. Harrer, "Statistik der Hinrichtungen in Luzern."

Conclusion

1. Jäggi, "Luzerner Verfahren wegen Zauberei und Hexerei."

Appendix: Selected Trial Documents

1. This phrase was omitted in Hoffmann-Krayer's transcription.

Bibliography

Archival Sources

Abbreviations:

StABS	**Staatsarchiv Basel-Stadt**
WAG 6	Finanz G 6 Wochenausgabenbuch 1423–1433
WAG 9	Finanz G 9 Wochenausgabenbuch 1452–1462
WAG 10	Finanz G 10 Wochenausgabenbuch 1462–1473
WAG 11	Finanz G 11 Wochenausgabenbuch 1473–1490
WAG 12	Finanz G 12 Wochenausgabenbuch 1490–1510
WAG 13	Finanz G 13 Wochenausgabenbuch 1510–1521
WAG 14	Finanz G 14 Wochenausgabenbuch 1521–1529
WAG 15	Finanz G 15 Wochenausgabenbuch 1530–1537
Criminalia 1	Criminalia 1. Gottesverleugnung, Abfall, Irrgeister, Separatisten, verächter des Wortes Gottes, ungereimte Prediger, (B) Wiedertäufer
Criminalia 4	Criminalia 4. Zauberei und aberglaübische Künste
Criminalia 6	Criminalia 6. Ungehorsam
Criminalia 21	Criminalia 21. Totschlag und andere verdächtige Todesfälle
Criminalia 34	Criminalia 34. Diebstahl
Urteilsbücher	Urteilsbücher, Schultheissengericht der mehreren Stadt (Gerichtsarchiv A series)
Kundschaften	Kundschaften, Schultheissengericht der mehreren Stadt (Gerichtsarchiv D series)
Leistungsbuch II	Ratsbücher A, 3 Leistungsbuch II: 1398–1473
StrPolAkt C 9	Straf- und Polizeiakten C 9 Gotteslästerung, Störung des Gottesdienstes 1496–1890
StrPolAkt C 19	Straf- und Polizeiakten C 19 Mord und Todschlag 1449–1713
Urfehdenbuch I	Ratsbücher O, 1 Urfehdenbuch I: 1397–1443
Urfehdenbuch II	Ratsbücher O, 2 Urfehdenbuch II: 1509–1523)
Urfehdenbuch III	Ratsbücher O, 3 Urfehdenbuch III: 1523–1529)
Urfehdenbuch IV	Ratsbücher O, 4 Urfehdenbuch IV: 1529–1532)
StALU	**Staatsarchiv Luzern**
RP	Ratsprotokolle 1381–1798
COD 8045–8920	Finanzwesen Bände: Umgeld, Wochenrechnungen
URK	Urkunden
AKT	Akten
StAN	**Staatsarchiv Nürnberg**
Diff-Akt	Rep. 4. Differentialakten 33c
RV	Rep. 60a Ratsverlässe
Stadtsrechungen	Rep. 54 Stadtsrechnungen
RB	Rep. 60b Ratsbücher
AStB	Rep. 52b Amts- und Standsbücher

Edited Primary Sources

Baader, Joseph. *Nürnberger Polizeiordnungen aus dem XIII. bis XV. Jahrhundert.* 1861. Reprint, Amsterdam: Editions RODOPI, 1966.

Buxtorf-Falkeisen, Carl. *Basler Zauber-Prozesse aus dem 14. und 15. Jahrhundert.* Basel: Schweighauserische Verlags-Buchhandlung, 1868.

Chène, Catherine. "Johannes Nider, *Formicarius* (livre II, chapitre 4 et livre V, chapitres 3, 4, et 7)." In *L'imaginaire du sabbat: Edition critque des textes les plus anciens (1430 c.–1440 c.)*, edited by Martine Ostorero, Agostino Paravicini Bagliani and Kathrin Utz Tremp, 122–43. Lausanne: Université de Lausanne, 1999.

Karl, Hegel, and Matthias, Lexer. *Chroniken der fränkischen Städte. Nürnberg*, edited by Historische Commission bei der königl. Academie der Wissenschaften. 5 vols, *Die Chroniken der deutschen Städte vom 14. bis ins 16. Jahrhundert.* Leipzig: Verlag von S. Hirzel, 1872.

Guggenbühl, Dietegen. *Mit Tieren und Teufeln: Sodomiten und Hexen unter Basler Jurisdiction in Stadt und Land 1399 bis 1799.* Basel: Verlag des Kantons Basel-Landschaft, 2002.

Hansen, Joseph. *Quellen und Untersuchungen zur Geschichte des Hexenwahns und der Hexenverfolgung im Mittelalter.* 1901. Reprint, Hildesheim: Georg Olms Verlag, 2003.

Harms, Bernard. *Der Stadthaushalt Basels im ausgehenden Mittelalter.* 3 vols, *Quellen und Studien zur basler Finanzgeschichte.* Tübingen: Kommissionsverlag der H. Laupp'schen Buchhandlung, 1909.

Hirschmann, Gerhard. *Johannes Müllner: Die Annalen der Reichsstadt Nürnberg von 1623.* Vol. 2. Nuremburg: Selbstverlag des Stadtrats zu Nürnberg, 1984.

Hoffmann-Krayer, E. *Luzerner Akten zum Hexen- und Zauberwesen.* Zurich: Buchdruckerei Emil Cotti's Wwe, 1900.

Jacobs, Jürgen Carl, and Heinz Rölleke, eds. *Das Tagebuch des Meister Franz Scharfrichter zu Nürnberg. Nachdruck der Buchausgabe von 1801.* Harenberg: Die bibliophilen Taschenbücher, 1980.

Kors, Alan Charles, and Edward Peters, eds. *Witchcraft in Europe 400-1700: A Documentary History.* 2nd ed. Philadelphia: University of Pennsylvania Press, 2001.

Kramer, Heinrich. *Nürnberger Hexenhammer 1491. Faksimile der Handschrift von 1491 aus dem Staatsarchiv Nürnberg, Nr. D 251.* Edited by Günter Jerouschek. Hildesheim: Georg Olms Verlag, 1992.

Levack, Brian P., ed. *The Witchcraft Sourcebook.* New York: Routledge, 2004.

Ostorero, Martine, Agostino Paravicini Bagliani, Kathrin Utz Tremp, and Catherine Chène, eds. *L'imaginaire du sabbat: Édition critique des textes les plus anciens (1430 c.–1440 c.).* Lausanne: Université de Lausanne, 1999.

Remy, Nicolas. *Demonolatry.* Trans. by E. A. Ashwin. Secaucus, New Jersey: University Books, 1974.

Rippmann, Dorothee. "Hexen im 15. und 16. Jahrhundert." In *Arbeit - Liebe - Streit: Texte zur Geschichte des Geschlechterverhältnisses und des Alltags, 15. bis 18. Jahrhundert*, edited by Dorothee Rippmann, Katharina Simon-Muscheid and Christian Simon, 159–222. Liestal: Verlag des Kantons Basel-Landschaft, 1996.

Sander, Paul. *Die reichsstädtische Haushaltung Nürnbergs dargestellt auf Grund ihres Zustands von 1431 bis 1440.* Leipzig: Druck und Verlag von B.G. Teubner, 1902.

Scheurl, Siegfried Frhr. von. "Näher am Original? Zur Verfassung der Reichsstadt Nürnberg 1516." *Mitteilungen des Vereins für Geschichte der Stadt Nürnberg* 86 (1999): 21–46.

Schnell, Johannes, ed. *Rechtsquellen von Basel Stadt und Land.* Basel: Bahnmaiers Buchhandlung (C. Detloff), 1856.

Schrieber, Martin, ed. *Die Nürnberger Ratsverlässe. Heft 2 1452–1471.* Neustadt a.d.A.: Verlag Degener & Co., 1995.

Schroeder, Friedrich-Christian, ed. *Die Peinliche Gerichtsordnung Kaiser Karls V. von 1532 (Carolina).* Stuttgart: Reclam, 2000.

Stahl, Irene, ed. *Die Nürnberger Ratsverlässe. Heft 1 1449–1450.* Neustadt a.d.A.: Verlag Degener & Co., 1983.

Wakefield, Walter, and A. P. Evans, eds. *Heresies of the High Middle Ages.* New York: Columbia University Press, 1965.

Wanner, Konrad, ed. *Die Rechtsquellen des Kantons Luzern.* 3 vols, *Sammlung Schweizerischer Rechtsquellen. III. Abteilung: Die Rechtsquellen des Kantons Luzern.* Aarau: Sauerländer, 1998.

Wittenwiler, Heinrich. *"Der Ring."* Trans. by Bernhard Sowinski. Stuttgart: Helfant Edition, 1988.

Secondary Literature

Albert, Thomas D. *Der gemeine Mann vor dem geistlichen Richter. Kirchliche Rechtsprechung in den Diözesen Basel, Chur und Konstanz vor der Reformation.* Stuttgart: Lucius & Lucius, 1998.

Andenmatten, Bernard, and Kathrin Utz Tremp. "De l'hérésie à la sorcellerie: l'inquisiteur Ulric de Torrenté OP (vers 1420–1445) et l'affermissement de l'inquisition en Suisse romande." *Zeitschrift für Schweizerische Kirchengeschichte* 86 (1992): 69–119.

Baader, Joseph. "Polizeiliche Massregelungen des Rates der Stadt Nürnberg gegen Luxus und Unsittlichkeit gerichtet." *Anzeiger für Kunde der deutschen Vorzeit. Organ des Germanischen Museum* (1862): 325–326.

———. "Zur Criminaljustiz der Nürnberger." *Anzeiger für Kunde der deutschen Vorzeit, Neue Folge. Organ des Germanischen Museum* 9 (1862): 364–365.

Bader, Guido. *Die Hexenprozesse in der Schweiz.* Affoltern a.A.: Buchdruckerei Dr. J. Weiss, 1945.

Bailey, Michael. *Battling Demons: Witchcraft, Heresy, and Reform in the Late Middle Ages.* University Park, Pennsylvania: Pennsylvania University Press, 2003.

———. "Medieval Concept of the Witches' Sabbath." *Exemplaria* 8, no. 2 (1998): 419–439.

———, and Edward Peters. "Sabbat of Demonologists: Basel 1431–1440." *The Historian* 65: 6 (2003): 1375–1395.

Baldauf, Dieter. *Die Folter. Eine deutsche Rechtsgeschichte.* Cologne: Böhlau, 2004.

Bart, Philippe. "Hexenverfolgungen in Der Innerschweiz 1670–1754." *Der Geschichtsfreund* 158 (2005): 5–161.

Baufeld, Christa. *Kleines frühneuhochdeutsches Wörterbuch. Lexik aus Dichtung und Fachliteratur des Frühneuhochdeutschen.* Tübingen: Max Niemeyer Verlag, 1996.

Behringer, Wolfgang. "Climatic Change and Witch-Hunting: The Impact of the Little Ice Age on Mentalities." *Climatic Change* 43 (1999): 335–351.

———. "Detecting the Ultimate Conspiracy, or how Waldensians became Witches." In *Conspiracies and Conspiracy Theory in Early Modern Europe: From the Waldensians to the French Revolution,* edited by Barry Coward and Julian Swann, 13–34. Aldershot: Ashgate, 2004.

———. *Hexenverfolgung in Bayern. Volksmagie, Glaubenseifer und Staatsräson in der Frühen Neuzeit.* Munich: R. Oldenbourg, 1988.

———. *Witches and Witch-Hunts: A Global History.* Cambridge: Polity Press, 2004.

Behringer, Wolfgang, Hartmut Lehmann, and Christian Pfister. "Kulturelle Konsequenzen der "Kleinen Eiszeit"? Eine Annäherung an die Thematik." In *Kulturelle Konsequenzen der "Kleinen Eiszeit". Cultural Consequences of the "Little Ice Age",* edited by Wolfgang Behringer, Hartmut Lehmann and Christian Pfister, 7–27. Göttingen: Vandenhoeck & Ruprecht, 2005.

Bendlage, Andrea. *Henkers Hetzbrüder. Das Strafverfolgungspersonal der Reichsstadt Nürnberg im 15. und 16. Jahrhundert.* Constance: UVK Verlagsgesellschaft, 2003.

Bendlage, Andrea, and Peter Schuster. "Hüter der Ordnung. Bürger, Rat und Polizei in Nürnberg im 15. und 16. Jahrhundert." *Mitteilungen des Vereins für Geschichte der Stadt Nürnberg* 82 (1995): 37–55.

Bendlage, Andrea, and Ulrich Henselmeyer. "Zur Monopolisierung des Strafrechts. Gesellschaftliche Relevanz und Reichweite obrigkeitlicher Normen in der Reichsstadt Nürnberg im 15. und 16. Jahrhundert." In *Herrschaftliches Strafen seit dem Hochmittelalter: Formen und Entwicklungsstufen,* edited by Hans Schlosser, Rolf Sprandel and Dietmar Willoweit, 311–29. Cologne: Böhlau, 2002.

Betteridge, Tom, ed. *Sodomy in Early Modern Europe.* Manchester: Manchester University Press, 2002.

Bever Edward. *The Realities of Witchcraft and Popular Magic in Early Modern Europe: Culture, Cognition, and Everyday Life.* Basingstoke: Palgrave Macmillan, 2008.

Bielmann, Jürg. *Die Bevoelkerung Basels vom Mittelalter bis zur Gegenwart. Begleitheft zur Ausstellung im Staatsarchiv Basel-Stadt vom 1. Februar bis 31. März 1974.* Basel: Herausgegeben vom Staatsarchiv Basel-Stadt, 1974.

Blauert, Andreas. "Die Erforschung der Anfänge der europäischen Hexenverfolgungen." In *Ketzer, Zauberer, Hexen. Die Anfänge der europäischen Hexenverfolgungen,* edited by Andreas Blauert, 11–42. Frankfurt a.M.: Suhrkamp Verlag, 1990.

———. *Frühe Hexenverfolgungen: Ketzer- Zauberei- und Hexenprozesse des 15. Jahrhunderts.* Hamburg: Junius Verlag, 1989.

———. "Hexenverfolgung in einer spätmittelalterlichen Gemeinde: Das Beispiel Kriens/Luzern um 1500." *Geschichte und Gesellschaft* 16, no. 1 (1990): 8–25.

———, ed. *Ketzer, Zauberer, Hexen. Die Anfänge der europäischen Hexenverfolgungen.* Frankfurt a.M.: Suhrkamp Verlag, 1990.

———. "Kriminaljustiz und Sittenreform als Krisenmanagement?" In *Mit den Waffen der Justiz: Zur Kriminalitätsgeschichte des Spätmittelalters und Frühen*

Neuzeit, edited by Andreas Blauert and Gerd Schwerhoff, 115–136. Frankfurt am Main: Fischer Taschenbuch Verlag, 1993.

——. *Das Urfehdewesen im deutschen Südwesten im Spätmittelalter und in der Frühen Neuzeit*. Tübingen: Bibliotheca Academica Verlag, 2000.

de Blécourt, Willem. "A Journey to Hell: Reconsidering the Livonian 'Werewolf.'" *Magic, Ritual, and Witchcraft* 2, no. 1 (2007): 49–67.

Bloch, Iwan. "Homosexualität in Köln am Ende des 15. Jahrhunderts." In *History of Homosexuality in Europe and America*, edited by Wayne R. Dynes and Stephen Donaldson, 1–9. New York: Garland Publishing, 1992.

Boes, Maria. "On Trial for Sodomy in Early Modern Germany." In *Sodomy in Early Modern Europe*, edited by Tom Betteridge, 27–45. Manchester: Manchester University Press, 2002.

Boos, Heinrich. *Geschichte der Stadt Basel im Mittelalter*. Basel: C. Detloff's Buchhandlung, 1877.

Borst, Arno. *Medieval Worlds: Barbarians, Heretics, and Artists in the Middle Ages*. Translated by Eric Hansen. Chicago: University of Chicago Press, 1992.

Briegleb, H. E. B. *Die Ausweisung der Juden von Nürnberg im Jahre 1499*. Leipzig: Druck von Julius Klinkhardt, 1868.

Buchholz, Werner. "Anfänge der Sozialdisziplinierung im Mittelalter. Die Reichsstadt Nürnberg als Beispiel." *Zeitschrift für Historische Forschung* 18 (1991): 129–147.

Bullough, Vern. "Postscript: Heresy, Witchcraft, and Sexuality." In *Sexual Practices and the Medieval Church* edited by Vern Bullough and James Brundage, 206–217. Buffalo: Prometheus Books, 1982.

Burghartz, Susanna. "Disziplinierung oder Konfliktregelung? Zur Funktion städtischer Gerichte im Spätmittelalter: Das Zürcher Ratsgericht." *Zeitschrift für Historische Forschung* 16 (1989): 385–407.

——. "Ehen vor Gericht. Die Basler Ehegerichtsprotokolle im 16. Jahrhundert." In *Eine Stadt der Frauen. Studien und Quellen zur Geschichte der Baslerinnen im späten Mittelalter und zu Beginn der Neuzeit (13.–17. Jahrhundert)*, edited by Heide Wunder, 167–187. Basel: Helbing & Lichtenhahn, 1995.

——. "The Equation of Women and Witches: A Case Study of Witchcraft Trials in Lucerne and Lausanne in the Fifteenth and Sixteenth Centuries." In *The German Underworld: Deviants and Outcasts in German History*, edited by Richard J. Evans, 57–74. London, New York, 1988.

——. *Leib, Ehre und Gut. Delinquenz in Zürich Ende des 14. Jahrhunderts*. Zurich: Chronos, 1990.

——. *Zeiten der Reinheit, Orte der Unzucht. Ehe und Sexualität in Basel während der Frühen Neuzeit*. Paderborn: Ferdinand Schöningh, 1999.

Chène, Catherine, and Martine Ostorero. "Démonologie et misogynie. L'émergence d'un discours spécifique sur la femme dans l'élaboration doctrinale du sabbat au XVe siècle." In *Les femmes dans la société européenne. Die Frauen in der europäischen Gesellschaft*, edited by Anne-Lise Head-König and Liliane Mottu-Weber, 171–196. Geneva: Société d'Histoire et d'Archéologie de Genève, 2000.

Clark, Stuart. *Thinking with Demons: The Idea of Witchcraft in Early Modern Europe*. Oxford: Clarendon Press, 1997.

Cohen, Esther. "Inquiring once more after the Inquisitorial Process." In *Die Entstehung des öffentlichen Strafrechts. Bestandsaufnahme eines europäischen*

Forschungsproblems, edited by Dietmar Willoweit, 41–59. Cologne: Böhlau, 1999.

Cohn, Norman. *Europe's Inner Demons: The Demonization of Christians in Medieval Christendom.* Rev. ed. Chicago: University of Chicago Press, 2000.

Crawford, Katherine. *European Sexualities, 1400–1800.* Cambridge: Cambridge University Press, 2007.

Dillinger, Johannes. *"Böse Leute" Hexenverfolgungen in Schwäbisch-Österreich und Kurtrier im Vergleich.* Trier: Spee, 1999.

——. "Hexenverfolgungen in Städten." In *Methoden und Konzepte der historischen Hexenforschung,* edited by Gunther Franz and Franz Irsigler, 129–165. Trier: Spee, 1998.

Douglas, Mary. *Purity and Danger: An Analysis of Concept of Pollution and Taboo.* New York: Praeger, 1966.

Dubler, Anne-Marie. "Fremde Handwerksgesellen in der Stadt Luzern des 15. Jahrhunderts." *Jahrbuch der Historischen Gesellschaft Luzern* 9 (1991): 41–76.

Duesterberg, Daniela. "Hexenproduktion - Materielle, Formelle und literarische Voraussetzungen. Dargestellt am Beispiel der freien Reichsstadt Nürnberg." Dissertation, Johann Wolfgang Goethe-Universität, 1983.

Endres, Rudolf. "Heinrich Institoris, sein Hexenhammer und der Nürnberger Rat." In *Der Hexenhammer. Entstehung und Umfeld des Malleus maleficarum von 1487,* edited by Peter Segl, 195–216. Cologne: Böhlau Verlag, 1988.

Evans, Richard J. *Rituals of Retribution: Capital Punishment in Germany, 1600–1987.* New York: Penguin Books, 1996.

Fehr, Hans. "Das Bahrrecht, insbesondere in der Schweiz." *Deutsches Jahrbuch für Volkskunde* 6 (1960): 85–90.

——. "Zur Erklärung von Folter und Hexenprozeß." *Zeitschrift für Schweizerische Geschichte* 24 (1944): 581–585.

Fischer, Fr. *Die Basler Hexenprozesse in dem 16ten und 17ten Jahrhundert.* Basel: Druck der Schweighauserischen Universitätsbuchdruckerei, 1840.

Fouquet, Gerhard. "Die Affäre Niklas Muffel. Die Hinrichtung eines Nürnberger Patriziers im Jahre 1469." *Vierteljahrschrift für Social- und Wirtschaftsgeschichte* 83, no. 4 (1996): 459–500.

Franck, Johannes. "Geschichte des Wortes Hexe." In *Quellen und Untersuchungen zur Geschichte des Hexenwahns und der Hexenverfolgung im Mittelalter,* 614–670. 1901. Reprint, Hildesheim: Georg Olms Verlag, 2003.

Fudge, Erica. "Monstrous Acts. Bestiality in Early Modern England." *History Today* 50, no. 8 (2000): 20–25.

Ginzburg, Carlo *The Night Battles: Witchcraft and Agrarian Cults in the Sixteenth and Seventeenth Centuries.* Trans. by John and Anne Tedeschi. Baltimore: Johns Hopkins University Press, 1983.

Glaser, Rüdiger. *Klimageschichte Mitteleuropas. 1000 Jahre Wetter, Klima, Katastrophen.* Darmstadt: Primus Verlag, 2001.

Glauser, Fritz. "Der Gotthardtransit von 1500 bis 1660. Seine Stellung im Alpentransit." *Schweizerische Zeitschrift für Geschichte* 29, no. 1 (1979): 16–52.

——. "Zur Verfassungstopographie des mittelalterlichen Luzern." In *Luzern 1178–1978. Beiträge zur Geschichte der Stadt,* 53–106. Lucerne: Verlag Stiftung Stadtjubiläum 800 Jahre Luzern, 1978.

Grimm, Jacob, and Wilhelm Grimm. *Deutsches Wörterbuch.* Leipzig: S. Hirzel, 1854–1960. Online edition: http://germazope.uni-trier.de/Projects/DWB

Groebner, Valentin. "Der verletzten Körper und die Stadt. Gewalttätigkeit und Gewalt in Nürnberg am Ende des 15. Jahrhunderts." In *Physische Gewalt. Studien zur Geschichte der Neuzeit*, edited by Thomas Lindenberger and Alf Lüdtke, 162–189. Frankfurt a.M.: Suhrkamp, 1995.

Guggisberg, Hans Rudolf. *Basel in the Sixteenth Century. Aspects of the City Republic before, during and after the Reformation.* St. Louis: Center for Reformation Research, 1982.

Günther, Bettina. "Sittlichkeitsdelikte in den Policeyordnungen der Reichsstädte Frankfurt am Main und Nürnberg (15.–17. Jahrhundert)." In *Policey und frühneuzeitliche Gesellschaft*, edited by Karl Härter, 121–148. Frankfurt a.M.: Vittorio Klostermann, 2000.

Hagemann, Hans-Rudolf. *Basler Rechtsleben in Mittelalter.* Basel, 1987.

——. "Basler Strafjustiz im Mittelalter." *Basler Juristische Mitteilungen* 5 (1979): 225–242.

Hansen, Joseph. *Zauberwahn, Inquisition und Hexenprozess im Mittelalter und die Entstehung der grossen Hexenverfolgung.* 1900. Reprint, Frankfurt a.M.: Eichborn Verlag, 1998.

Harmening, Dieter. "Zauberinnen und Hexen. Vom Waldel des Zaubereibegriffs im späten Mittelalter." In *Ketzer, Zauberer, Hexen. Die Anfänge der europäischen Hexenverfolgungen*, edited by Andreas Blauert, 68–90. Frankfurt a.M.: Suhrkamp Verlag, 1990.

Harrer, Michael. "Statistik der Hinrichtungen in Luzern von 1551 bis 1798." In *Richtstätte und Wasenplatz in Emmenbrücke (16.–19. Jahrhundert). Archäologische und historische Untersuchungen zur Geschichte von Strafrechtspflege und Tierhaltung in Luzern*, edited by Jürg Manser, 233–242. Basel: Schweizerischer Burgenverein, 1992.

Harrington, Joel. *Reordering Marriage and Society in Reformation Germany.* Cambridge: Cambridge University Press, 1995.

Henningsen, Gustav. *The Witches' Advocate: Basque Witchcraft and the Spanish Inquisition (1609–1614).* Reno: University of Nevada Press, 1980.

Henselmeyer, Ulrich. "Alltagskriminalität und ratsherrliche Gewalt. Niedergerichtliche Strafverfolgungspraxis des Nürnberger Rates in der ersten Hälfte des 15. Jahrhunderts." In *Neue Wege strafrechtsgeschichtlicher Forschung*, edited by Hans Schlosser and Dietmar Willoweit, 155–174. Cologne: Böhlau Verlag, 1999.

——. *Ratsherren und andere Delinquenten. Die Rechtsprechungspraxis bei geringfügigen Delikten im spätmittelalterlichen Nürnberg.* Constance: UVK Verlagsgesellschaft, 2002.

Hergemöller, Bernd-Ulrich. "Homosexuelle als spätmittelalterliche Randgruppe." *Forum Homosexualität und Literatur* 2 (1987): 59–91.

——. "Die unsprechliche stumme Sünde in Kölner Akten des ausgehenden Mittelalters." *Geschichte in Köln* 22 (1987): 5–51.

Herzig, Tamar. "The Demons' Reaction to Sodomy: Witchcraft and Homosexuality in Gianfrancesco Pico Della Mirandola's *Strix*." *Sixteenth Century Journal* 34, no. 1 (2003): 53–72.

Heusler, Andreas. *Verfassungsgeschichte der Stadt Basel im Mittelalter.* Basel: Bahnmaier's Buchhandlung (C. Detloff), 1860.

Hirschmann, Gerhard. "Zeitalter des Markgrafen Albrecht Achilles." In *Nürnberg – Geschichte einer europäischen Stadt*, edited by Gerhard Pfeiffer, 115–120. Munich: C. H. Beck, 1971.

His, Rudolf. *Das Strafrecht des deutschen Mittelalters*. 2 vols. Aalen: Scientia Verlag, 1964.

——. *Geschichte des deutschen Strafrechts bis zur Karolina*. Munich: R. Oldenbourg Verlag, 1967.

Hoffmann, Carl A. "Der Stadtverweis als Sanktionsmittel in der Reichsstadt Augsburg zu Beginn der Neuzeit." In *Neue Wege strafrechtsgeschichtlicher Forschung*, edited by Hans Schlosser and Dietmar Willoweit, 193–237. Cologne: Böhlau, 1999.

Horsley, Richard. "Who Were the Witches? The Social Roles of the Accused in the European Witch Trials." In *Articles on Witchcraft, Magic and Demonology*, edited by Brian P. Levack, vol. 10, 169–196. New York: Garland, 1992.

Hsia, R. Po-chia. *The Myth of Ritual Murder: Jews and Magic in Reformation Germany.* New Haven: Yale University Press, 1988.

——. *Social Discipline in the Reformation: Central Europe 1550–1750.* London: Routledge, 1989.

——. *Trent 1475: Stories of a Ritual Murder Trial.* New Haven: Yale University Press, 1992.

Jäggi, Stefan. "Hexen im Rontal und im Habsburgeramt." *Rontaler Brattig* (2004): 73–76.

——. "Luzerner Verfahren wegen Zauberei und Hexerei bis zur Mitte des 16. Jahrhunderts." *Schweizerische Zeitschrift für Geschichte* 52, no. 2 (2002): 143–150.

——. "Waldbruder, Prophet, Astrologe. Ein Luzerner Eremit am Ende des 16. Jahrhunderts." *Geschichtsfreund* 158 (2005): 163–185.

Jerouschek, Günter. "Die Herausbildung des peinlichen Inquisitionsprozesses im Spätmittelalter und in der frühen Neuzeit." *Zeitschrift für die gesamte Strafrechtswissenschaft* 104 (1992): 329–360.

——. "'Mit aller Schärpffe angegriffen undt gemartert.' Überlegungen zur Folter als Institut des gemeinrechtlichen Strafverfahrens." In *"Zur Erhaltung guter Ordnung." Beiträge zur Geschichte von Recht und Justiz. Festschrift für Wolfgang Sellert zum 65. Geburtstag*, edited by Jost Hausmann and Thomas Krause, 351–375. Cologne: Böhlau, 2000.

Kellenbenz, Hermann. "Gewerbe und Handel am Ausgang des Mittelalters." In *Nürnberg - Geschichte einer europäischen Stadt*, edited by Gerhard Pfeiffer, 176–186. Munich: C. H. Beck, 1971.

Kieckhefer, Richard. *European Witch Trials: Their Foundations in Popular and Learned Culture, 1300–1500.* London: Routledge & Kegan Paul, 1976.

Kleefeld, Traudl, Hans Gräser, and Gernot Stepper. *Hexenverfolgung im Markgraftum Brandenburg-Ansbach und in der Herrschaft Sugenheim mit Quellen aus der Amtsstadt Crailsheim.* Edited by Gerhard Rechter, Robert Schuh and Werner Bürger, *Mittelfränkische Studien im Auftrag des Historischen Vereins für Mittelfranken.* Ansbach: Selbstverlag des Historischen Vereins für Mittelfranken, 2001.

Kleinöder-Strobel, Susanna. *Die Verfolgung von Zauberei und Hexerei in den fränkischen Markgraftümern im 16. Jahrhundert*: Mohr Siebeck, 2002.

Knapp, Hermann. *Das alte Nürnberger Kriminalrecht. Nach Rats-Urkunden erlautert.* Berlin: J. Guttentag, Verlagsbuchhandlung, 1896.

——. "Das alte Nürnberger Kriminalverfahren bis zur Einführung der Karolina." *Zeitschrift für die gesamte Strafrechtswissenschaft* 12 (1892): 200–276, 473–552.

Knapp, Hermann. *Das Lochgefängnis, Tortur und Richtung in Alt-Nürnberg. Auf Grund urkundlicher Forschung.* Nuremberg: Heerdegen-Barbeck, 1907.

Körner, Martin. "Luzern als Finanzplatz im 16. Jahrhundert." In *Luzern 1178–1978. Beiträge zur Geschichte der Stadt,* 217–32. Lucerne: Verlag Stiftung Stadtjubiläum 800 Jahre Luzern, 1978.

Kroeschell, Karl. *Deutsche Rechtsgeschichte.* Vol. 2. Opladen: Westdeutscher Verlag, 1989.

Kümmell, Juliane. *Bäuerliche Gesellschaft und städtische Herrschaft im Spätmittelalter. Zum Verhältnis von Stadt und Land im Fall Basel/Waldenburg 1300–1535.* Constance: Wolfgang Hartung-Gorre, 1983.

Kunstmann, Hartmut. *Zauberwahn und Hexenprozess in der Reichsstadt Nürnberg.* Nuremberg: Schriftenreihe des Stadtarchivs Nürnberg, 1970.

Kurmann, Josef. *Die politische Führungsschicht in Luzern 1450–1500.* Lucerne: Verlag Raeber, 1976.

Landolt, Oliver. ""Mit dem Für zuo ir richten und si zuo Bulfer verbrennen" Zauberwahn und Hexenverfolgungen im spätmittelalterlichen Schaffhausen." *Schaffhauser Beiträge zur Geschichte* 78 (2004): 161–185.

Langbein, John H. *Prosecuting Crime in the Renaissance: England, Germany, France.* Cambridge, MA, 1974.

——. *Torture and the Law of Proof.* Chicago: University of Chicago Press, 1977.

Lea, Henry Charles. *Torture.* Edited by Edward Peters, *Sources of Medieval History.* Philadelphia: University of Pennsylvania Press, 1973.

Leiser, Wolfgang. "Nürnbergs Rechtsleben." In *Nürnberg - Geschichte einer europäischen Stadt,* edited by Gerhard Pfeiffer, 171–6. Munich: C. H. Beck, 1971.

Lembke, Sven. "Folter und gerichtliches Geständnis. Über den Zusammenhang von Gewalt, Schmerz und Wahrheit im 14. und 15. Jahrhundert." In *Das Quälen des Körpers. Eine historische Anthropologie der Folter,* edited by Peter Burschel, Götz Distelrath and Sven Lembke, 171–199. Cologne: Böhlau, 2000.

Leutenbauer, Siegfried. *Hexerei- und Zaubereidelikt in der Literatur von 1450 bis 1550. Mit Hinweisen auf die Praxis im Herzogtum Bayern.* Berlin: J. Schweitzer Verlag, 1972.

Levack, Brian P. "Crime and the Law." In *Palgrave Advances in Witchcraft Historiography,* edited by Jonathan Barry and Owen Davies, 146–163. Basingstoke: Palgrave Macmillan, 2007.

Maier, Christoph. "Regiment und Rechtschaffenheit: Regelungen des öffentlichen "Benehmens" in Basel 1415–1460." Lizentiatsarbeit, Basel, 1985.

Martin, Helmut. *Verbrechen und Straf in Spiegel der spätmittelalterlichen Chronistik Nürnbergs.* Cologne: Böhlau Verlag, 1996.

Martin, Ruth. *Witchcraft and the Inquisition in Venice, 1550–1650.* Oxford: Basil Blackwell, 1989.

Maxwell-Stuart, P.G. " 'Wild, Filthie, Execrabill, Detestabill, and Unnatural Sin': Bestiality in Early Modern Scotland." In *Sodomy in Early Modern Europe,* edited by Tom Betteridge, 82–93. Manchester: Manchester University Press, 2002.

Merback, Mitchell B. *The Thief, the Cross, and the Wheel: Pain and the Spectacle of Punishment in Medieval and Renaissance Europe.* London: Reaktion, 1999.

Metzger, Karl. *Die Verbrechen und ihre Straffolgen im Basler Recht des späteren Mittelalters I. Teil: Die Verbrechen und ihre Straffolgen im allgemeinen.* Basel: Verlag Helbing & Lichtenhahn, 1931.

Midelfort, H. C. Erik. *Witch Hunting in Southwestern Germany 1562–1684: The Social and Intellectual Foundations.* Stanford: Stanford University Press, 1972.

Modestin, Georg. *Le diable chez l'évêque: Chasse aux sorciers dans le diocèse de Lausanne (vers 1460).* Lausanne: Université de Lausanne, 1999.

——. *Ketzer in der Stadt. Der Prozess gegen die Straßburger Waldenser von 1400.* Hanover: Hahnsche Buchhandlung, 2007.

Monter, E. William. "Sodomy and Heresy in Early Modern Switzerland." In *The Gay Past: A Collection of Historical Essays,* edited by Salvatore J. Licata and Robert P. Petersen, 41–55. New York: Harrington Park Press, Inc., 1985.

——. "Sodomy: The Fateful Accident." In *History of Homosexuality in Europe and America,* edited by Wayne R. Dynes and Stephen Donaldson, 192–215. New York: Garland Publishing, 1992.

——. *Witchcraft in France and Switzerland. The Borderlands During the Reformation.* Ithaca: Cornell University Press, 1976.

Mormando, Franco. *The Preacher's Demons: Bernardino of Siena and the Social Underworld of Early Renaissance Italy.* Chicago: University of Chicago Press, 1999.

Muchembled, Robert. *Popular Culture and Elite Culture in France 1400–1750.* Baton Rouge: Louisiana State University Press, 1985.

Müller, Arnd. *Geschichte der Juden in Nürnberg 1146–1945.* Nuremberg: Selbstverlag der Stadtbibliothek, 1968.

Mummenhoff, H. C. Ernst. "Die Juden in Nürnberg bis zu ihrer Austreibung im Jahre 1499." In *Aufsätze und Vorträge zur Nürnberger Ortsgeschichte,* 301–334. Nuremberg: Ernst Fromman und Sohn, 1931.

Naphy, William G. *Sex Crimes from Renaissance to Enlightenment.* Stroud: Tempus, 2002.

——. "Sodomy in Early Modern Geneva: Various Definitions, Diverse Verdicts." In *Sodomy in Early Modern Europe,* edited by Tom Betteridge, 94–111. Manchester: Manchester University Press, 2002.

Ochs, Peter. *Geschichte der Stadt und Landschaft Basel.* 9 vols. Berlin: Georg Jacob Decker, 1786.

Ostorero, Martine. *"Folâtrer avec les démons" Sabbat et chasse aux sorciers à Vevey (1448).* Lausanne: Université de Lausanne, 1995.

——. "Itinéraire d'un inquisiteur gâté: Ponce Feugeyron, les juifs et le sabbat des sorciers." *Médiévales* 43 (2002): 103–117.

——. "Les chasses aux sorciers dans le Pays de Vaud (1430–1530). Bilan des recherches." *Schweizerische Zeitschrift für Geschichte* 52, no. 2 (2002): 109–114.

——. "Le procès d'Aymonet Maugetaz d'Épresses, en 1438." In *L'imaginaire du sabbat. Edition critique des textes les plus anciens (1430 c.–1440 c.),* edited by Martine Ostorero, Agostino Paravicini Bagliani and Kathrin Utz Tremp, 339–353. Lausanne: Université de Lausanne, 1999.

Paravy, Pierrette. "Claude Tholosan: Ut magorum et maleficiorum errores..." In *L'imaginaire du sabbat. Edition critique des textes les plus anciens (1430 c.–1440 c.),* edited by Martine Ostorero, Agostino Paravicini Bagliani and Kathrin Utz Tremp, 355. Lausanne: Université de Lausanne, 1999.

——. "Zur Genesis der Hexenverfolgungen in Mittelalter: Der Traktat des Claude Tholosan, Richter in der Dauphiné (um 1436)." In *Ketzer, Zauberer, Hexen. Die Anfänge der europäischen Hexenverfolgungen,* edited by Andreas Blauert, 118–159. Frankfurt a.M.: Suhrkamp Verlag, 1990.

Peters, Edward. *Torture*. Oxford: Basil Blackwell, 1985.

Pfeiffer, Gerhard, ed. *Nürnberg - Geschichte einer europäischen Stadt*. Munich: Verlag C. H. Beck, 1971.

Puff, Helmut. "Localizing Sodomy. The Priest and Sodomite in Pre-Reformation Germany and Switzerland." *Journal of the History of Sexuality* 2 (1997): 165–195.

——. *Sodomy in Reformation Germany and Switzerland, 1400–1600*. Chicago: University of Chicago Press, 2003.

——. "A State of Sin: Switzerland and the Early Modern Imaginary." In *Queer Masculinities, 1550–1800: Siting Same-Sex Desire in the Early Modern World*, edited by Katherine O'Donnell and Michael O'Rourke, 94–105. Basingstoke: Palgrave Macmillan, 2006.

Reicke, Emil. *Geschichte der Reichsstadt Nürnberg von dem ersten urkundlichen Nachweis ihres Bestehens bis zu ihrem Uebergang an das Königreich Bayern (1806)*. Nuremberg: Verlag der Joh. Phil. Raw'schen Verlagsbuchhundlung, 1896.

Reinle, Christine. "Zur Rechtspraxis gegenüber Homosexuellen. Eine Fallstudie aus dem Regensburg des 15. Jahrhunderts." *Zeitschrift für Geschichtswissenschaft* 4 (1996): 307–326.

Rippmann, Dorothee. *Bauern und Städter: Stadt-Land-Beziehung im 15. Jahrhundert*. Basel: Verlag Helbing & Lichtenhahn, 1990.

——. "Hexen im 15. und 16. Jahrhundert." In *Arbeit - Liebe - Streit: Texte zur Geschichte des Geschlechterverhältnisses und des Alltags, 15. bis 18. Jahrhundert*, edited by Dorothee Rippmann, Katharina Simon-Muscheid and Christian Simon, 159–222. Liestal: Verlag des Kantons Basel-Landschaft, 1996.

——. "Hexenverfolgungen und soziale Unrast. Der Forschungsstand zum Basler Raum (Nordwestschweiz) im Spätmittelalter." *Schweizerische Zeitschrift für Geschichte* 52, no. 2 (2002): 151–156.

Rocke, Michael. *Forbidden Friendships: Homosexuality and Male Culture in Renaissance Florence*. Oxford: Oxford University Press, 1996.

Roper, Lyndal. *The Holy Household. Women and Morals in Reformation Augsburg*. Oxford: Clarendon Press, 1989.

——. *Witch Craze: Terror and Fantasy in Baroque Germany*. New Haven: Yale University Press, 2004.

Rowlands, Alison. *Witchcraft Narratives in Germany: Rothenburg, 1561–1652*. Manchester: Manchester University Press, 2003.

Ruf, Franz. "Acht und Ortsverweis im alten Land- u. Stadgericht Nürnberg." *Mitteilungen des Vereins für Geschichte der Stadt Nürnberg* 46 (1955): 1–139.

Ruggiero, Guido. *Binding Passions: Tales of Magic, Marriage, and Power at the End of the Renaissance*. Oxford: Oxford University Press, 1993.

Russell, Jeffrey B., and Mark W. Wyndham. "Witchcraft and the Demonization of Heresy." In *Articles on Witchcraft, Magic and Demonology*, edited by Brian P. Levack, vol. 2, 305–336. New York: Garland Publishing, 1992.

Salisbury, Joyce E. *The Beast Within: Animals in the Middle Ages*. New York: Routledge, 1994.

Sander, Paul. *Die reichsstädtische Haushaltung Nürnbergs dargestellt auf Grund ihres Zustands von 1431 bis 1440*. Leipzig: Druck und Verlag von B.G. Teubner, 1902.

Schacher, Joseph. *Das Hexenwesen im Kanton Luzern nach den Prozessen von Luzern und Sursee 1400–1675.* Lucerne: Druck Räber & Cie., 1947.

Schatzmann, Niklaus. "Hexenprozesse in der Leventina und die Anfänge der Hexenverfolgung auf der Alpensüdseite (1431–1459)." *Schweizerische Zeitschrift für Geschichte* 52, no. 2 (2002): 138–142.

———. *Verdorrende Bäume und Brote wie Kuhfladen. Hexenprozesse in der Leventina 1431–1459 und die Anfänge der Hexenverfolgung auf der Alpensüdseite.* Zurich: Chronos, 2003.

Scheurl, Siegfried Frhr. von. "Näher am Original? Zur Verfassung der Reichsstadt Nürnberg 1516." *Mitteilungen des Vereins für Geschichte der Stadt Nürnberg* 86 (1999): 21–46.

Schmauder, Andreas, ed. *Frühe Hexenverfolgung in Ravensburg und am Bodensee.* Constance: UVK Verlagsgesellschaft, 2001.

Schmidt, Eberhard. *Inquisitionsprozess und Rezeption: Studien zur Geschichte des Strafverfahrens in Deutschland vom 13. bis 16. Jahrhundert.* Leipzig: Weicher, 1940.

Schmidt, Heinrich R. "Die Christianisierung des Sozialverhaltens als permanente Reformation. Aus der Praxis reformierter Sittengerichte in der Schweiz während der frühen Neuzeit." In *Kommunalisierung und Christianisierung,* edited by Peter Blickle and Johannes Kunisch, 113–163. Berlin, 1989.

Schneider-Lastin, Wolfram, and Helmut Puff. ""Vnd solt man alle die so das tuend verbrennen, es bliben nit funffzig mannen jn Basel." Homosexualität in der deutschen Schweiz im Spätmittelalter." In *Lust, Angst und Provokation. Homosexualität in der Gesellschaft,* edited by Helmut Puff, 79–103. Göttingen, 1993.

Schnelbögl, Fritz. "Zwischen Zollern und Wittelsbachern." In *Nürnberg – Geschichte einer europäischen Stadt,* edited by Gerhard Pfeiffer, 120–127. Munich: C. H. Beck, 1971.

Schneller, Joseph. "Das Hexenwesen im sechszehnten Jahrhundert (Nach den Thurmbucher Lucerns)." *Geschichtsfreund* 23 (1868): 351–370.

Schnyder, Werner. "Reich und Arm im spätmittelalterlichen Luzern." *Geschichtsfreund* 120 (1967): 51–86.

Schnyder, Wilhelm, Karl Meyer, and Peter Xavier Weber. *Geschichte des Kantons Luzern von der Urzeit bis zum Jahre 1500.* Edited by Herausgegeben im Auftrage des Regierungsrates des Kantons Luzern. Lucerne: Druck und Verlag Räber & Cie, 1932.

Schoeps, Julius H. "Justizfolter und Geständis. Der Trienter Ritualmordprozeß von 1475." *Zeitschrift für Religions- und Geistesgeschichte* 49, no. 4 (1997): 377–381.

Schönberg, Gustav. "Basels Bevölkerungszahl im 15. Jahrhundert." *Jahrbücher für Nationalökonomie und Statistik* 40 (volume 6 of new series) (1883): 344–380.

Schorer, Reinhold. "Die Strafherren - Ein selbständiges Organ der Rechtspflege in der Reichsstadt Augsburg in der Frühen Neuzeit." In *Neue Wege strafrechtsgeschichtlicher Forschung,* edited by Hans Schlosser and Dietmar Willoweit, 175–191. Cologne: Böhlau, 1999.

Schulze, Winfried. "Gerhard Oestreichs Begriff 'Sozialdisziplinierung' in der Frühen Neuzeit." *Zeitschrift für Historische Forschung* 14, no. 3 (1992): 265–320.

Schuster, Beate. *Die freien Frauen. Dirnen und Frauenhäuser im 15. und 16. Jahrhundert.* Frankfurt a.M., 1991.

Schuster, Peter. *Eine Stadt vor Gericht: Recht und Alltag im spätmittelalterlichen Konstanz.* Paderborn: Schöningh, 2000.

———. "Hinrichtungsrituale in der Frühen Neuzeit. Anfragen aus dem Mittelalter." In *Justiz = Justice = Justicia? Rahmenbedingungen von Strafjustiz im frühneuzeitlichen Europa,* edited by Harriet Rudolph and Helga Schnabel-Schüle, 213–233. Trier: Kliomedia, 2003.

Schüßler, Martin. "Statistische Untersuchung des Verbrechens in Nürnberg im Zeitraum von 1285 bis 1400." *Zeitschrift der Savigny-Stiftung für Rechtsgeschichte, Germ. Abt.* 108 (1991): 117–193.

Schwerhoff, Gerd. "Blasphemie vor den Schranken der städtischen Justiz: Basel, Köln und Nürnberg im Vergleich (14–17 Jahrhundert)." *Ius commune. Zeitschrift für europäische Rechtsgeschichte* 25 (1998): 39–120.

———. "Devianz in der alteuropäischen Gesellschaft. Umrisse einer historischen Kriminalitätsforschung." *Zeitschrift für Historische Forschung* (1992): 384–414.

———. "Falsches Spiel. Zur kriminalhistorischen Auswertung der spätmittelalterlichen Nürnberger Achtbücher." *Mitteilungen des Vereins für Geschichte der Stadt Nürnberg* 82 (1995): 23–35.

———. "Kriminalitätsgeschichte im deutschen Sprachraum. Zum Profil eines 'verspäteten' Forschungszweiges." In *Kriminalitätsgeschichte. Beiträge zur Sozial- und Kulturgeschichte der Vormoderne,* edited by Gerd Schwerhoff and Andreas Blauert, 21–67. Constance: Universitätsverlag Konstanz, 2000.

———. *Köln im Kreuzverhör: Kriminalität, Herrschaft und Gesellschaft in einer frühneuzeitlichen Stadt.* Bonn: Bouvier, 1991.

———. *Zungen wie Schwerter. Blasphemie in alteuropäischen Gesellschaften 1200–1650.* Constance: UVK, 2005.

Scribner, Robert W. "The Mordbrenner Fear in Sixteenth-Century Germany: Political Paranoia or the Revenge of the Outcast?" In *The German Underworld: Deviants and Outcasts in German History,* edited by Richard J. Evans, 29–56. London: Routledge, 1988.

———. *Popular Culture and Popular Movements in Reformation Germany.* London: Hambledon Press, 1987.

Segesser, Philipp Anton von *Rechtsgeschichte der Stadt und Republik Luzern.* 5 vols. Lucerne, 1850–1858.

Sieber-Lehmann, Claudius. *Spätmittelalterlicher Nationalismus. Die Burgunderkriege am Oberrhein und in der Eidgenossenschaft.* Göttingen: Vandenhoeck & Ruprecht, 1995.

Silverman, Lisa. *Tortured Subjects: Pain, Truth, and the Body in Early Modern France.* Chicago: University of Chicago Press, 2001.

Simon-Muscheid, Katharina. "Gewalt und Ehre im spätmittelalterlichen Handwerk am Beispiel Basels." *Zeitschrift für Historische Forschung* 18, no. 1 (1991): 1–31.

Soman, Alfred. *Sorcellerie et justice criminelle: Le Parlement de Paris (16e–18e siècles).* Aldershot: Variorum, 1992.

Sprandel, Rolf. "Die Strafrechtswirklichkeit im Spiegel der spätmittelalterlichen Chronistik. Ein Überblick über den Forschungsstand des Würzburger

Teilprojekts." In *Neue Wege strafrechtsgeschichtlicher Forschung*, edited by Hans Schlosser and Dietmar Willoweit, 147–154. Cologne: Böhlau, 1999.

Staehelin, Adrian. "Sittenzucht und Sittengerichtsbarkeit in Basel." *Zeitschrift der Savigny-Stiftung für Rechtsgeschichte, Germ.Abt.* 85 (1968): 78–103.

——. "Von der Folter im Basler Strafrecht." *Basler Stadtbuch: Jahrbuch für Kultur und Geschichte* (1965): 100–116.

Stokes, Laura. "Experiments in Pain: Reason and the Development of Judicial Torture." In *Ideas and Cultural Margins in Early Modern Germany: Essays in Honor of H.C. Erik Midelfort*, edited by Marjorie E. Plummer and Robin Barnes, 239–254. Aldershot, Hampshire: Ashgate, 2009.

——. "Prelude: Early Witch-Hunting in Germany and Switzerland" *Magic, Ritual, and Witchcraft* 4:1 (2009): 54–61.

Strauss, Gerald. *Nuremberg in the Sixteenth Century*. New York: John Wiley & Sons, 1966.

Terrier, Isabelle, and Charlotte Touati. "Procès de sorcellerie à Neuchâtel au XVᵉ siècle. Quelques aspects." *Schweizerische Zeitschrift für Geschichte* 52, no. 2 (2002): 133–137.

Teuteberg, René. *Basler Geschichte*. Basel: Christoph Merian Verlag, 1986.

Tlusty, B. Ann. *Bacchus and Civic Order: The Culture of Drink in Early Modern Germany*. Charlottesville, VA: University Press of Virginia, 2001.

Tschacher, Werner. *Der Formicarius des Johannes Nider von 1437/38: Studien zu den Anfängen der europäischen Hexenverfolgungen im Spätmittelalter*. Aachen: Shaker Verlag, 2000.

Unverhau, Dagmar. "Akkusationsprozeß - Inquisitionsprozeß. Indikatoren für die Intensität der Hexenverfolgung in Schleswig-Holstein? Überlegungen und Untersuchungen zu einer Typologie der Hexenprozesse." In *Hexenprozesse. Deutsche und skandinavische Beiträge*, edited by Christian Degn, Hartmut Lehmann and Dagmar Unverhau, 59–143. Neumünster: Karl Wachholtz Verlag, 1983.

Utz Tremp, Kathrin. "Von der Häresie zur Hexerei. Waldenser- und Hexenverfolgungen im heutigen Kanton Freiburg (1399–1442)." *Schweizerische Zeitschrift für Geschichte* 52, no. 2 (2002): 115–121.

——. *Waldenser, Wiedergänger, Hexen und Rebellen: Biographien zu den Waldenserprozessen von Freiburg im Üchtland (1399 und 1430)*. Freiburg: Universitätsverlag Freiburg Schweiz, 1999.

van Dülmen, Richard. *Theatre of Horror: Crime and Punishment in Early Modern Germany*. Translated by Elisabeth Neu. Cambridge: Polity Press, 1990.

Wackernagel, Rudolf. *Geschichte der Stadt Basel*. 3 vols. Basel, 1907–1924.

Waite, Gary K. *Heresy, Magic, and Witchcraft in Early Modern Europe*. Houndmills, Basingstoke, Hampshire: Palgrave Macmillan, 2003.

Waldmann, Daniel. "Die Entstehung der Nürnberger Reformation von 1479 (1484) und die Quellen ihrer prozessrechtlichen Vorschriften." *Mitteilung des Vereins für Geschichte der Stadt Nürnberg* 18 (1908): 1–98.

Wiltenburg, Joy. "True Crime: The Origins of Modern Sensationalism." *American Historical Review* 109, no. 5 (2004): 1377–1404.

Wunder, Heide, ed. *Eine Stadt der Frauen. Studien und Quellen zur Geschichte der Baslerinnen im späten Mittelalter und zu Beginn der Neuzeit (13–17 Jahrhundert)*. Basel: Helbing & Lichtenhahn, 1995.

Zagolla, Robert. "Die Folter: Mythos und Realität eines rechtsgeschichtlichen Phänomens." In *Realität und Mythos. Hexenverfolgung und Rezeptionsgeschichte,* edited by Burghart Schmidt and Katrin Moeller, 122–149. Hamburg: DOBU, 2003.

——. *In Namen der Wahrheit. Folter in Deutschland vom Mittelalter bis heute.* Berlin: Berlin-Brandenburg, 2006.

Index